Contrapunto

SUNY Series in
Power and Political Economy

Marvin E. Olsen, Editor

Contrapunto

The Informal Sector Debate in Latin America

❏

Edited by
Cathy A. Rakowski

STATE UNIVERSITY OF NEW YORK PRESS

Production by Ruth Fisher
Marketing by Bernadette LaManna

Published by
State University of New York Press, Albany

For information, address the State University of New York Press,
State University Plaza, Albany, NY 12246

Library of Congress Cataloging-in-Publication Data

Contrapunto : the informal sector debate in Latin America / edited by
    Cathy A. Rakowski.
        p.   cm. — (SUNY series in power and political economy)
    Includes bibliographical references and index.
    ISBN 0–7914–1905–3 (hardcover). — ISBN 0–7914–1906–1 (pbk.)
    1. Informal sector (Economics)—Latin America.   I. Rakowski,
    Cathy A. II. Series.
    HD2346.L38C66   1994
    330—dc20   93–26767
                                                                        CIP

10 9 8 7 6 5 4 3 2 1

*This volume is dedicated to the memory of
Marvin E. Olsen—mentor, colleague, dear friend*

Contents

Tables and Figures

Tables

Figures

Acknowledgments

I take this opportunity to thank Vanessa Cartaya for her astute assistance in editing several chapters, and Gustavo Márquez, Ray Bromley, Doug Uzzell, and María Otero for many hours of conversation on the issues. The contributors showed incredible patience and gave freely of their time, exchanging and revising manuscripts to "contrapunto-ize" chapters. Stanley E. Welch, a graduate student at Ohio State University, provided invaluable assistance with proofreading, style correction, and tracking down missing bibliographic information.

A thank you also goes to the publications office at the United Nations, Kumarian Press, ACCION International, The American Journal of Sociology, and the U.S. Department of Labor for permission to revise and use material previously published by them.

Part I

Overview

❏ Chapter 1

Introduction: What Debate?

Cathy A. Rakowski

Contrapunto n. Counterpoint, harmony.

Velázquez Spanish and English Dictionary, 1974

Counterpoint n. The combination of two or more independent melodies into a single harmonic texture in which each retains its linear character, vt. Use of contrast or interplay of elements in a work . . . to set off or emphasize by juxtaposition; set in contrast . . . (as in) opposing themes.

Webster's Ninth New Collegiate Dictionary, 1987

Introduction

This volume[1] is about the informal sector, informality, and the informals—the people who engage in informal activities. It also is about the people who study, interpret, intervene in, promote, or attempt to regulate the sector. These include academics, politicians, planners and policy makers, economists, sociologists and anthropologists, labor unions and industrialists, development practitioners, representatives of private voluntary associations, nongovernmental organizations and international aid agencies, associations of informals, and so forth. It is about power, powerlessness, and empowerment; theory, ideology, objectivity, values, and politics; basic research, applied research, program evaluation, and policy making; subordination, exploitation, entrepreneurship, and opportunity; and about poverty and the cre-

3

ation and accumulation of wealth. It discusses controversial issues of an as-yet unresolved debate that began in the early 1970s—issues regarding what constitutes "work"; which types of "work" should be valued; which types of production and producers contribute to local, urban, rural, national, and international development; and who should share in the benefits ensuing from and privileges and subsidies that seek to stimulate development.

In keeping with the diversity of uses of these terms in the literature and among contributors, whenever the terms *informal sector, informal economy, informality,* or *informals* appear, they encompass any or all of the following: small-scale firms, workshops, and microenterprises with low capital inputs where production levels depend on intensive use of labor; nonprofessional self-employed, subcontracted put-out workers, disguised wage workers; unprotected or only partially protected work, illegal contractual arrangements, not fully regulated or registered or extralegal activities; activities that escape standard fiscal and accounting mechanisms; domestic service; cooperatives and associated activities with little or no separation between labor and ownership of the means of production; casual trade, street vendors, and market sellers, regardless of the source of goods; direct subsistence production. *Informalization* refers to the circumventing of regulations, benefits, payment of taxes, and so on by employers and the unequal and selective application of such by the state.

This book is concerned not so much with where the "truth" lies (if there is *a* truth), as with clarifying and comparing the different inputs to and outcomes of policy and intervention strategies; organizing and revealing the implications of competing paradigms that influence policy and intervention; and in particular, with reconciling the diverse roles of informal activities in economic development and of the state in organizing, regulating, promoting, or repressing these activities as part of its development strategy.

The book has both academic and applied objectives.

1. For academics, chapters are intended to provide an overview of conceptual and methodological issues and findings from selected empirical research.

2. For development practitioners and policy makers, chapters are meant to help clarify differing ideological positions, the links between macro and micro level issues, the relative advantages and disadvantages of distinct approaches and actors, and the constraints to policy formulation and implementation.

3. The book's strength is its emphasis of an analytic and theoretical, rather than empirical, treatment of the issues.

Organizing the Debate

All authors address one or more of the following issues in their chapters:

1. In what ways do concepts, operationalization, sources of data, and research objectives influence findings and policy?

2. How does the heterogeneous nature of activities labeled *informal* affect policy making and research?

3. How are research, policy formulation, and programs affected by involvement of public agencies, international donor agencies, nongovernmental organizations, local business leaders, grassroots groups, academic researchers, or others?

4. What specific programs, policies, economic conjunctures, or other factors have had a significant impact (intended or unintended, positive or negative) on the evolution of the informal sector and the role it plays or could play in development?

These issues pull together bits and pieces of the long-standing debate about the informal sector, its role in economic growth and development, and its relationship to the lives and well-being of real people—the latter a common concern shared by authors.

What Debate?

The informal sector debate emerged from disagreement over how Third World economies should develop and at what pace, the role state planning and investment or international funding and technical advising should play in economic development; and the relative importance and costs to the pace of economic development of addressing social problems such as poverty, rural-urban migration, rapid urbanization, and so forth. Each author in this volume contributes a strategic perspective to the debate, providing a necessary link between (what might otherwise have been merely) an academic exercise and the day-to-day realities of policy makers, practitioners, and informals.

Part One of this volume presents three background papers. Moser and Rakowski provide overviews of the issues at the core of the debate, comparing the periods 1970–1983 and post-1983. De Oliveira and Roberts (sociologists) evaluate the contextual factors that influenced changing labor markets from 1940 to 1989—including factors external and internal to Latin American countries.

In this chapter and her earlier work, Moser (an anthropologist and consultant who was among the earliest voices to enter the debate) argues that the early debate emerged from studies of employment, unemployment, and poverty and focused on whether or not—and under what conditions—the activities identified as an informal sector could generate economic growth and employment. She discusses how progress on addressing this question got bogged down on three problems: the first conceptual or definitional (is the "sector" synonymous with poverty? one half of a dichotomy or a segment on a continuum of activities?); the second methodological (how to operationalize and conduct research on the sector—survey and census data sets, case studies, ethnographic research); and the third focusing on the type of linkages with modern activities (e.g., independent, subordinate). She argues that the third issue is the most important for policy making and is itself dependent upon definition and methods. Thus, Moser's chapter gives voice to the critical issues between 1970 and 1983 and underscores their relevance for understanding the relationship between the state, capital-intensive development strategies, and the persistence of the informal sector.

The following chapter by Rakowski updates the general debate through 1993. She argues that one critical shift was from a view of the informal sector as resulting from the failure of development paradigms to a view of the informal sector as a potentially rational and efficient opportunity for genuine development. (She links this shift to the increasing exposure given the ideas of Hernando de Soto and to the greater visibility of NGO—nongovernmental organization—and other microenterprise programs.) The relevant academic and policy questions then became (a) which informal activities generate economic growth and employment, (b) which serve as a buffer against unemployment, and (c) what policies promote which informal activities? It is argued that this shift contributed to clarification of the different roles of the informal sector and encouraged debaters to talk with—not past—each other and avoid getting bogged down in an argument over semantics and labels. Another change discussed in this chapter is the growing attention allocated to people ("informals") as opposed to a sector (e.g., subcontracted workers, workers—entrepreneurs—and owners of microenterprises, the under- and unemployed). The resulting policy debate, says Rakowski, split into a focus at the macro level on economic (reactivation) issues and how state bureaucracies hinder entrepreneurship and at the micro level on the best means for promoting microenterprise development (e.g., through maximalist or minimalist service approaches).

De Oliveira and Roberts provide evidence of the economic context within which the debate originated and changed over time. They argue that shifts in the debate are explained in great part by the changing nature of industrialization, the changing characteristics of labor demand and supply, and the way the role of the informal sector varies under different economic and policy conditions. They use selected case studies—especially Mexico—to illustrate the variability of the context, but also point to common factors—nature of production, regulatory environment, and human capital variables, among others—that influence the demand and supply of labor and, hence, the role of the informal sector.

Subsequent parts of the volume focus almost exclusively on contemporary issues. Part Two presents the debate on macro policy issues and between macro level and micro level approaches. The section begins with Liedholm's (an economist) concise explanation of the types of government policies meant to promote investment and economic growth. He shows how these, unintentionally, disadvantage microenterprises, thereby limiting the informal sector's potential for economic growth. Liedholm, whose work has focused primarily on Africa, raises questions too often ignored in academic research and policy discussions in Latin America: the impact of the supply and demand sides of markets on microenterprise production of goods and services, the irony that measures implemented by the state to protect local ventures from foreign competition can create obstacles to efficient, small firms, and the problem of inadequate markets as an important obstacle to economic growth based on microenterprise development.

Whereas Liedholm focuses on the impact of state policies on firms, Franks (an economist and Latin Americanist) focuses on whether or not state policies will fail to achieve their intended objectives if macroeconomic models exclude informal sector responses to those policies. He criticizes the generally accepted practice of developing macroeconomic models only for the "modern" sector when an overwhelming amount of employment and production concentrates in the informal sector. Thus, both Liedholm and Franks agree that policy makers need to understand the interaction between the informal sector and macroeconomic policies (whether or not they are intended to impact the sector) if they are to assess and influence the role of the informal sector in development. Franks's engaging chapter extends to their logical conclusion two arguments, that informal firms are (a) an opportunity and (b) a problem for crisis economies. If both perspectives are to some degree correct, then there could exist an "optimal" level of informality that could be manipulated through policy implementation.

Portes's (a sociologist and one of the most influential academic voices in the debate) chapter focuses on the role of the informal sector under crisis conditions and in the transition from import substitution industrialization to export-oriented industrialization. His chapter brings into the debate a consideration of linkages between local conditions and global factors. Portes raises the question of whether or not labor standards (protection, benefits) should be enforced in developing economies. The first issue, he says, is that export-oriented firms require flexibility in employment to maximize competitiveness; in the face of rigid standards, firms and states both tend to "informalize" by only selectively applying accepted standards. The second is that failure to enforce standards can lead to a downward spiral in wages and work conditions for workers across the globe. The debate, as Portes sees it, is not *if* the state and firms should enforce labor standards, but *what* standards are critical and nonnegotiable and at what point (and under what conditions) can standards be upgraded.

Bromley's (a geographer and well-known debater since the 1970s) assessment of the contribution of Hernando de Soto and the Instituto Libertad y Democracia presents the other side of the regulatory policy–labor standards debate. He says that de Soto argued against state intervention and regulation, preferring to leave wages, benefits, prices, supply of raw materials, and so on to market determination. He assesses the origin of these ideas, the impact of concrete policies and programs based on them, and their popularity among both conservatives (pro-privatization, debureaucratization, and a free-market economy) and liberals (pro-poverty alleviation and grassroots initiatives). Bromley's discussion of de Soto clarifies broader concerns among those who advocate neo-liberal economic policies and state withdrawal of "interference in the market."

Márquez's (economist and consultant) chapter, written from an insider's perspective, pulls together most of the preceding themes by explaining how they became popularized, for example, how PREALC (an ILO employment policy body in Latin America) became committed to a specific conceptualization of the informal sector. He also explains the shift among economists and policy makers in Latin America from an exclusively macro level approach to one that includes micro level policies; summarizes arguments from the debate that have the greatest practical relevance for policy making; grounds these in the concrete experiences and changing economic context faced by policy makers and their economic advisors in Latin America; and most important, reconciles what appear to be contradictory policy recommendations and research findings. For Márquez, the arguments of the debate are not inherently important. What is important is making sense of the evidence and recommendations and retaining what seems useful and feasible for macroeconomic and social welfare planning.

Part Three of the volume provides an in-depth look at two micro level controversies: (a) what—if any—role should be played by the state versus NGOs in microenterprise development (Otero) and (b) what type of programs will be most successful at promoting growth, productivity, and employment in microenterprises (McKean). Otero (Washington director of ACCION International) zeros in on the critical issue of whether or not state intervention in microenterprise development will be framed by political and regulatory (e.g., increasing revenues) concerns. She lays out the reasons for and the advantages and disadvantages of state participation and explains three possible roles for the state. Her chapter is evidence of a shift in the NGO position from one that opposed state intervention (because of the danger of politicizing programs) to one supporting some kind of intervention (as a means to reach a larger population and guarantee the appropriate policy environment).

McKean (program and policy specialist at the Agency for International Development) takes a more critical look at the relative success of NGO experiences and the conditions (economic context, NGO organization, type of beneficiaries) that influence outcome. The major debates on which she focuses are (a) under what conditions and for whom are minimalist (credit only) or maximalist (credit, training, and some other services) the best strategy for microenterprise development, and (b) whether industry sectors and subsectors are important factors for microenterprise support strategies (an issue also discussed by Márquez). She evaluates the role played in program success by competition, markets for goods and services, and the capacity of individuals to benefit from programs.

Part Four of the volume takes a closer look at the issues of poverty, planning, and power. Cartaya (sociologist, labor market consultant and former planner) is critical of the widely held assumption that informality and poverty are synonymous. She presents evidence that the relative demand and supply of labor intervene in the link between poverty and informality, contributing to a relationship that is conditional and complex—not linear. That is, informality and poverty are associated only under certain conditions and for certain types of workers and households. Cartaya's work picks up on a theme common to many chapters—that the economic context must be considered when assessing the characteristics of poverty and employment (informal or modern). She asserts that these different conditions influence not only the role of the informal sector in economic development, but also that of the "modern" sector. This point can help to reconcile opposing arguments that either the informal sector or modern industrial activities is the most important strategy to achieve economic growth and increase productivity and employment.

The preceding chapters all consider to some degree the question of where funding and programs should concentrate and who should benefit. Implicit is the notion of power and the potential for a zero-sum game among the diverse actors. Uzzell (an anthropologist who greatly influenced the early research of Hernando de Soto and the Instituto Libertad y Democracia) addresses the issue of power explicitly. For Uzzell, the important issues are whether informality is deviant or normative and who has power in development planning and regulation (who benefits? whose interests are served? who pays?). He rejects as obfuscatory the common definitions and debates surrounding the informal sector and critiques the way in which they intersect with power issues. He questions the role and usefulness of research and formal planning on the informal sector. He argues the informal sector represents a rational and normative strategy for most actors and criticizes formal planning as not "reality based" and acting largely as a mechanism for maintaining the status quo, in contradiction to its expressed purpose of directing and achieving change.

Finally, the concluding chapter by Rakowski pulls together points of agreement among contributors and highlights the main policy issues emerging from the book. It suggests the direction for future debate, proposes guidelines for policies and programs, and summarizes the debate on the role of the state.

NOTES

1. The idea for this volume dates from my 1982 frustration in working with the diverse definitions (and implicit ideologies) of "the informal sector" for policy tasks I had been assigned while a consultant in Venezuela. Many conversations with Gustavo Márquez and Vanessa Cartaya convinced us of the need for public dialogue on the "debate." Marv Olsen encouraged me to pull together the debate in book form. I am grateful to all three persons for their encouragement and to Alejandro Portes for both his enthusiastic support of the idea and contributing the first paper (an act that sealed my commitment to the project).

❏ Chapter 2

The Informal Sector Debate, Part 1: 1970–1983

Caroline O. N. Moser

Introduction

Since it was first introduced (Hart 1973; ILO 1970, 1972), the use of the term *informal sector* has become commonplace. This produced a growth industry of studies that have sought, at various levels and in a diversity of contexts, to define it, describe it, analyze it, and propose policy solutions to assist its development—obviously varying widely in scope, standard, and applicability.

The critical issue underlying this review is the relationship between conceptual definitions, research methodologies, and policy proposals for the period of 1970–1983. The conceptual definition of the urban economy (such as dualist or nondualist) largely determines both the area of study and the research methodology utilized. The types of

This is a revised and abridged version of "The Informal Sector Reworked: Viability and Vulnerability in Urban Development," *Regional Development Dialogue* 5, no. 2 (Autumn 1984): 135–178. The original article was written as a review of debates between 1970 and 1980. Its purpose was to assist researchers about to undertake informal sector studies at that time. Although it is somewhat dated, it nevertheless relates to a rich body of literature, now largely unknown to those embarking on informal sector research in the 1990s. I wish to thank the United Nations Publications Board for permission to publish this revised version of the article.

questions asked determine the range of answers given. This, in turn, sets the parameters of the arena for policy formulation (and in so doing, frequently reinforces a priori conceptual categories). Thus, conceptual definitions, empirical studies, and policy proposals are interlinked and must be considered in relation to each other.

In this review, the existence and proliferation of small-scale enterprises in the informal sector (ignoring definitional problems for the moment) is taken as empirically given. The importance of the informal sector concept is a consequence of the fact that, under the prevailing conditions of twentieth century capitalism, small-scale forms of production are not disappearing (a marked difference from the process of capitalist development that occurred in nineteenth century Europe). The informal sector debate is concerned therefore not only with the reasons for its persistence but also with its capacity to generate growth and employment.

The fundamental question underlying the whole informal sector debate has concerned "the ability or inability of small-scale enterprises to generate not only employment but also autonomous economic growth, and consequently the utility of policy recommendations directed at the expansion of productive activities in the informal sector." The debate over the nature of growth in this sector—evolutionary or involutionary—was "largely related to differences in definitions as to the nature of the relationship between large- and small-scale enterprises" with the dualist approach assuming it is benign, and the petty commodity production approach assuming it is exploitative. These contrasting views "lead to two opposite sets of policy measures, with 'dualists' advocating the development of closer links between the two sectors through subcontracting and credit, and the 'petty commodity production school' advocating the increasing autonomy of petty commodity producers and the cutting of links with large-scale capitalist enterprises" (Moser 1978, p. 1061).

Between 1978 and 1983 considerable evidence either supported or refuted these theoretical assumptions within particular empirical contexts. The critical question in each case concerned the identification of the specific conditions and constraints under which the informal sector operates: autonomy or dependence, evolution or involution, benign or exploitative relationship with the formal sector (see Table 2.1).

This chapter summarizes the major thrusts of the debate between 1978 and 1983. It is divided into three sections. The first section provides a brief resume of the theoretical developments that led to the adoption of the informal sector concept by international agencies and national governments seeking policy solutions to alleviate unemployment in Third World cities. The second section examines studies con-

Table 2.1 Summary of the Key Issues Under Debate, 1970–1983

Definitional debate:

Definition as function of measurement technique
Problem versus solution
Dichotomy versus continuum
Sector versus segmented labor market
Mode of production versus scale of operation
Occupational category versus way of organizing production

Cause and function:

Survival strategy during crisis, for poor and those with low human capital
Absorb labor surplus due to failure of development paradigms
Labor market segmentation to keep labor costs low

Capacity to generate employment, income, and growth:

Entrepreneurship versus survival strategy
Internal versus external constraints to growth
Nature of growth: involutionary versus evolutionary

Nature of links to modern sector:

Autonomous versus dependent-subordinate
Benign versus exploitative

Approach to policy: neo-liberal versus neo-Marxist

cerned with the validity of the informal sector concept, indicating the manner in which an essentially descriptive category has come to be identified as an explanatory variable, capable of generating policy solutions. The third section presents conclusions.

Background to the Informal Sector Debate

Unprecedented rates of population growth in many Third World cities between 1950 and 1980 focused attention on the question of employment. Growth produced two important problems; first, the natural rate of population growth, aggravated by migration of large numbers of peasants from the rural areas, meant that the rate of urbanization far outstripped that of industrialization under the prevailing conditions of capitalist economic development; and second, the inability of the industrialization process to absorb into the urban productive labor force the large numbers of unskilled, illiterate workers, rural and urban born, resulted in immense poverty and unemployment for considerable proportions of the urban population.

Recognition of the scale of the problem resulted in widespread reappraisal of the adequacy of existing development models. The "accelerated growth" model, which essentially dominated development planning for the first two decades after the Second World War, assumed that large-scale industrialization would create investment capital and save foreign exchange through import substitution faster than other policies. A policy designed to maximize the GNP would, therefore, provide resources to develop the whole economy. Industrial expansion based largely on import substitution would increase wage-sector employment, and the "filter down" effect would lead ultimately to the redistribution of resources and income throughout society. This dualist model of an economy divided into "traditional" and "modern" sectors provided the rationale for the gradual but inevitable elimination of inequality and the social and economic aspects of poverty. This model predicted that social aspects of rapid urbanization, including such problems as squatter settlements and unemployment, were temporary and would pass with time. Furthermore, with "modernization" migrant workers from rural areas would gradually become assimilated into the city. With "increased participation in the urban structure and increased assimilation of urban norms" migrants would shift from a "marginal position towards full integration," moving from "peripheral occupations in an 'exaggerated' tertiary sector to industrial wage employment" (Moser 1978, p. 1042).

The Intervention of the ILO

By the mid-1960s the level of poverty and unemployment in Third World countries was a preoccupation. Accelerated growth strategies based on maximizing the GNP were not leading to desired levels of income redistribution, because of the particular characteristics of capital-intensive import-substitution policies. The fact that the "filter down" effect was not operating quickly enough within the prevailing political structure resulted in a search for alternative means to achieve redistribution with growth (Chenery et al. 1974). The ILO took the initiative in the search for viable alternatives by openly recognizing that unemployment was not simply a cyclical phenomenon but "chronic and intractable in nearly every developing country" and by committing governments to adopt "active full-employment policies."[1] The ILO undertook a series of studies at the country, city, and sector levels in which the policy emphasis shifted from the formulation of development strategy based on economic growth per se (with employment obtained as a residual) to a strategy focusing on employment as a major policy objective in its own right. In their diagnosis of the problem and the methodological basis from which policy recommendations were derived, the initial ILO studies utilized both categories and perceptions derived largely from the experience of developed economies. Thus, the ILO Colombia report based its somewhat utopian recommendation to create 5 million jobs for "a full employment strategy" on the fact that 30–40 percent of the urban labor force was in a position of open or disguised unemployment or open or disguised underemployment.[2]

These tabulations highlighted the problem of evaluating employment in a Third World context with concepts of measurement intended for advanced economies. Ultimately the concept and measurement of unemployment is dependent on the concept of employment; it is only in those contexts where a reason exists to register as unemployed (such as for the payment of social security benefits) that a rigorous recording of statistics has some measure of accuracy. Other definitions of *employment* or *unemployment* tend to be arbitrary, because only in those countries where unemployment benefits are provided can the adult population afford not to work. The problem is one of employment not unemployment.

Recognition of low levels of unemployment in the absence of unemployment insurance and other benefits resulted in the identification of the "working poor" as the target group requiring specific attention. In its search for conceptual categories more appropriate to the Third World context, the ILO adopted the informal sector concept to describe work in small-scale activities, largely escaping recognition, enumeration, regulation, or government protection. In Kenya the ILO found employment in the informal sector—though regarded as stagnant and unproductive—was competitive, labor intensive, utilized locally produced goods, and developed its own skills and technology in small family or locally owned units. This accounted for some 30 percent of those employed, and the development of this sector—then restricted and harassed—would be the solution to Kenya's employment problem and to increasing its growth. Another importance of the ILO Kenya Report was its emphasis on the *productive* role of this sector, leading to the conclusion that: "From being the Cinderella of underdevelopment the 'informal sector' could thus become a major source of future growth" (Leys 1975).

Definitional Problems

Since the utility of the informal sector concept was first recognized, researchers and policy makers have applied it to a diversity of empirical data and in many different contexts. What resulted was complete confusion about what was meant by the *informal sector*, regarded at times as synonymous with "the urban poor, or with people living in slums or squatter settlements, or with the immigrant populations of cities." Certain occupations have been treated as belonging to the informal sector, and those concerned with housing at times regarded the informal sector as synonymous with "the improvement of housing in informal areas" (Moser 1978, p. 1051). Thus, the "target group" included heterogeneous sets of activities and people without clearly identifiable or analytically useful common characteristics.

The most important definitional distinctions within the dualist framework include those of Hart, Mazumdar, Weeks, the ILO Kenya Report, and Sethuraman.

Hart's (1973) original dualist dichotomy was based on the distinction between wage earning and self-employment with the key variable being the degree of rationalization of work. Although based on a dichotomy of the characteristics of urban enterprises, his definition of the target group remained unclarified and included informal income-generating activities, the unorganized sector, and self-employed individuals.

Mazumdar (1976) based his dichotomy on the urban labor market rather than enterprises, with the informal sector "unprotected" in contrast to the formal "protected" sector. The basic distinction was the fact that employment in the formal sector was protected, so that wage levels and working conditions were not available to job seekers unless they managed to cross the barriers to entry created by both the trade unions and government.

Weeks (1975), like Mazumdar, emphasized the role of the state. His two-sector distinction focused on "the organizational characteristics of exchange relationships and the position of economic activity *vis-à-vis* the State." The formal sector, which includes government and private activities, is officially recognized, nurtured, and regulated by the state through such mechanisms as tariff and quota protection, import tax rebates, selective monetary controls, and licensing measures. The informal sector operates outside the system of benefits or access to formal credit institutions.

The ILO two-sector dichotomy of informal and formal sectors was based on the characteristics of enterprises. Informal sector enterprises showed the following attributes: ease of entry, reliance on indigenous resources, family ownership of enterprises, small-scale operation, labor intensive and adapted technology, skills acquired outside the formal school system, and unregulated and competitive markets. Of all the definitions of the informal sector, this one has been the most popular and widely used.

The work of S. V. Sethuraman (1976a; 1976b; 1981) provided the working definition, methodological approach, and policy guidelines for much of the international agency research on the subject between 1970–1983, especially in Latin America: "small-scale units engaged in the production and distribution of goods and services with the primary objective of generating employment and incomes to their participants notwithstanding the constraints on capital, both physical and human, and knowhow" (Sethuraman 1981, p. 17).

Sethuraman's redefinition was based on the recognition that the characteristics identified by the Kenya Mission did not constitute a definition; the problem was one of multiple criteria, such that "each criterion can be used to define a universe of its own."[3] His choice of the "activity or enterprise as the basic unit of dichotomization implies that the urban economy is viewed as a continuum of enterprises engaged in the production of goods and services" (Sethuraman 1981, p. 15). Activities can be sorted out on the basis of one or more of the characteristics: mode of production, form of organization, and scale of operation. Informal sector enterprises can be interpreted as "belonging to the lower end of the urban continuum of enterprises." Thus the informal sector would be "expected, in principle, to overcome the capital and skill constraints over time and thus assimilate themselves with enterprises." The feature that divides informal sector units and small enterprises "is their orientation; whereas the former is motivated primarily by employment creation, the latter is concerned primarily with profit maximization" (Sethuraman 1981, p. 17).

Sethuraman's definition had analytical significance and led to the conclusion that the value added per worker—the level of labor productivity—provides an attractive single measure to distinguish the two subsystems within urban economies, with the formal sector showing high labor productivity and the informal sector low labor productivity. This subcategorization within a dualist framework was intended to identify more "dynamic" areas within the informal sector so that policy measures be directed specifically to them. All depended on "what information is collected from the informal sector and how it is analyzed," particularly information on the nature of the relationship between the informal and formal sectors (Sinclair 1976).

Major Conceptual and Policy Issues

The ILO Kenya Report concluded that the informal sector is capable of both creating more jobs and growing faster than the formal sector and that the "bulk of employment in the informal sector far from being only marginally productive is economically efficient and profit making" (ILO 1972, p. 5). Similarly, Weeks argued that there were considerable advantages in having an evolving and dynamic low-wage sector in less developed countries, not only because accumulation was higher there than in the formal sector, but because the informal sector had an important contribution to make in three areas. It could produce a significant proportion of consumer goods for consumption by the lowest income groups, thereby reducing dependence in industrialization policy on import "reproduction." Informal sector workshops could provide a source of indigenous capital goods. And greater relative growth in the informal sector as compared to the formal sector could mean a shift toward labor-intensive industrialization. In theory this would increase the incremental employment/output ratio, while ensuring a more efficient utilization of capital (Moser 1978, p. 1055).

On the basis of such recommendations, the informal sector came to be viewed as the solution to Third World employment problems, and policy-oriented studies increasingly advocated the direct intervention of the state in implementing reforms and fiscal measures designed to promote informal sector growth. Within the informal sector itself, at a prescriptive level the problem was seen as one of identifying the dynamic areas of the economy, presupposing one can tell them in advance, and then implementing training programs and credit loan schemes, to assist them in their self-generating capacity for growth.

The popularity of the informal sector concept with the ILO and other international agencies that occurred, Bromley argued, was due to the fact it "embodied policy implications which were convenient for international organizations and politically middle-of-the-road governments. Support of the informal sector appeared to offer the possibility of 'helping the poor without any major threat to the rich.'" This represented a "compromise between pressures for the redistribution of income and wealth and the desire for stability on the part of economic and political elites" (1978a, p. 1036).

Bromley maintained that "the marketing of ideas is as important as their quality in determining what degree of diffusion is eventually obtained . . . the intellectual validity of the concept was, for many people, secondary to its policy implications" (1978, p. 1036). The debate was between liberal neo-classical evolutionary views that policies can be formulated to bring the "benefits" of development to the poor and the radical neo-Marxist views that only a sharp change can improve the situation (Moser 1978); policy discussions reflected different conceptions of the structure and functioning of the socioeconomic system and the role of the state within it (Bromley 1978a, p. 1037). It is important to examine how far this became the dominant determinant of the positions taken by different interpretations of the informal sector.

Independence and the Informal Sector

Critics of the ILO concept of an independent informal sector capable of growth argued that the level of capital accumulation possible is constrained by structural factors in the total socioeconomic system. Small-scale enterprises tend to be subordinate and dependent, and the linkages between small-scale and large-scale enterprises are not benign but exploitative. Diverse studies of small-scale enterprises and entrepreneurs showed how seemingly independent enterprises really operate within a complex system of dependent relationships. An excellent example was provided by Birkbeck's study of garbage pickers in Cali, Colombia.

Birkbeck explains how, although working independently, the garbage picker is part of the recuperative raw material production system that flourishes where raw materials such as paper, steel, and plastics are expensive or in short supply. "With the growth of the market of recuperated raw materials, capital-intensive companies have not only devoted themselves to industrial and commercial wastes but have also had their eye on domestic waste" (Birkbeck 1979, p. 161). Because of the great difficulty of subjecting domestic waste to capital-intensive processes or recuperation, the garbage picker is used in work whose survival depends on the lack of technical changes in the recycling business.

Birkbeck argues that pickers' poverty derives from the fact that they work for the factory but are not part it and describes how the garbage recycling business is characterized by a hierarchy of vertical links that extend from factory to garbage picker, via small buyer, satellite warehouse, and central warehouse, with each level differentiated by the size of economic unit. He explains that the lack of direct link between picker and factory is intentional. First, it effectively fractionalizes its labor force and severely impedes any attempt at true collective wage bargaining; second, it lets the factory avoid problems that arise due to the fluctuations of the market and to provide the necessary flexibility to cope with changing demand. The combination of piecework and "independence" of the suppliers of waste paper keeps efficiency high and costs low. The income of the garbage picker is low, not only because of the nature of recuperation, but also because of external factors relating to the international supply and demand for waste paper related to its price in comparison to pulp, a naturally preferable material. The garbage picker must be paid according to the price of pulp. This hierarchical system is set up to keep the price of waste paper low and ensure continued waste paper collection. Thus, policy cannot seek to incorporate the garbage picker into the industrial sector, since he or she is already part of it. Neither can their share of the income generated by recuperation be increased because of the structural constraints that operate in determining income. The garbage picker may be the "near-perfect example of the enterprising individual" but it will not get him or her far (Birkbeck 1979, pp. 179–182).

Dependence and Petty Commodity Production

Birkbeck's case study indicated the importance of understanding the nature of linkages within the urban economy. Dissatisfaction with a priori dualist models resulted in an alternative framework emphasizing a continuum of productive activities. Based on Marx's theory of different modes of production and their mutual articulation, this contained a theoretical apparatus for explaining the internal dynamics of a particular form of production, the conditions necessary for its existence, and the contradictions that lead to its eventual elimination, including both the social and the technical relations of production. The vast majority of small-scale enterprises identified as informal fit into the category of "petty commodity production," a form of production that exists at the margins of the capitalist mode of production but is integrated into and subordinate to it.

The petty commodity production approach conceptualizes economic activities in terms of a continuum[4] of productive activities. This places the essence of analysis in the identification of complex linkages and dependent relationships between and within production and distribution systems and hence the potential for evolutionary as against involutionary growth within the productive sector. It allows for the more accurate identification of illusory self-employment and disguised wage employment and for the complexities of linkages between the small-scale enterprise and the "capitalist sector."

Within this conceptual framework a diversity of studies tried to define and categorize the labor market and the nature of small-scale enterprises more accurately (with implications for class analysis).[5] Concern with the inadequacy of the wage-employment–self-employment dichotomy led Bromley and Gerry to develop the category of "casual" work and to conceive of a continuum stretching from stable wage work to true self-employment, with particular focus on the intermediate categories and transitional processes along this continuum. Casual work was divided into four broad and occasionally overlapping ideal categories of short-term wage work, disguised wage-work, dependent work, and true self-employment. Therefore they maintained that "these four categories of casual work are in fact alternative relations of production as they affect the individual worker. In turn they have ramifications at the aggregate level in terms of the types and structure of enterprises (firms) and the composition and nature of social classes." And they claim categorizing activities into stable wage work and casual work, and the division of casual work into four main categories, "forms the basis for a focus on relationships between large and small firms and between the State and the labour process" (Bromley and Gerry 1979, pp. 5–7).

A similar concern with the self-employed–wage labor dichotomy led MacEwen Scott (1977, 1979) to argue for a shift in analysis from fundamental occupational categories to forms of production in the urban economy. She argued against separating classes of labor from the forms of production on which they were based and for examining relations of production within manufacturing, construction, transport, and commerce. Using empirical material from Lima, Peru, she distinguished between artisan, petty commodity, and capitalist production and identified the mechanism whereby self-employment is converted into wage labor. "If by self-employment we are referring basically to a situation of economic independence then it is autonomy over the production process which is crucial and ownership of the means of production lies at its base." The critical factor is the loss by the worker of the ability to acquire the means of production by one's own efforts and dependence on external agents, including merchants or industrial capitalists for their provision. This dependence subordinates the worker to capital and results in loss of independence as a producer. "The subordination takes three forms: loss of access to markets; loss of control over the labour process; and extraction of surplus" (MacEwen Scott 1979, p. 121).

MacEwen Scott also recognized that discrepancies emerge between real and perceived situations of economic independence and argues that this is partly a result of the form of remuneration, especially the practice of "payment by results," which gives the worker a "feeling of freedom to decide when, where, and how hard" to work. This is, she says, a reflection of the fact that "subjection to capital is only partial," and the worker still owns some of the means of production and "thus has a material basis for a bourgeois consciousness" (MacEwen Scott 1979, p. 121).

Benign and Exploitative Relationships

A critical area of inquiry relates to the linkages between the informal and formal sectors, and between small- and large-scale enterprises—an examination of the benign-exploitative hypothesis. Two works in particular illustrate the debate between 1970–1980. In an early paper, Tokman (1978) outlines, at a conceptual level, the two approaches. One assumed that benign relationships between sectors prevail; the second assumed that subordination is the main characteristic of informal activities. To these he added a third, an intermediate conceptual framework of heterogeneous subordination that implied a subordinate relationship for the sector as a whole, but resulting from different processes occurring within it. He suggested that a declining share in income in the sector as a whole should be expected that—with the expansion of labor supply for the sector—would result in involutionary growth.

Schmitz (1982a) rigorously examines growth constraints in small-scale manufacturing (including up to ten workers). He stated that growth constraints as discussed in the literature are grouped into two categories: those of an internal nature (entrepreneurship and management) and those of an external nature (access to resources and exploitation by larger enterprises). He questioned the extent to which lack of motivation-drive-adaptability, organizational skills, or technical skills constrains enterprises. The inventiveness and responsiveness of small-scale enterprises is well known; limits on advance planning can equally be seen as the result of the markets in which they operate or shortages of resources. Schmitz argues that factors internal to the enterprise are as much a source of strength as of weakness, whereas on the question of skills, he suggests that a thorough knowledge of the production process tends to be the strong point, with learning by doing an integral part of the small producers' struggle for survival or expansion.

External factors can be examined in terms of two sets of arguments. First comes the question of "exploitation," as exemplified by Leys: "What the informal sector does is to provide the formal sector with goods and services at very low prices, which makes possible the high profits of the 'formal' sector" (1975, pp. 267–268). Portes adds that the informal sector subsidizes part of the costs of formal capitalist enterprises because some needs of formal workers are met by goods and services produced by unpaid or cheaply paid informal labor (1978,

p. 37). But Schmitz criticizes this important debate on the grounds that it has "rarely, if ever, been subjected to detailed empirical examination . . . such an investigation would have to begin with a list of the material needs of the industrial worker and his family and examine how these needs were satisfied" (1982a, p. 433).

The "cheap wage goods issue" is critical, as it concerns the function of the informal sector. The evidence suggested the need to distinguish between different economic systems or levels of industrialization and the need for far greater clarification of two more issues: First, why is the level of remuneration of petty producers so low (if it is forced on them by the greater efficiency of expanding capitalist production, then clearly there is no subsidy or exploitation) and, second, if extreme competition among petty producers forces them to use unpaid family labor or underpaid wage labor, then mechanisms exist that prevent the petty producer from accumulating the surplus. Schmitz argued that this loss of surplus does not necessarily result in cheaper wage goods for the worker because it may be retained by the buyer or intermediary. Therefore, Schmitz concluded it is more useful to focus squarely on the question of whether the small producer can retain the surplus and to separate this question from that of the cost of the reproduction of the industrial labor force, because both of these are, at the empirical level, very complex questions.

The second constraint examined by Schmitz is that of subcontracting, widely practiced in the construction industry in Dakar, Lima, and Manila and also in footwear and clothing in Calcutta (Lebrun and Gerry 1975; MacEwen Scott 1979; Stretton 1979; Bose 1978). Its importance relates to the extent to which small producers are independent or simply an extension of the production network of large firms working as disguised wage labor. Although critical of Lenin's view that small producers become anachronistic, most clearly belied by the Japanese experience (Watanabe 1971), Schmitz concludes that "very little is known about the growth potential of small subcontractors in less developed countries because of the difficulties in carrying out research—e.g., small subcontractors and outworkers usually are not registered and do not appear in official statistics (Schmitz 1982a, p. 437).

The third constraint, access to markets, is another area where empirical reality does not always coincide with the perceived wisdom. Barriers lie in the preexistence of very advanced technologies and the control large firms exercise over product markets, raw materials, and credit. Improving communications does give distributional advantages to branded standardized products of large firms, especially through advertising, but there are regional and sectoral exceptions that are important to recognize. Three examples provide different experience. Schmitz (1982a) shows that where seasonal markets are unpredictable, small firms are a strategy to cope with the enormous flexibility required in production. Bose (1978) suggests the market for small producers is effectively controlled by large firms. Finally, Langdon (1975) finds that small firms were struggling to survive despite a growing market for their product, while multinational companies were expanding due to expensive marketing to promote "taste transfer." Such transfer resulted in higher prices, generated industrialization inappropriate to the local resource base and employment needs, and established patterns of demand that small-scale indigenous industrialists could not meet directly (Langdon 1975).

In his discussion of the fourth constraint, the technological gap, Schmitz points to physical distance between small producers and suppliers of technology to explain why producers are confronted with the technological gap in some branches and places more than others; the successful use of secondhand equipment depends on local availability of machines, spare parts, and repair services. Fifth, access to raw material is stressed as a critical constraint on the growth of small-scale enterprises because of the bargaining difficulties of small producers, their lack of working capital, and also government's discrimination against small firms in the allocation of raw materials (Gerry 1974, 1978a, 1978b; Mars 1977; Steel 1977). Easier access to credit, the sixth constraint, has been a favorite among policy makers (Fowler 1978; PREALC 1979). But do "higher interest rates paid by the small producers and their difficulties in gaining access to credit merely reflect an underlying reality of unstable and risky conditions of production (and hence repayment defaults)" or are they "due to distortions in the views and practices of those in charge of the credit institutions?" (Schmitz 1982a, p. 441).

The final constraint, government discrimination, requires the examination of the growth potential of the small producer in a political context, which raises deeper questions about the power structure of the country; in particular about the role of the state, the social classes it is based on, and the connections with international capital. These issues are unlikely to be examined by reports addressed to a government, as was the case with the ILO Kenya Mission. Nevertheless, this can have dangerous consequences when optimistic recommendations, made for political purposes, are later replicated. This suggests that the optimistic view is justified when in reality the data collected can neither confirm nor contradict the view, because of the methodology of data collection. In the last instance Schmitz concludes, "the issue is not whether small enterprises have growth and employment potential, but under what conditions" (1982a, p. 445).

Evolution or Involution

Many of Schmitz's conclusions are equally applicable to manufacturing and the distributive and service sector. The nature of the linkages is complex to identify and may change over time, requiring longitudinal studies. An eight-year case study of a retail market illustrates this. In 1970 detailed categorization of retail market enterprises selling staples, fruits, and vegetables in one of the poorest markets in the city of Bogotá, Colombia, indicated a heterogeneous group of workers with differential access to sources. Amid the overall involutionary situation it was possible to identify those "healthy" entrepreneurs, mostly younger single men, more likely to accumulate sufficient resources to expand their enterprises either within or outside the market. A restudy of the market in 1978 indicated that of the 56 percent of the sellers who had left it during the eight-year period, only 10 percent had done so for an alternative or better job, with 90 percent leaving due to ill-health, death, or involvency. Of the 44 percent still in the market, 42 percent had declined in their scale of enterprise, 42 percent had remained static, while only in the remaining 15 percent was there any indication of expansion of the market enterprise (Moser 1980). Analysis of the lack of expansion of the majority of enterprises at different levels shows the complexity of interpretation required, if mechanisms to help the growth of small-scale enterprises are to be identified. At the individual level expansion is prevented by personal constraints at different points in individual life cycles. When people live close to the margins of survival, they lack sufficient capital to cushion themselves against crises and are pushed into insolvency by any small incident. Education, medical expenses, and rent are the biggest drains on the resources of the poor and influence the amount of working capital available and the growth potential of enterprises (Moser 1980, p. 376).

City-level economic trends showed that although wage employment remained static during the 1970–1978 period, younger, more skilled men finding it increasingly difficult to find wage employment, moved into self-employment in marketing. Because of external economic constraints (such as increased competition from unemployment and rural-urban migration), the function of the market was gradually changing from its traditional role as a "refuge occupation" that absorbs the labor surplus, the old, unskilled, and women. These groups were rendered uncompetitive and forced out through insolvency and were replaced by younger, more "skilled," professional men. During a period of massive inflation a decline in consumer purchasing power was reflected in the reduction of market stalls selling high-profit "opportunist" produce in favor of those more basic commodities with regular demand such as vegetables and staples.

Do wider causal constraints provide sufficient explanation of the dynamics of productive enterprises at this level and of the extent to which the relationship between these and larger-scale enterprises are exploitative or benign? Because such small-scale enterprises are part of a continuum of productive activities, the analysis should consider the changes in their direct and indirect linkages with large-scale retail enterprises and their dependent relationships within the wholesale marketing system of Bogotá over the eight-year period. The following three factors appear most important. First, the rationalization of the wholesale marketing system and introduction of a modernized wholesale market resulted in increased travel time and transport costs, while increased monopolization of price fixing reduced the profit margins of the small-scale retailer. Second, labor legislation requiring large companies to invest 4 percent of their payroll into a fund providing a family subsidy to workers resulted in the development of a private sector welfare system, clinics, and particularly the large-scale development of so-called non-profit-making supermarket consortiums controlling 30 percent of food-stuff retailing in the city. This provides another example of the increasing penetration of merchant capital into the distribution sector that, because of efficiency and access to large-scale capital, took over large areas of the market. Third, the increasing land values in the area where the market is located, due to its close proximity to the central business district, changed the class composition of the area, and because the low-income population use retail markets, this had a detrimental impact on spending power in the market. The dependent subordinate relationship between the lowest level of petty retailing and the wider capitalist marketing structures meant that, with decreasing access to resources and the growth of monopolistic practices, the level of activity in the market became involutionary able "only to reproduce the existing conditions and scale of operations frequently at the expense of its cost of labor (such as the increased use of unpaid family labor) and living standard (such as longer working hours)." This is in direct contradiction to the informal sector approach, which categorizes two separate sectors each with an autonomous potential for growth. Focus on the flow of labor between these "autonomous" sectors tends to underestimate the importance of the articulation of subordination-domination relationships within the capitalist system. "As it becomes increasingly profitable for large-scale capital to penetrate into the different areas of wholesale and retail markets of fresh foodstuffs (including supermarkets), fewer petty producers make the transition to small capitalist production. For a small number the process is one of proletarianisation . . . for the vast majority no alternative to dependent selling exists." This leads to further impoverishment and marginalization (Moser 1980, pp. 383–385).

This detailed review of selected studies indicates the manner in which a priori assumptions concerning the informal sector and its capacity to generate growth and employment were effectively challenged on conceptual grounds. This reveals the limitations of broad generalizations and the dangers of sweeping assumptions when identifying the functions of the informal sector in a specific context and underlines the critical influence of the methodological approach adopted in data collection.

Conclusion

The early debate on the informal sector concluded that it is likely to play an important role under conditions where it provides cheap inputs and goods that large-scale national or foreign capital cannot produce profitably. Small-scale artisan production survives most often in areas with difficult communication or markets that are unprofitable for large-scale production. Similarly, small retailers, traders, and shops survive until the size of the market makes it sufficiently lucrative for supermarkets. A small scale is more important under those economies not yet fully industrialized or where the constraints and costs of the internal communication network result in the survival of local markets for small-scale production.[6] Small-scale enterprises also are more likely to survive where the market is unpredictable due to seasonal or fashion fluctuations or where the product produced has such a localized demand that it is not seen as sufficiently profitable to shift to an international technology.

Researchers also argue that, if small-scale production is highly competitive, producing goods below their real value through the use of longer working hours and unpaid family labor, to understand the reasons for their survival it is important to establish where the surplus goes. Does it help keep the price of labor low, thus subsidizing part of the cost of formal capitalist enterprises, enabling them to reenforce comparatively low wages, or does it simply increase the profits of intermediaries? Studies point to the fact that the extent to which the production of cheap, highly competitive goods for the low-income market is significantly important in keeping the price of labor low is dependent on what part of the worker's budget is spent on industrialized goods, as against those produced in the informal sector.[7] Not only the size of the industrialized labor force, but the size of the city, may well be important determinants of this.

The capacity of small-scale enterprises to survive in an involutionary manner by means of self-exploitation, resulting in an ability to persist even in downward swings in the business cycle, was found to have implications in terms of its importance in maintaining the reserve army of labor (Quijano 1974) and ensuring a flexible supply of skilled labor that can be drawn into the capitalist system at different phases of the business cycle.[8] The degree to which this reduces wage costs and limits the bargaining strength of organized labor must be considered in relation to the size of the labor surplus.

The proliferation of small-scale enterprises was believed to be a direct consequence of the role of the state and large-scale capital, as well as the interrelationship between the two, in specific economies. Because it functions outside the area of state intervention, small-scale enterprise was thought able to provide a convenient complement to large-scale production. The capacity (in enterprises with less than ten or fifteen workers) to avoid social security payments, minimum wage legislation, regulations concerning work conditions, hours, and age or gender restrictions was found to result in increased outwork and subcontractual contracts, with national level factors an important determinant here. An important conclusion of the debate of the 1970s and early 1980s was that under specific conditions it would be in the interest of large-scale capital, national as well as international, to promote the informal sector as a more profitable method of expansion that avoids overheads by utilizing outworkers while controlling raw materials and markets. In addition, competitive pressures at the international level were identified as resulting in increasing fragmentation of the labor force in certain sectors, with the reappearance of small-scale production as an ancillary to that at the large scale, with technology accordingly broken down into smaller components. Finally, identifying with accuracy the social relations of production in a specific context was deemed critical to understand the diversity of exploitation within the informal sector and its particular function within the city, regional, national, or even international economy.

NOTES

1. Applied through the ILO Employment Policy Convention No. 122.

2. Open unemployment includes persons without work and seeking it; disguised unemployment, persons without work who would probably seek it if unemployment were much lower; open underemployment, persons working less than 32 hours per week and seeking to work longer; disguised under-

employment, people working less than 32 hours per week who would probably seek longer hours if the opportunity were available (ILO 1970).

3. McNeil (1983), in his critique of this problem, identifies the informal sector as a plythetic class involving a cluster of attributes and proposes a methodology of factor analysis as an alternative to treating the informal sector as a monothetic class.

4. MacEwen Scott (1977) defines *petty commodity production* as containing three crucial elements: production of commodities for the market (for exchange value rather than use value); small-scale production (factors associated with this include volume of output, size of work force, size of capital, and level of technology); ownership of the means of production by the direct producer (with very low division of labor within the enterprises).

5. For a discussion of the implications of petty commodity production for analysis of class and class consciousness, see LeBrun and Gerry (1975), Portes (1978), Moser (1978), Kennedy (1979), Gerry and Birkbeck (1979), Middleton (1979), and Bujra (1982), among others.

6. King's (1974) work on the "moving frontier" examines the manner in which the diversification of artisan society has resulted in small-scale enterprise production and broad distribution of a range of cheaper household products and raised the standard of living of peasant and urban families (Moser 1978, p. 1058). As the market becomes more firmly established it will attract larger, more capitalist activities, and this initiates a process of growth and destruction (Bienefeld 1975).

7. For general descriptions of this and the following characteristics of the informal sector in Third World cities, see Portes (1978), Roberts (1978), and Sandbrook (1982).

8. A very well-known seasonal example of this is provided by the construction sector in tropical areas (Moser 1982).

❏ Chapter 3

The Informal Sector Debate, Part 2: 1984-1993

Cathy A. Rakowski

Introduction

The informal sector debate evolved significantly between 1984 and 1993. The main features of the debate have been the continued salience of early issues and the emergence of new issues tied to worldwide economic and political restructuring and a world recession. An important change has been the shift away from an expanding informal sector as a problem for development (or an indicator of the failure of development paradigms) to an emphasis on the informal sector as an asset or solution to economic crisis and poverty. In the spotlight are questions regarding the potential of certain informal activities to generate economic growth and the effectiveness of macroeconomic and poverty alleviation policies and programs. Increasingly popular in Latin America (and among bilateral and multilateral aid agencies) is the notion that informal activities might be a necessary stage or long-term component of developing market economies or even a potentially cost-effective path to "genuine" economic and social development. The latter notion is compatible with the 1990s' emphasis on promoting democratization, efficiency, privatization, poverty alleviation, and grassroots initiatives.

Ongoing "debates" remain over definitional concepts and methodology (Roberts 1991; Portes and Sassen-Koob 1987; Biggs, Grindle, and Snodgrass 1988), but the relative importance and focus have changed. In the 1970s, much energy was expended arguing over terminology and whether the informal sector was half of a dichotomy (economic dualism) or part of a continuum. Methods of study (survey analysis, case studies, ethnographic research) and limitations of existing techniques also dominated discussion. In the 1980s, research energy shifted to understanding the phenomenon regardless of what it was called (Peattie 1987). As a result, by 1993, a multiplicity of terms were used virtually interchangeably. These include *informality* (operating outside or on the margins of the regulatory context), *informal activity, self-employment, subcontracting, microenterprise, informal sector, the underground* or *black market economy* and *casual work*. Previously popular terms like *economic dualism, continuum, petty commodity production, marginality,* and *traditional sector* have fallen from favor. The people who engage in informal activities are equally likely to be called *the poor, unprotected workers, informals, entrepreneurs,* and occasionally, *petty producers* and *casual labor.* More important, research now considers the role of right- and left-wing ideologies in conceptualization and policy formulation (Annis and Franks 1989; Cameron 1989b). And, conversely, some policy analysts argue that the growth of the informal sector can reshape work, social organization, state-society relations, and have an impact on policy implementation and state authority (Franks this volume; Cameron 1989b).

Other important changes took place. The informal sector debate described by Moser was almost exclusively the domain of development economists and academic social scientists. They were joined in the 1980s by private voluntary agencies, community organizers, business leaders, politicians and political parties, and social planners. The debate once took place primarily in consultant reports, United Nations documents, scholarly publications, and at universities, think tanks, professional meetings or in government macroeconomic planning offices. In the 1980s it was extended to a broader arena—the popular press, television, chambers of commerce and business organizations, labor unions, legislative bodies, the offices of international donor agencies, and private voluntary organizations. In part, the growing popularity of the informal sector concept is a result of a convergence of interest in poverty issues and the need for improved policy instruments (Tokman 1987a; Tendler 1988; Peattie 1987). In Latin America, this popularity was reinforced by economic crisis, expanding poverty, and scarcity of financial resources and by cultural, political, and ideological factors such as imported concepts like "underground economy" and "black market," democratization, and a conservative international policy environment (Tokman 1987a, 1987b, 1989; Mezzera 1991; Pérez Sáinz 1991). But popularity has not translated into agreement regarding the nature of the informal sector or the policy needed to support genuine development. Rather, research and policy making have become more specialized—focusing on different segments of the informal sector (or specific activities and industry sectors) with somewhat different origins, potentials and policy needs. As a result, several broad analytical and policy approaches seek to explain the sector. The informal sector concept helped bridge these diverse approaches, but it was unable to integrate them (Peattie 1987, pp. 851–857).[1] The task of this chapter is to outline these broad approaches and show points of convergence and divergence among them (see Table 3.1 on page 34). In so doing, it provides an overview of the critical features of the debate as it has evolved since 1983.

Making Sense of the Dominant Approaches

Many observers identify the debate since 1980 as one between structuralist and legal(ist) schools of thought (Annis and Franks 1989; Tokman 1990). The structuralist school includes the ILO labor market approach (Moser 1978, 1984; Ghersi 1991) that dominated research and policy in the 1970s as well as the neo-Marxists and dependency theorists, whereas the legalist school tends to be (but is not always) a neo-liberal approach (Cartaya 1987; Murphy 1990) that includes broader economic issues such as the functioning of the market, competitiveness, entrepreneurship, and so forth.[2] Essentially, the structuralist school focuses on "cleavages in economic and social composition between formal and informal economies" and "infers that the proper role of the state is to help equalize differences." The legalist school argues that "cleavages are not structural but legal, bureaucratic, of state making" (Annis and Franks 1989, p. 10). A logical starting point for our comparison is the ILO position—more commonly known in Latin America as the *PREALC approach*.

The ILO-PREALC (Structuralist) Approach

Most advocates of the ILO-PREALC version of the informal sector concept find definitional questions unimportant, because the existence of the sector is as obvious as the existence of a Third World or a middle class. This version of the concept has encouraged a social democratic and reformist agenda through promotion of appropriate technologies, indigenous enterprise, local self-help, and an important government role in supporting informal sector enterprises (Bromley 1990, p. 338).

Table 3.1 Comparison of Selected Aspects of the Four Major Approaches, 1984–1993

DIMENSION	ILO-PREALC	UNDERGROUND	LEGALIST	MICROENTERPRISE
1. Approach	1. Structuralist	1. Structuralist and legalist	1. Legalist	1. Mixed
2. Unit of study	2. Surveys, size + type employment	2. Subcontracting, conditions of work not regulated, not legal, status of labor, form of managment	2. Small firms, entrepreneurs	2. Entrepreneur group, community
3. Theoretical model and methods	3. Segmentation, case studies, surveys	3. Production chains, firm linkages	3. Neo-liberal	3. Atheoretical or neo-liberal, case study
4. Origin of sector	4. Nature of development	4. Nature of capitalism, informalization	4. Excessive legal cost, bureaucratization, poverty	4. Poverty
5. Nature of Sector	5. Dualistic, marginal, heterogeneous	5. Subordinate, heterogeneous	5. Rational, moral, dualistic	5. Rational
6. Function	6. Survival strategy, absorb surplus labor	6. Keep labor cost low, competitiveness high	6. Survival strategy, avoid costs	6. Survival strategy
7. Focus	7. Nature of linkages, industrialization, labor market change	7. Nature of production economy	7. Cost of regulation, firm organization	7. The poor
8. Role of sector in development	8. Safety net for crisis, income for poor, capable of growth	8. Accumulate capital, impoverish workers, capable of growth	8. Create wealth, reduce costs, democratize	8. Create jobs and income, supply goods and services
9. Agenda	9. Social democratic reform, macroeconomic policy	9. Academic theory, empirical knowledge	9. Policy: legalize	9. Growth of firm + income, poverty alleviation, empower poor, massify programs
10. Role of state	10. Stimulate macroeconomy, social welfare, support entrepreneurship	10. Application of labor standards	10. Reform institutions promote small firm	10. Appropriate policy environment for massification, support NGO work

PREALC (Employment Program for Latin America and the Caribbean) is a policy-oriented organization and think tank composed primarily of economists. Its approach is illustrated in its publications (PREALC 1987a, 1990), the writings of its long-time director Victor Tokman (1987a, 1987b, 1989, 1990, 1991), and the publications of staff and collaborators like Jaime Mezzera (1987, 1990, 1991), Gustavo Márquez (this volume; Márquez and Portela 1991), Daniel Carbonetto (1984), and Vanessa Cartaya (this volume, 1990b; Cartaya and García 1988; Cartaya and Márquez 1990). Despite widespread criticism, proponents of the ILO-PREALC approach continue to use a dualistic definitional concept[3] (usually modern-informal) linked to size (small), type of employment or way of doing things–organizing production (self-employment, family firms, low levels of capital, unsophisticated technology), and outcomes (low productivity, poverty). Research focuses on linkages between labor market growth, the nature of industrialization (e.g., capital intensive), rural-urban migration, growth in the urban labor force and poverty (Tokman 1987a, 1987b; Mezzera 1990, 1991; Pérez Sáinz 1991).[4]

The contemporary ILO-PREALC approach emphasizes labor market segmentation models over human capital models as tools for analyzing labor markets (Mezzera 1990; Márquez and Portela 1991). Case studies of productive units complement census and survey analyses. Cost of legalizing enterprises and the content of laws and regulations are considered important contextual variables that influence (but do not cause) informality (which is "a certain form of production within a structural context characterized by an excess labor supply and a low demand for well-paid jobs") (Tokman 1990, p. 22).

Few PREALC analysts refer to informal activities as *traditional* although critics argue this is implicit in the modern-informal point of segmentation used in labor market analyses (Portes 1989b). Finally, the *heterogeneous nature* of the informal sector is emphasized (Tokman 1989; Márquez, this volume; PREALC 1987a, 1990; Mezzera 1991). Causes of heterogeneity are posited to include economic conditions (prosperity, recession) and policies (structural adjustment, welfare subsidies, etc.). Studies include income segmentation and comparisons across industry sectors and subsectors (e.g., manufacturing, services and commerce) and between informals (the self -employed, entrepreneurs, microenterprise workers, domestic servants) and productive units (microenterprises).

This approach identifies at least two strata of informal activities—the survival strategies of the permanent poor (people with deficient human capital or tracked into marginal jobs because of their characteristics) and the "conjunctural" unemployed (who have lost jobs or whose incomes have declined due to economic crisis and structural adjustment policies) (Tokman 1987a, 1987b; Mezzera 1987, 1990, 1991; Márquez and Portela 1991). Therefore, PREALC argues that the informal sector acted as a social welfare and unemployment "safety net" in countries that have no welfare system. A third, small group—entrepreneurs with growth potential—includes individuals from both strata.

The PREALC approach proposes that the *primary* path to development and to poverty alleviation is macroeconomic policy that emphasizes expanding modern sector employment and incomes. But—as pointed out by Márquez (this volume), a complementary package of mutually reinforcing policies are advocated to address the myriad factors that affect job creation, productivity, and income (Tokman 1989, 1990; Mezzera 1987, 1990; Márquez and Portela 1991; Carbonetto 1984).

The Underground Economy (Structuralist) Approach

The underground economy approach combines structuralism—neo-Marxist focus on economic restructuring and class cleavages—with legalism—selective compliance with or avoidance of regulations and laws. It has been called alternately *the black market approach, the world-systems approach,* and even the *Portes approach* (Cartaya 1987, 1988; Berger 1988; Murphy 1990).[5] Because the term *underground* is used in several writings, this is the label used here.

The underground approach evolved among academics in the noneconomic social sciences. Policy relevance has not been of primary concern, but rather contributing to empirical knowledge and social science theory.

Underground proponents reject economic dualism and focus on the way in which forms of production, productive units, technologies, and workers are integrated into local, regional and international economies. Underground language includes terms like *industrial restructuring,"* the *internationalization of capital,* and *flexible specialization; informal economy* is preferred over *informal sector.* Research on the underground assesses relations of production (especially mechanisms for subordinating labor), circuits of accumulation (e.g., linkages between informal activities and large firms), class cleavages, and the (re)organization of production under changing economic, institutional, social, and legal conditions, flexible specialization, libertarianism, and exploitation and greed. Research includes labor market analyses (using survey and census data) and case studies of specific industries and their workers (Portes and Sassen-Koob 1987, p. 31; Portes, Castells, and Benton 1989; Benería and Roldán 1987; Roldán 1985; Fernández-Kelly 1983; Armstrong and McGee 1985). Because "informal economic processes cut across the whole social structure," research focuses on the "social dynamics underlying the production of such conditions" (Castells and Portes 1989, p. 12).

Despite a long-standing debate between Tokman and Portes (Tokman 1987b; Portes 1989b), there are many points of agreement between the underground approach and the PREALC approach. Both focus on forms of production, identify economic restructuring or crises as factors in the expansion of informality and its changing role in the 1980s, and accept the heterogeneity of the informal economy. For the underground, this includes activities like direct subsistence, small-scale production and trade and subcontracting to semiclandestine enterprises and homeworkers (Portes and Sassen-Koob 1987). Both see a link between informality and impoverishment of workers (although they differ on important details): "the informal economy is not a set of survival strategies performed by destitute people on the margins of society. . . . It is a specific form of relationships of production, while poverty is an attribute linked to the process of distribution" (Castells and Portes 1989, p. 12).

Both approaches conclude that informality is the "expression of the uneven nature of capitalist development" in peripheral societies (Peattie 1990; Portes and Sassen-Koob 1987; Castells and Portes 1989; Portes, Castells, and Benton 1989; Feldman 1991). Finally, both agree that informal economies can be growth economies under certain conditions: technological advancement, an export orientation, and relative autonomy (when not integrated into vertical hierarchies of subcontracting) (Portes, Castells and Benton 1989, pp. 302–303). Although not policy oriented, underground proponents agree with the advisability of a heterogeneous policy package and the need for state intervention to reduce inequalities, limit exploitation, and support entrepreneurial endeavors (Tokman 1989; Portes, Castells, and Benton 1989).

The underground approach also differs from the PREALC approach in important respects, including attributing subcontracting to greed, interpretation of the consequence of linkages with the "formal" sector (exploitation), and assessment of the nature of segmentation and the direction of future economic change (more subcontracting and noncompliance with labor regulations). More important, they emphasize that informality is present both in peripheral and in advanced economies and that peripheral economies are themselves "modern"; both informal and formal activities are features of capitalism that fulfill necessary functions for the accumulation of capital, including the disenfranchisement of organized labor (Castells and Portes 1989, p. 11). Thus, the underground approach rejects the notion of social marginality implicit in the PREALC approach. Firms "go underground"—large firms subcontract to small firms, large firms engage in illegal hiring practices—to lower costs associated with protective labor legislation, and the defining feature of informality is lack of regulation "by the institutions of society, in a legal and social environment in which similar activities are regulated" (p. 12). "Informalization"—a concept coined by the proponents of this approach—is a mechanism to reverse the costly process of proletarianization and weaken the rights of workers and unions with the acquiescence of the state in the interest of renewed economic growth (Roberts 1991; Portes, Castells, and Benton 1989, pp. 298, 308; Castells and Portes 1989, pp. 26–27; Safa 1987; Portes this volume). For this reason, workers in the informal sector are "downgraded labor"—they receive few benefits and low wages and have poor working conditions.

States support informalization because it grants competitive advantage. Economic activities can be informalized *passively* when state regulation is extended selectively (e.g., to large firms, but not to small-scale firms) or *actively* when some firms and private interests gain a market advantage by avoiding some state controls (e.g., subcontracting of production to small firms or the hiring of a casual labor force not subject to stability and benefits) (Portes, Castells, and Benton 1989, p. 299; Castells and Portes 1989, pp. 26–27).

In what is not merely an argument over semantics, proponents of the underground approach claim the informal sector represents not a segment of the labor market (as PREALC argues), but a segment of the *economy* (Portes and Sassen-Koob 1987, p. 31). An informal sector is maintained and grows through "the juxtaposition of *extensive labor legislation* . . . and an *abundant labor supply*" (Portes and Sassen-Koob 1987, p. 38). This can be contrasted with the PREALC position that "laws are not the cause of informality . . . operating outside the margin of the law is the result of a certain form of production within a structural context characterized by an excess labor supply and a low demand for well paid jobs" (Tokman 1990, p. 22).

Despite significant overlap in their positions, underground proponents have been highly critical of the PREALC definition of the informal sector as small scale, easy entry, a "way of doing things." The underground approach proposes "informality" should be conceptualized alternately as a "status of labor" (undeclared and noncontractual, lacking benefits, paid less than minimum wage, etc.), "conditions of work" (hazardous, unprotected [Portes and Sassen-Koob 1987; Castells and Portes 1989]), "form of management of some firms" (fiscal fraud, unrecorded payments), and as the "nature" of work (extralegal [Castells and Portes 1989]). This conceptualization has important policy implications for the welfare of workers (Portes, this volume). But a critical shortcoming is the impossibility of operationalizing the concept for aggregate analyses—censuses and surveys include no variables with this information. Therefore, case studies—expensive, time consuming—are needed.[6]

Peattie is dissatisfied with both PREALC and the underground approach. She says research should focus on the "real world" for grounding policy and action. In this "real world," there would be institutions instead of "the economy," entrepreneurs and firms instead of industries and sectors, employers and workers with "particular purposes and characteristics" instead of labor and labor markets; and the "state would be just another actor to be studied." Economic modeling and academic theorizing only contribute to the "fuzziness" of the informal sector concept (Peattie 1990, pp. 32–34). Underground case studies of specific production chains and conditions behind restructuring and employment practices fulfill her mandate and revealed that informality is not limited to peripheral economies, but is typical of advanced economies as well.

The Legalist or ILD-de Soto Approach

Issues of regulation and extralegality are at the heart of "new stars" in the debate—the Peruvian Hernando de Soto and the think tank primarily of economists and lawyers he founded (the ILD–Instituto Libertad y Democracia). This approach is neo-liberal and does not rely on economic modeling or academic research. Terms like *moral, efficient, rational* and *democratic* season publications. It purports to be based on the real world economics Peattie advocates—the study of entrepreneurs and the institutional constraints that make informality a rational economic strategy. Methods (criticized as "sloppy") include surveys, interviews, document analysis, case studies of subsectors, and "real-world experiments" (Rossini and Thomas 1990; ILD 1990b). Frequently cited is their step-by-step analysis of staff experience in trying to set up a legal sewing workshop (de Soto 1989).

Legalists differ with the PREALC and underground approaches in their assessment of the primary causes and outcomes of informality and in the role of the informal sector in economic growth. They agree with PREALC that informality is encouraged by rural-urban migration. It is "survival strategies"—"a safety valve for societal tensions" (de Soto 1989, p. 243)—undertaken by the poor with "ingenuity and entrepreneurial spirit" (Bromley 1990, p. 328; Main 1989). The informals are *forced* into extralegality (and poverty) because of discriminatory state regulations and costs that advantage powerful economic interest groups that compete unfairly with informals who have no property rights and no access to credit. Whereas the underground approach sees informalization originating in large firms' attempts to evade costs, legalists see informalization originating in small-scale entrepreneur's efforts to avoid costs. Dualism is between privileged and nonprivileged enterprises (Márquez and Portela 1991, p. 8) with legality a privilege of those with political and economic power. Informality is the people's "spontaneous and creative response to the state's incapacity to satisfy the basic needs of the impoverished masses" and to the system that has "traditionally made them victims of a kind of legal and economic apartheid" (de Soto 1989, pp. xiv–xv). This legalist approach has had a profound impact on the public image of the informal sector and on policy (Bromley, this volume; Biggs, Grindle, and Snodgrass 1988; Jenkins 1988).

The legalist concepts of *informality, informal activities, informals,* or *informal sector* and *entrepreneurs* (used interchangeably) share with the PREALC approach notions of dualism and the marginalization of certain actors or activities. In contrast to the underground focus on production chains and subordinated subcontracting, legalists emphasize income generating efforts and expenditure saving activities. Although they discard the assumption that informals are always poor, de Soto frequently refers to the informals as *the poor.*

Legalists reject the notion that the problems of Latin American economies are the result of external factors like imperialism. They see in the informals the hope for competitive capitalist development if only the state will get out of the market and eliminate the bureaucratic maze and costs associated with legalizing business operations. The informals-poor are the backbone of a country's economy, risking all their assets in daily transactions, providing vital services and enhancing a nation's human resources through the development of craft and entrepreneurial skills and increased capacity to educate themselves and their children. They help reduce imports and indebtedness by providing goods and services and constructing necessary infrastructure (housing, markets, transportation systems) (Bromley, this volume; de Soto 1989). In other words, they create wealth—albeit unrecognized officially as such—and represent a genuine path to development. They also hold the key to true democracy as they rebel against state favoritism (de Soto 1988, pp. 29–31); they are not "passive objects in need of assistance programs" (de Soto 1989, p. 242). If their "entrepreneurial spirit were legalized and nurtured rather than fettered and suppressed . . . a burst of competitive energy would be released, living standards would start rising, international trade would increase, developing countries could service their huge and debilitating external debts more easily" (Main 1989, p. 15).

The preceding passages make clear why one of the major criticisms of this approach is that it romanticizes the self-employed and owners of microenterprises.[7] It also does not consider the exploitation of unprotected microenterprise employees; and, although there may be elements of truth in the legalist discussion of overregulation, bribes, and costs, the notion that an unregulated economy offers a "magical solution" to Latin America's problem of underdevelopment is pure speculation (Portes 1991). The legalist position overlooks the fact that inefficiency and bureaucratization exist in advanced economies, too (Bromley 1990, p. 334; Portes, this volume).

A notion shared by the underground and legalist approaches is that of selective informality—firms and informals break only specific (unfair, exceedingly disadvantageous) laws and regulations (de Soto 1989, p. 12; Portes, this volume). Legalists also agree with PREALC on some characteristics of informal activities—including the small scale of operation, rudimentary technology, and that informality is a way of organizing production—as a consequence of state regulations and their costs (Márquez and Portela 1991, p. 8; Bromley, this volume), not as a result of the human capital characteristics of individuals or labor market segmentation (de Soto 1989, p. 185).

Legalists and underground proponents also share the notion that dealing with growing and persistent informalization has contributed to ambivalent or contradictory behavior on the part of the state. The underground calls this the *informalization of the state* through the selective application of rules and regulations whereas the legalists refer to it as the state's conscious acts to defend the status quo and respond to privileged interest groups or state dependence on the informal sector to supply goods and services the state cannot or will not.[8] Therefore, the state tolerates small, extralegal firms (though some may be harassed) and even stimulates some informal activities as a way to resolve potential social conflicts or promote political patronage.[9]

The legalist approach has had a profound impact in numerous settings, and ILD-like think tanks have been established in other Latin American countries and in some African countries (Jenkins 1988). Documents emphasize what Hopenhayn (1987) calls the *solidarity economy* characterized by social conscience, organizational culture, capacity for action, popular creativity, mutual aid, dedication, and innovation—the means to moral, democratic development in civil society (Razeto Migliaro 1986) and stabilizing political systems (Kilby 1988). This "hides" economic causes of informality like limited demand for labor, lack of access to capital and markets, and exploitation of informals by large firms.

Portes provides one of the strongest criticisms of the legalist approach by pointing to weaknesses in its argument that regulation and labor protection disadvantage small firms, not large firms, and that the state favors large firms. Portes counters that small firms manage to survive by taking (unfair?) advantage of state regulations that apply to large firms. Thus, legality is a *burden* for large firms, not a *privilege*. Additionally, the legalist support for removal of regulation and labor protection could hurt small firms by making large firms more agile and competitive relative to informals (Portes 1991). Many of the most profitable activities would cease being profitable were markets liberalized (Jenkins 1988, p. 231). Furthermore, there are discriminatory divisions within the informal sector (Jenkins 1988, p. 227) and these are not addressed by the legalist approach. For instance, labor market and income segmentation studies carried out by PREALC and others suggest that microenterprise workers are the most disadvantaged and exploited segment of the labor force—by keeping wages low, avoiding compliance with labor benefits, and using unpaid family labor, small firms achieve competitive advantage. Thus, many analysts—including Portes, Márquez, and McKean in this volume—find morally questionable support for a form of production based on the exploitation of workers.

Recent research by PREALC seriously questions the legalist claim that the costs of legality and nonlegal status disadvantage small firms. Studies of such costs in various Latin American cities found they vary widely across settings as did the advantages and disadvantages of size or legality. Only certain costs were important obstacles to legality (Mesa-Lago 1990). Even informal entrepreneurs express fear legalization would be the first step in the introduction of new taxes and control (Bromley 1992).

The importance of the work of de Soto and other legalists is that it draws attention away from the characteristics of workers, activities, and exclusively economic factors in development and toward the role of institutions, power and politics in development: "A country's entrepreneurial reserves do not automatically function properly, they do so only if prevailing institutions allow them to" (de Soto 1989, p. 244; 1988, p. 16; Bromley 1990).

Entrepreneurship, support for microenterprise development, poverty alleviation, and popular initiatives are concepts associated with other approaches to the discussion of informality. These concepts have been reinforced by the growing visibility in the 1980s of nongovernmental organizations, international donor agencies, and private business groups that target poverty alleviation through small enterprise development (Sullivan 1987; Levitsky 1988; Liedholm and Mead 1987; SEEP Network 1988; Kilby 1988; GEMINI 1990–; ACCION International and the Calmeadow Foundation 1988). These organizations have become important participants in the informal sector debate in the 1980s and in some places the success of their programs has influenced development policy. Although not formally organized into an analytical or policy "approach," to facilitate discussion they will be referred to as the *microenterprise development approach*.

The Microenterprise Development Approach

The "proponents" of this "approach" are action oriented, disinterested in conceptual issues, and only marginally concerned with theories of the origin of microenterprises (considered synonymous with *informal sector, poverty*, and *entrepreneurship*). Typically neo-liberal, they feel comfortable with legalist arguments that reinforce their own sense of faith and confidence in the ability of the poor to defend themselves and survive. They seek to level the playing field, expand jobs and improve productivity and income; some aim to empower individual entrepreneurs, groups, or communities. Their focus is practical and they promote, fund, and carry out programs that address the needs of the poor. Many base needs assessments and program design on "participatory research"—knowledge acquired through interaction with informals—and evaluations of the success of past programs.

Although these organizations have no formal label, their umbrella organizations, pamphlets, evaluations, instructional manuals, and papers are most easily identified by the use of the term *microenterprise*[10] and by their focus on practical action for social and economic change. Practical action typically includes credit programs, "solidarity groups," and entrepreneurship training in management, marketing, and accounting. This is the language of efficiency and of the individual pursuit of self interest, rather than a language of rights of the weak or of justice (Pruegl 1989).

Though they represent the types of micro level interventions long advocated by PREALC, NGOs and PVOs engaged in microenterprise development have been quick to embrace many of the ideas of the legalist school, especially de Soto. Some observers have gone so far as to say they see de Soto as a "potential savior"[11] and his informal sector as the "new economic hero" (Márquez and Portela 1991, p. 2; Bromley 1990, p. 330) that provides a sounder basis for development than "skeptical bureaucracies and traffickers in privileges" and behind whose products and services lie "sophisticated calculations and risk-taking ability" (de Soto 1989, p. 243).

Because microenterprise promotion is practical, it incorporates those elements of each approach that can contribute to poverty alleviation. This is illustrated clearly by a pamphlet published by ACCION International (circa 1986) that combines de Soto's arguments with elements of both the PREALC and underground approaches:

> The informal sector is the vast market economy that has developed in Third World cities without imported economic models, government subsidies, or foreign aid. Its tenacious growth, despite enormous obstacles, gives new meaning to the term 'free enterprise' in Latin America . . . all micro-businesses are labor-intensive, small-scale and usually family owned and operated. Capital inputs are minimal, . . . enterprises rely . . . on indigenous resources and markets . . . transactions take place outside economic mainstream; they are not taxed, licensed, safety-inspected or . . . registered in national income accounts.
>
> Micro-businesses create jobs . . . increase national income . . . provide vocational training . . . supply needed goods and services . . . promote a broad distribution of wealth (as a basis for economic democracy . . . particularly for women and the unskilled . . .). Far from obstructing development, the informal sector represents the single most generative source of new jobs and income for the majority of the population . . .

Microenterprise promotion evolved from poverty alleviation activities dating from the 1960s. Some programs started as charitable and disaster relief operations (Korten 1987); others were founded specifically to bring multinational corporate funds to the aid of Latin America's urban poor (GEMINI 1990–). Some started as Christian youth movements and peace corps equivalents hoping to contribute to a better world (Korten 1987; MO).[12] International groups predominated in the 1960s, but by the late 1970s, groups were equally likely to be of international or local origin. Local groups often had international financial support.

Charitable and welfare organizations started with short-term goals, but their work turned out to be never ending. As a result, many found their organizational structure "institutionalizing" and their staff "professionalizing." From direct assistance and welfare, they were transformed over time into organizations that focused on "helping the poor help themselves." By the early 1970s, their work concentrated on supporting self-help initiatives and grassroots economic projects (Korten 1987; MO). Some encountered state resistance because they competed for international funds or undercut clientilistic programs with political ends.

Rural-urban migration in Latin America increased concentration of NGO activities in urban areas in the late 1970s. Activities included health, vocational training, day care, community organization (along democratic principles), self-help housing, and community development (construction of infrastructure, provision of basic services, etc.). After the United Nations' International Women's conference in Mexico City in 1975, many NGOs targeted women for the first time (MO).

The shift to support for income generating activities was a natural outgrowth of collective and cumulative experience in helping organize community groups. But different strategies were required in urban settings, where there were no cooperative systems for land owners or agrarian reform programs; gradually programs began to target individuals as well as groups. Growth in the informal sector in neighborhoods where NGO activities concentrated heightened awareness of unregulated, low resource survival strategies of the poor, especially female household heads (MO).

The idea of empowering the poor through social welfare and economic projects grew out of experience. NGOs found clients excluded from formal credit systems and disadvantaged by lack of training and productive inputs. NGOs gradually shifted programs in the direction of promoting access to resources. Initially, the political contexts in which NGOs operated and their negative experience with government supported programs encouraged them to keep their distance from state agencies. Thus, NGOs created a niche where they did not compete with governments or multi- and bilateral agencies (MO).

Credit and technical service programs required different technical and financial skills than community development programs (Korten 1987; Klein, Keeley and Carlisle 1991; MO). To facilitate the transition, NGOs established a pattern of dialogue and networking among themselves[13] (gradually incorporating donor agencies) and found through experience that exchange of information was critical to improving the impact of their work. Program evaluation also helped (see McKean, this volume), but networking overcame the limited access to funding for research and program evaluation and for staff training (Drabek 1987; Bromley 1992).

As the 1980s drew to a close, NGOs expanded their role due to the amount of unmet need and assumed a role of catalyst for micro and macro level policies (Korten 1987). They set up a dialogue with governments and the private sector (Paul 1988; Otero, this volume) and joined with the private sector—business leaders, foundations, corporations—for the express goal of "massification" (applying the NGO method and philosophy on a broader scale to help increasing numbers of entrepreneurs and poor families) (Bejar 1987; Korten 1987). As Otero (this volume) points out, massification and overcoming institutional obstacles demand government and private sector collaboration (Padrón, Castro, Neumann, and Rodriguez 1991).[14] Through dialogue with the state and the private sector, NGOs' essentially atheoretical, pragmatic approach to poverty alleviation has managed to displace some the overly theoretical macroeconomic models of PREALC and strengthened the influence of the neo-liberal legalists.

There are criticisms of the microenterprise approach. One criticism is that they engage in a menu approach to policy and programs to support microenterprise development: deregulation, tax reform, access to credit, technical assistance, economic efficiency, education and training, linkages between formal and informal sectors, and so on. (Sullivan 1987; Levitsky 1988). Although there is substantial agreement among approaches on the need for policy changes to accelerate growth and improve the welfare of the poor, there is disagreement on how to go about this and how to accomplish policies of great magnitude. For instance, should or can the informals be incorporated into formal sectors (e.g., legalized, taxed)? Should they be provided special privileges and subsidies even if it is unlikely that they can graduate to formal status? Priorities need to be established. But differences of opinion on appropriate policies are rampant among those who promote small enterprises, including voluntary organizations, foundations, and international agents (Bromley 1990, p. 345). Proponents of microenterprise promotion have not achieved consensus on a comprehensive strategy for economic development and poverty alleviation.

Final Comments

The preceding discussion reveals several important trends. Over time, the language of the informal sector debate has become simpler and the conceptual framework and discussion of theory less muddled and academic. Proponents of different approaches appear to "speak to" each other's concerns and critiques in their publications, pamphlets and program designs. In part, this may be explained by the natural evolution of ideas and methods over time and by improved access to the growing body of informal sector literature. Certainly, the importance of the informal sector as a policy phenomenon created a demand for analyses and policy recommendations framed in terms easily understood and applied by planners and policy makers. In dialogue with each other, proponents of opposing approaches have had to simplify and focus issues, arguments, and concepts to make them understandable to each other. These changes can contribute to a more flexible and comprehensive approach for analyzing complex socioeconomic systems.

Important disagreements make difficult an integrated approach. One issue is whether the state should be involved in supporting small firms (e.g., through credit and training) as argued by PREALC and NGOs or large firms (through macroeconomic policies) as also argued by PREALC, should withdraw from intervening in the market as argued by the legalists (deregulation, debureaucratization and privatization), should change its form of intervention to make it more equitable as suggested by the underground approach (uniform application of labor standards), or focus on providing an appropriate institutional environment for democracy and a market economy (as Peattie and microenterprise proponents would suggest).

Also not resolved is whether or not ignoring small enterprises for decision making and policy formulation produces diseconomies, waste, inefficiency, and hardship without concrete benefits to larger scale enterprises (Bromley 1985, p. 330). There is some evidence that microenterprise intervention can be inefficient, discriminatory, susceptible to paternalism, favoritism, corruption, and victimization, which would support the need to regulate broader economic, social, and physical environmental conditions (which affect numbers, types, and sizes of microenterprises), rather than support or constrain microenterprises on a selective basis (Bromley 1985, p. 333; Liedholm and Mead 1987).

Promotion of the informal sector has implications for changing the balance of power, for long-range planning, for implementation of programs and plans, for the legitimacy of the state. Bringing informals into the policy arena and supporting microenterprises may lead to empowerment and democratization, but not necessarily to a more rational and competitive economy. Informals may become merely one more officially recognized interest group able to gain special privileges that disadvantage other groups. Cameron (1989b) finds that the informals are pragmatic and support those groups and institutions that provide the goods and services they need to survive. Including informals in decision making may require advocacy programs and government efforts for building grassroots constituencies (Sullivan 1987), and it is unlikely that state officials will reduce their patronage potential or give up their authority and privileges (Jenkins 1988, p. 224).

Some ideological differences among approaches may be insurmountable. Is the problem one of directing scarce resources at amelioration of poverty or is it one of low productivity requiring human capital and technical change (Biggs, Grindle, and Snodgrass 1988, p. 141)? Should the most dynamic firms be promoted or the playing field be leveled? Would support for the formal or informal sector be a better means of creating jobs and increasing production? Some argue that informal work may be rational and efficient in the short run, but in the long run economic and social gains may depend on achieving higher productivity through more efficient units of production that draw labor into sectors with better protection of property and contractual rights and higher wages and benefits (Biggs, Grindle, and Snodgrass 1988, pp. 141–142).

Finally, can development occur through consensus and can consensus be achieved in socioeconomic systems through a coalition of support encouraged by the active leadership of policy makers? Or will development and poverty alleviation depend on a centralized, technocratic, authoritarian regime that may have to use coercion to introduce significant policy changes (Biggs, Grindle, and Snodgrass 1988, pp. 163–165)?

These are issues which will be debated through the 1990s.[15]

NOTES

1. In her much cited 1987 article, Peattie concludes that the concept should be relegated to "an item in the history and sociology of ideas" that contributed to the identification of problems in the functioning of a complex economy, gave standing to a variety of economic activities that otherwise would probably have been ignored in policy, and opened a space for considerations that might be called *political* or *moral*. She cautions that lumping diverse activities together and separating them conceptually from others to which they are linked will make it harder to carry out analyses and arrive at useful conclusions. But Peattie's is pretty much a lone voice; definitional issues simply are no longer considered critical and are treated as distractions to understanding informal activities and addressing the needs of the poor and the economies in which they operate. Ironically, her comment on the concept as a "real phenomenon" in policy and planning has attracted attention, rather than her central argument that the term is not useful, is "fuzzy," obscures analysis of central issues, and is counterproductive for research and policy formulation. In fact, there is support for integrating diverse approaches into a multifaceted, comprehensive approach. See Bejar (1987) and Hopenhayn (1987).

2. Ghersi (1991) also identifies a cultural approach—"the British social anthropologists."

3. Márquez (this volume) argues that their commitment to a dualistic terminology is explained by the way in which the concept is operationalized.

Operationalization is determined by the assumptions underlying census and survey instruments (e.g., a market economy) and the limited range of variables for measuring economic activity (e.g., enterprise size, industry sector, worker classification).

4. PREALC has focused much of its research on large urban areas. Moser (1984) and Long and Roberts (1978) find ample evidence of informality in secondary cities and towns, and Liedholm and Mead (1987) argue that informality in Africa is more widespread in rural areas.

5. In the early 1980s, Manuel Castells, Alejandro Portes, and a group of Latin American sociologists organized a working group to study and discuss case studies of the informal sector in different settings, primarily in Latin America. The group expanded gradually over time to include graduate students and European sociologists studying "black markets" and underground economies in Europe and the United States. Two conferences were organized by Portes and held at Harper's Ferry. The second conference culminated in an edited volume: Alejandro Portes, Manuel Castells, and Lauren A. Benton, eds., *The Informal Economy: Studies in Advanced and Less Developed Countries* (Baltimore: Johns Hopkins Press, 1989).

6. Many underground analysts resort to some variation on the PREALC form of operationalization (e.g., self-employment, unpaid family workers, and size of enterprise) to estimate the relative importance of informality (see Portes and Sassen-Koob 1987).

7. During a lecture to the Venezuelan Chamber of Commerce in 1986, de Soto revealed that "entrepreneurs" interviewed by ILD staff tended to identify themselves as "workers" (not capitalists) who preferred stable wage employment.

8. Interestingly, de Soto both argues that informality is widespread (responsible for 42.6 percent of all housing in Lima, 93 percent of the urban transport fleet, built 83 percent of all public markets) and that it is "traditional" and "institutionalized." He cites records from as early as 1920 referring to efforts to control land invasions and the state's acceptance of invasions as an accepted means of acquiring property (de Soto 1989, pp. 37–52). In fact, street trading was first addressed in law and policy in 1594 and numerous laws between 1915 and the 1970s cite efforts to regulate vending (pp. 75–78). In 1965 the state legally recognized minibus operators, in 1971 informal transportation systems and organizations were incorporated into the design of transportation policy, and by the 1980s, organizations of informals had their own political candidates (pp. 78–87, 110–117).

9. Bromley (1985) addresses the issue of informalization when he discusses the "paradoxical relation between official repression and the evident functionality of small enterprises." He cites the following factors encouraging repression: (1) elites and governments hold negative stereotypes of the poor, (2) unionized workers and political parties have been disinterested in the prob-

lems of petty entrepreneurs, (3) governments may use sporadic repression to impress elites although in fact doing nothing serious to eliminate informal enterprises, (4) persecution may concentrate on enterprises that are unacceptable or unimportant to the urban economy and on those targeted by pressure or interest groups, and (5) governments may not understand the importance of these activities or the linkages between microenterprises and large firms subcontracting to them (pp. 328–329).

10. Pruegl (1989) argues that "microentrepreneurs" are not a self-identifying class (as de Soto would have them be), but a "construction of international development practitioners; part of the vocabulary used in an ongoing discourse in development practice which is dominated by a liberal theology."

11. See numerous references to de Soto in the publications of the SEEP network, ACCION International, the World Bank, U.S. Agency for International Development, Inter-American Development Bank, among others.

12. Insight into microenterprise promotion also was provided by conversations (1984–1990) with William Burrus, executive director of ACCION International, and staff members of CESAP (Centro de Servicio al Acción Popular) in Venezuela. During long phone conversations, María Otero provided valuable information on the history and evolution of NGOs and PVOs. Ideas that should be attributed to her are cited as MO in the text.

13. The two best known networks are SEEP (through PACT at the United Nations) and the Committee of Donor Agencies for Small Enterprise Development housed at the World Bank.

14. Private foundations also have entered the informal sector debate. Some, like the Carvajal Foundation in Colombia and Mendoza Foundation in Venezuela provide training, credit, and technical assistance to microentrepreneurs. Others, like the Friedrich Ebert Foundation's research organization ILDIS (with offices in several countries) fund, carry out, and disseminate research findings through conferences and publications.

15. Exciting empirical research is underway in diverse economic and political contexts. As of April 1993, research efforts include consideration of the impact of cutbacks in financial support for microenterprise programs, on the combined impact on informality of the aging of the population (as a result of increasing life expectancies) and the contraction of state employment (e.g., as older workers are pushed out of employment or families need funds to cover health care of the elderly, informal activities expand), on the characteristics and work history of traders and street vendors (to assess whether or not these fit the characteristics described by Hernando de Soto for Lima), and on the impact of NAFTA (trade liberalization) on informal activities.

Chapter 4

The Many Roles of the Informal Sector in Development: Evidence from Urban Labor Market Research, 1940-1989

Orlandina de Oliveira and Bryan Roberts

Introduction

In this chapter, we explore the role of the informal sector in economic development through a study of urban labor markets in Latin America. Although the estimated share of informal sector employment has remained relatively constant since the 1940s at a third or more of urban employment,[1] research evidence indicates the role of the informal sector in the urban economy has altered with changes in the demand for and supply of labor. Changes in demand occurred as Latin America passed through different phases of industrialization accompanied by growth of service employment, particularly producer and social services. Changes in supply have been equally important and are due to increasing levels of education, declining rates of rural-urban migration, and increasing female participation in the labor market.

This chapter draws upon two approaches to analyze the informal sector, each of which gives a different emphasis to demand and supply side factors (see the PREALC approach and the Underground approach, preceding chapter). One approach focuses on the characteristics of enterprises and defines the informal sector as very small-scale enterprise—the self-employed, owners and workers, unpaid family workers, and in some analyses, domestic servants (PREALC 1976).[2] The other approach emphasizes state regulation and defines the informal sector as employment that is unprotected by existing labor legislation in such matters as minimum wage, social security benefits, contracts, or health and safety ordinances (Portes and Sassen-Koob 1987). There is an overlap between the workers and enterprises included in these definitions.[3]

The focus on the characteristics of informal enterprise addresses the demand side of the labor market and employer policies. Employer policies that give rise to informal enterprises arise from a variety of sources: economic restructuring aimed at reducing labor or capital costs by subcontracting parts of the production of goods or services to small-scale enterprise or domestic workers; and the structure of product markets in which large firms dominate most of the market, but leave specialized niches for small firms to meet more volatile and less profitable parts of the market.

State regulation or intervention is, in contrast, mainly a supply side variable. It distorts the supply of labor by creating a division between protected formal workers with relatively high wages and unprotected informal workers with low wages (World Bank 1990b). Employers have no incentive to create formal employment because of the premium paid to protected workers, whereas there are incentives to informalize in order to avoid the fiscal burden imposed by labor legislation (see Portes, this volume). State regulation can also affect the supply of labor directly, by providing disincentives to enter paid work at low prices, as is the case of some types of unemployment benefit schemes (see Davies and Elias 1990 for the British case). These disincentives reduce the supply of labor in general, but especially to informal firms (where low pay is likely to be concentrated). Conversely, of particular relevance in Latin America, the lack of unemployment benefits or other welfare payments compels people to find or generate income, however low, and this increases the supply of labor in general.

The demand and supply side approaches can be applied to an analysis of the characteristics of urban labor in Latin America, including the gender structure of the labor force. This chapter examines the factors that produce change in gendered labor market structure (both the supply and demand sides), including household responsibilities and social norms. For instance, firms may accommodate to the available supply of labor and what employers get for their wages depends not only on human capital variables, such as education and work skills, but on the preferences and constraints of men and women in terms of type of work and working time patterns.

The following two sections contrast two broad, overlapping periods. The first is that of import-substitution industrialization (approximately 1940–1980). The second is the contemporary one (1970s–present) of debt-related austerity characterized in some Latin American countries by a shift to export-oriented industrialization. For each period, the chapter outlines the demand and supply factors in the labor market that affect the informal sector, concentrating, on the demand side, on factors affecting the structure of urban employment, and on the supply side, on changes in participation rates by gender.

Labor Markets and Import Substitution Industrialization

Overview

In the period from 1940 through the 1970s, import-substitution industrialization predominated in Latin America and was, to a great extent, internally financed through an "alliance" of state, national capital, and multinational corporations. Starting with the basic goods industries, manufacturing was relatively labor intensive in this period, using imported technology that changed little from year to year. Factory workers gained importance among the working class, as did rail and port workers, while craft workers were displaced by factory competition. The skills demanded by new jobs remained basically craft skills and did not break sharply with previous working-class traditions. The parallel gradual decline of craft production was accompanied by the emergence of a specialized repair service sector, especially small-scale workshops of shoemakers, mechanics, electricians, and others.

In the countries studied, factory workers reached the peak of their relative importance in the 1940s and 1950s. By 1960, a greater proportion of workers in manufacturing were employed in medium- and large-scale—rather than small—enterprises, and factory employment in enterprises of 100 or more people constituted half or more of the total industrial labor force in countries such as Brazil, Colombia, and Chile (Cardoso and Reyna 1968). In the late 1960s, manufacturing expanded to include consumer durable, capital, and intermediate goods production. Production became increasingly capital intensive and dependent on advanced technology.

The import substitution phase marks substantial growth in the Latin American economies and employment opportunities that favored men. There was a rise in real incomes benefitting urban workers. Traditional services like sales and domestic service decreased in importance as employment rose in producer, social, and administrative services (office workers, teachers, health workers, other salaried professionals and technicians) and other modern urban services, such as car repair.[4] Between 1970 and 1980 in Brazil, the most dynamic sectors for employment creation were producer services (11.6 percent annual rate of growth), electricity and water (14.3 percent), and manufacturing (7.5 percent). In contrast, personal services and commerce in Brazil expanded at lower rates (4.8 percent and 6.0 percent respectively).[5]

In the 1960s, most Latin American governments began substantial, centralized economic development programs to modernize agriculture, raise educational levels, provide health care, renovate and extend economic infrastructure, and improve the fiscal capacity of the state. On a world level, this was a "development" decade during which advanced industrial countries provided funds and technical assistance through international or bilateral agencies to assist Latin American governments' development programs. The end result of internal and external pressures to modernize was a substantial increase in state employment in administration, state financed development agencies, public enterprises, and social services, such as health and education. By 1980, Latin American states had become an important source of urban employment.

Census data available for several countries partially illustrate the quantitative importance of public employment to the formal employment sector. About 1980, public employment represented 33.8 percent of formal urban employment in Argentina, 29.3 percent in Brazil, 21.2 percent in Colombia (1982), and 49.1 percent in Peru (1981) (Echeverría 1983; Saldanha, Mais and Camargo 1983). This increase was particularly significant in the nonmanual strata of all countries. By 1981, the public sector employed 66 percent of nonmanual workers in Peru and 51 percent in Argentina (refer to Table 4.1).

The period 1940–1980 experienced a substantial increase in nonmanual employment throughout the region, from approximately 22 percent of the urban labor force to 35 percent. This increase was due to growth in public service employment and technological changes that replaced manual workers with machines and increased demand for technical and administrative workers. In Mexico, for instance, managerial, technical, and administrative workers grew from 11 percent of industrial workers in 1940 to 24 percent in 1980 (census data).

Demand Side Implications

Rapid urbanization through the 1970s was associated with increases in formal wage labor, not informal labor, reducing the relative impor-

Table 4.1 Occupational Stratification in Latin America, 1940–1980

	1940	1950	1960	1970	1980
Higher Nonmanual Strata					
Employers, independent professionals	4.4	5.2	1.9	2.6	2.4
Managers, salaried prof-technical personnel	2.2	4.2	8.2	10.1	13.5
Total	**6.6**	**9.4**	**10.1**	**12.7**	**15.9**
Lower Nonmanual Strata					
Office workers	8.4	10.0	11.1	11.7	13. 2
Sales clerks	6.8	6.0	5.8	6.8	5.8
Total	**15.2**	**16.0**	**16.9**	**18.5**	**19.0**
Small-Scale Entrepreneurs					
Commerce	0.8	2.3	1.5	1.2	1. 3
Other (manufacturing, services)	0.0	.2	1.1	1.3	1.2
Total	**0.8**	**2.5**	**2.6**	**2.5**	**2.5**
Self-Employed					
Commerce	9.5	7.1	7.5	6.6	5.8
Other	19.0	12.7	13.0	10.8	12. 8
Total	**28.5**	**19.8**	**20.5**	**17.4**	**18.6**
Wage Workers					
Transport	6.1	3.8	4.5	3.7	2.7
Construction	5.4	7.0	7.1	7.8	7.1
Industry	20.1	19.2	19.1	16.3	16.5
Services	4.3	11.3	9.7	11.6	10.1
Total	**35.9**	**41.3**	**40.4**	**39.4**	**36.4**
Domestic Servants	13.0	11.0	9.5	9.5	7.6
Total	**100.0**	**100.0**	**100.0**	**100.0**	**100.0**
Agriculture as % of active population	61.6	52.5	46.7	39.5	30. 6

Source: Calculations taken from the national censuses of Argentina, Brazil, Chile, Colombia, Mexico, and Peru. The years are approximate: 1940 includes figures from the 1914 Argentine census because the next Argentine census was in 1947, which is included in the 1950 figures; the figures for 1980 do not include Colombia.

tance of self-employed and unpaid family workers. Despite the increasing importance of formal enterprise both for employment and economic growth, informal enterprise made its own contribution to economic growth. The rapid expansion of urban economies and wage work created a substantial market for diverse goods and services; non-manual workers purchased factory produced consumer goods and personal services such as domestic and craft services.[6] Manual workers in the formal sector often lived in squatter or other irregular settlements. Low-income and squatter populations use informal sector firms to construct their houses, purchase goods from small local stores, and buy or repair shoes, clothing, radios, and other consumer items in informal workshops (Portes and Walton 1981; Portes and Sassen-Koob 1987; Roberts 1978).

The continuing importance of the informal sector is reflected in employment trends. The proportion of small-scale entrepreneurs and the self-employed in the urban labor force declined between from 29 percent in 1940 to 21 percent in 1980. Manufacturing workshops, construction-related firms, and repair shops were the fastest growing small-scale enterprises in these years. Growth in these activities is associated with growth of formal employment and the consumption patterns of formal sector workers.

Several studies suggest that the role of the informal sector was greater outside major metropolitan areas. Cities such as Huancayo in Peru (just over 100,000 inhabitants in 1970) or Zamora in Mexico (of similar size) were places in which almost all employment was in enterprises of fewer than ten people (Long and Roberts 1985; Verdusco 1990). Small-scale enterprise also was more important in cities whose production focused on basic goods like shoes, clothing, furniture, food processing (Arias and Roberts 1985). These studies show ease of entry for certain branches of production (little capital or advanced technology needed). Furthermore, the opportunities for subcontracting work from large-scale enterprises was greater in these basic goods industries. For instance, in Guadalajara, Mexico, small-scale manufacturing was more common than in Monterrey or Mexico City. This was due to the concentration in Guadalajara of shoes, clothing, and construction-related industries (Arias and Roberts 1984).

From the demand side, the economic contribution of the informal sector up to the 1970s appears based on uneven urban development apparent within cities and between cities. Smaller urban centers showed a greater proportion of their work force in informal enterprises, as self-employed workers or workers in small enterprises, whereas large-scale enterprises concentrated employment in major metropolitan centers. In the smaller urban centers, workshops and the self-employed serviced the goods supplied from the metropolitan centers, such as cars or trucks, and met part of the local demand for food and clothing.

This does not imply that, among the metropolitan areas of Latin America, there were not considerable differences in the importance of the informal sector. For instance, differences are found between the metropolitan areas of the economically more developed regions of the south-center of Brazil and those of the poorer regions of the north. Telles (1988) compares Sao Paulo, with 12.7 percent of its workforce in informal employment, with the northeastern cities of Fortaleza and Recife in which 26 percent and 22 percent of the work force are informally employed.[7]

In Latin American metropolitan centers, the makeshift character of urban expansion, particularly the lack of formal housing and transport, accounted for much of the demand for small-scale enterprise among low-income populations. The incomes of the metropolitan middle classes were high enough to create a market for personal services like car and house repairs and domestic service, but not high enough to present an attractive market for formal sector provision of such services.

Supply Side Factors

The increase in state employment described in the previous section had both direct and indirect consequences for the status of both non-manual and manual urban employment. Latin American governments in the period up to the 1970s became active agents in stabilizing and formalizing urban labor markets, creating clear-cut categories of workers with different entitlement and contracts. Social security benefits, such as health care and pension rights, were extended first to state employees and applied mainly to white-collar employees. Key manual worker groups, such as railroad and energy sector workers—often state employees—received such benefits next (Mesa Lago 1978, 1983, 1986). In the 1950s and 1960s, benefits were extended to other sectors of the urban working class, especially those in large-scale formal enterprises.[8] Regulation of the labor market also increased, resulting in labor codes that provided some job security and established minimum wages and health and safety requirements. These codes frequently went unenforced, but they created a distinction between formal and informal employment that became an increasingly significant feature of urban labor markets in the 1970s and 1980s. Furthermore, the outcome of legislation was to make social security dependent on employment rather than a universal citizen right. The provision of a general welfare safety net in case of unemployment was left to individuals, families, and communities, through mutual assistance and kinship obligations, particularly the unpaid caring work of women.

Various studies cite escape from costs of labor market regulation and fiscal obligations as factors in the creation and economic success of informal enterprises (Roberts 1975; Benería and Roldán 1987; MacEwen Scott 1991). Small-scale entrepreneurs worked so close to the margins of profitability, often in markets experiencing sharp fluctuation, that savings on overhead, such as fiscal and social security obligations, were an important survival strategy.[9] In contrast, large-scale operators were enmeshed in sophisticated credit, marketing, and supply networks that necessitated legal status and made difficult avoiding these obligations.

Despite this evidence of economic dualism, other data suggest that labor market segmentation was not pronounced in the years before 1970. Despite high levels of rural-urban migration from 1940 to the 1970s, there is no evidence of rising levels of unemployment in the cities or of a growing, economically marginal population unable to find adequate employment. Therefore, little evidence supports the argument that the supply of labor to the urban economies outpaced economic growth. For instance, Gregory (1985) provides data from Mexico showing that for most of this period real levels of income rose for almost all urban occupational strata. He found differences between income levels adequately accounted for by differences in human capital variables, such as education or work experience.

By the 1970s, studies in Mexico reported only marginal differences in income between informal and formal sector workers, once human capital variables were accounted for (Roberts 1989a; Selby, Murphy, and Lorenzen 1990; Escobar 1988). Escobar's (1986, 1988) analyses indicate some of the reasons for the small differences in income. The informal sector of small-scale enterprises in Guadalajara served as a training ground for workers, many of whom subsequently move to large-scale enterprises. These male workers were urban natives who found their first wage job in, for instance, a neighborhood shoe workshop and moved later to one of the large city shoe factories. Subsequently, they might return to the small-scale sector where hours of work were more flexible and where there were greater opportunities to earn extra income through self-employed piecework than through fixed factory wages.

MacEwen Scott's (1991) detailed analysis of the Lima labor market in the early 1970s also shows the heterogeneity of informal sector earnings. Owners of workshops earned many times more than their

least skilled workers, particularly when the latter were women, and
the self-employed earned as much as wage workers in larger enterprises. Income was highest in craft occupations, such as jewelers, car-
penters, electricians, and among drivers, many of whom were in the
informal sector. In contrast, other common informal occupations, such
as street peddlers and laundry workers had incomes that were only
half that of the craft occupations. In Lima, gender was a major factor
depressing incomes, with women and occupations in which women
were concentrated having lowest incomes.

Throughout Latin America, working-class heterogeneity was
considerable in this period because it was common for workers of different types to be present in the same household: workers in the manufacturing sector and service workers, white and blue collar workers, or
workers formally and informally employed. Studies in Mexico City
and Guadalajara indicated that, in households headed by manual
workers, the sons were usually manual workers, whereas daughters
and wives—when they worked for a wage—worked in a variety of
occupations, contributing to the heterogeneity just mentioned (García,
Muñoz, and Oliveira 1981; González de la Rocha 1986).

An important factor moderating the supply of labor up to the
1970s was the low activity rate of women.[10] The available data for 1950
show that women's economic participation rates were very low—an
average of 18.2 percent for the region (PREALC 1982). In the decade
1950–1960, female paid work increased little and in only five of twenty
countries. However, these five included the largest countries, Brazil
and Mexico (Pantelides 1976). Female participation rates remained
constant in Argentina and Colombia and declined in Chile.

In the decades between 1960 and 1980, female participation rates
increased more rapidly, particularly in Brazil, Mexico and Colombia.
In these countries, by 1980 between 26 percent and 28 percent of
women aged 10 and older participated in their respective labor forces
(CEPAL 1989). This increase was due to urbanization, higher female
activity rates in cities, the creation of low-level, nonmanual occupations in the public and private sector, and increased informal jobs for
women.

Women's employment in manufacturing did not increase to the
same extent as it did in the nonmanual services, and it differed among
countries. In Argentina, Chile, Brazil, and Peru, women's employment
in industry declined between 1960 and 1980, mainly due to declines in
craft industry (CEPAL 1986). Female manufacturing employment
increased in Mexico from 1950 to 1970 due to the expansion of assembly operations by multinational companies, the persistence of industries (such as the garment industry) that traditionally were heavy users

of female labor, and the spread of domestic out-work (de Oliveira and
García 1988). Brazil showed a slight expansion of both female manufacturing workers and craft workers between 1970 and 1980.

Social Inequality and Heterogeneity: 1970-1989

Overview

In the 1970s, a set of factors changed the context of both supply and
demand in the urban labor market. The supply of workers increased
rapidly as a result of migration and the delayed effect of the high rates
of natural increase in earlier periods and as a result of increasing
female participation rates. The manufacturing sector's capacity to
absorb labor fell due to economic recession and restructuring (e.g., the
shift from import-substitution toward export-oriented industrialization).

Changes in the world economy combined with indebtedness.
Latin American countries became strongly dependent on external
finance and had to reduce trade barriers, increasing opportunities to
export manufactures through subcontracting or integrated production
arrangements with foreign firms (Gereffi 1989). Competition from
imports weakened previously protected industrial sectors, while producer service industries grew to meet the complex credit, marketing
and technical needs of the open economy. The result is a shift in the
balance of formal employment toward technologically advanced sectors with different labor demands than manufacturing and commercial sectors serving protected internal markets. As external creditors
imposed austerity and privatization policies, the state lost importance
as an employer and provider of welfare (Canak 1989). Though cities
increased in complexity and costs of urban subsistence rose, governments reduced or withdrew urban subsidies.

The impact of this situation on labor markets will be illustrated in
detail by research on three Mexican urban centers, supplemented by
contrasting evidence from other settings.

Demand Side Factors

In the 1980s, formal sector demand for informal sector products and
services probably weakened. This is partly due to formal sector
restructuring toward new industries less likely to subcontract informally produced goods or services; for example, producer service

industries or electronics manufacturing with strict quality control practices subcontract only to capital-intensive small-scale firms. Also, deregulation of labor allows formal sector firms greater flexibility over hiring, eliminating the need to informalize some labor through internal mechanisms (illegal contractual practices), or externally (subcontracting) (Marshall 1987; Michon 1987; Roberts 1989b).

In this period, free trade policies promoted a flood of cheaply manufactured goods from countries where labor was cheaper or more productive. These are basic goods—shoes, textiles, cheap utensils—that compete directly with those produced by informal workshops. The limited possibility of expansion of informal manufacturing resulted in rising open unemployment in several countries (Portes 1989a).

The austerity policies of the 1980s had important consequences for consumption demand. A reduction in real income among all groups, especially the urban middle classes, led to fewer purchasers for the goods and services that the informal economy provided, leading to a restructuring of this sector.[11]

Data from Mexico and Central America provide eloquent evidence of employment consequences of the 1980s' crisis. In the three major metropolitan areas of Mexico, informal employment increased particularly in repair services and commerce (SPP 1979; INEGI 1988; Escobar 1988; González de la Rocha 1988). Informal employment in Mexico (entrepreneurs, self-employed, unpaid family workers, domestic service) was estimated at 33 percent of the urban labor force in 1987 compared to 24 percent in 1980 (ECLAC 1989, Table 20). By 1989, the urban labor markets of most Central American countries also were highly informalized, even when domestic service is excluded: 33 percent in Guatemala City, 48 percent in Managua, 29.9 percent in Tegucigalpa, 28 percent in San Salvador, and 23 percent in San Jose (Pérez Sáinz and Menjívar 1991).[12] Costa Rica, whose economy had been less affected than most by the recession of the 1980s, was the only Central American country to not experience increasing informalization in the 1980s.

Evidence from a study of firms registered in Jalisco state, Mexico, in 1981 suggests the Mexican economic crisis affected smaller, often family-based, firms most, driving them out of business or into informality (Alba and Roberts 1990); 384 out of 604 firms legally registered in 1981 were not registered in 1985 although many continued operations clandestinely and with fewer workers. Informants from both small-scale firms and large enterprises concurred in seeing the recession as having hit the small-scale firms hardest (Alba and Roberts 1990).

Escobar's (1988) study of the effects of the crisis on small workshops in Guadalajara arrived at the same conclusion. Before the crisis, he noted formalization of workshops through contracting of wage workers and compliance with labor laws; during the crisis workshops informalized employment conditions and pay declined drastically. Real wages in workshops dropped 40 percent between 1982 and 1985 compared with a 22.5 percent decline in the legal minimum wage. Some workshops went clandestine by moving location. Others, faced with rising prices of raw materials and a diminishing market, became more dependent on middlemen for credit.

The recession-induced restructuring of economies like that of Mexico, sharply increased polarization and segmentation of labor markets but in diverse ways. Large-scale manufacturing firms in Jalisco state in 1989, especially exporters, were most optimistic about economic prospects, but small-scale firms were pessimistic and complained of the negative impact of the new trade liberalization measures (Alba and Roberts 1990). However, turnover in large-scale firms was high; and employers complained of labor shortages, especially for skilled workers, and firms hired a slightly higher percentage of labor on temporary contracts than their equivalents had in 1981 (Alba and Roberts 1990). In Guadalajara (Jalisco's capitol), the new high technology industries, particularly in electronics, employed higher proportions of women than the older industries—such as shoes, steel and engineering—which were laying off workers.

The change in industrial structure through export-oriented industrialization altered the spatial distribution of formal employment. Carrillo's (1989) study of the restructuring of the Mexican automobile industry demonstrates how. Mexico increased its automobile production considerably until the crisis of the early 1980s when internal demand dropped sharply. The recovery of the industry was based on exports which accounted for nearly 40 percent of all cars produced in 1986. The 140 assembly plants that export auto parts and vehicles were located in the border region and, by 1987, employed 60,000 workers. Characteristics of employment in the north contrast sharply with those of automobile factories in central Mexico which produce mainly for the internal market. Women were a much higher percentage of the northern labor force, especially in auto parts production. Union affiliation was lower in the north, and the unions were less sensitive to the demands of members and not as successful in negotiating advantageous collective contracts as their counterparts in central Mexico. Wages were much lower in the north than in the center for similar positions (Carrillo 1989). Carrillo notes that restructuring involved the latest production techniques, including flexible production, and workers were expected to exercise initiative despite being paid less than their equivalents in the center of the country.[13]

The stagnation of traditional manufacturing industry, associated with an absolute decline in formal job opportunities for men, was geographically concentrated in the old centers of this industry, especially Mexico City. In northern zones like Monterrey, the loss of jobs in heavy manufacturing was partly compensated for by new *maquiladora* (assembly plant) plants. The *maquiladora* labor force in Mexico has been traditionally female (72 percent of 143,918 workers in 1983) (Carrillo and Hernández 1985); by 1988, men were about 38 percent of the *maquiladora* labor force of 325,400—49 percent in traditional manufacturing plants and 34 percent in new computerized production plants (INEGI 1989a; Wilson 1989). Thus industrial restructuring has implications for gender composition and geographical distribution of formal employment in Mexico.

The consequences of these trends in Mexico are increases in informal enterprise in major metropolitan areas. In the three metropolitan areas of Mexico City, Monterrey and Guadalajara, self-employment increased between 1976 and 1987, and the rise in self-employment and unpaid family workers was sharpest in Guadalajara.

Employment restructuring took place within industry sectors (INEGI 1988; SPP 1979) with sharp declines in the proportion of the labor force in manufacturing—from 30 percent to 24 percent between 1976 and 1987 in Mexico City and from 39 percent to 29 percent in Monterrey. In both cities, the proportion of employment in producer services and administration rose—from 24 percent to 28 percent in Mexico City and from 12.6 percent to 21 percent in Monterrey. Guadalajara's manufacturing employment remained proportionately stable from 1976 to 1987 (at 29 percent); but includes considerable craft-type production, included domestic out-working—compatible with the trend toward self-employment.

A pilot study of informal enterprises in Mexico City carried out in 1987–1988 (INEGI 1989b) reveals the nature of restructuring in urban economies. This survey took as its population all enterprises (including the self-employed) with six or fewer people selected from the government's third trimester urban employment survey. The employment structure of these enterprises was 8.4 percent owners, 37.4 percent employees or unpaid labor, and 54.2 percent self-employed workers (including out-workers, independent artisans, street vendors working on consignment, and so on).

Entrepreneurs were asked whether they fulfilled certain requirements: registration with fiscal authorities, with local government, with a relevant *cámara* (industrial association), with the health inspectorate when required, or payment of social security taxes. Half complied with fiscal registration. However, only 15 percent of enterprises legally bound to register with the Instituto Mexicano de Seguro Social (Social Security Administration) said they did so. The most frequent reason for noncompliance was ignorance of the law (not costs or disapproval of regulation).

The general picture that emerged was of a sector that evidenced little potential for economic growth, with few links to the formal sector and little appreciable capital. Almost all enterprises were self-financed, with friends and relatives being the only other appreciable source of funds (less than 1 percent used bank or other formal credits), and few made recent investments in the business. In comparison with their equivalents in the 1983 national income and consumption survey, these enterprises evidenced a decline in investments during the recession.

There was no evidence of widespread subcontracting of firms (less than 1 percent were subcontracted and only 4.3 percent subcontracted to others). Taxes were only 1 percent of the outlay of even the smallest businesses and wages were a relatively minor outlay (12 percent for firms with employees). The major expense was raw materials. When asked about the difficulties they faced, entrepreneurs overwhelmingly stressed competition, lack of customers, and the expense of materials. Despite the popularity of the notion, neither the costs of labor or bureaucratic regulation were cited as important by more than 6 percent.

Central American case studies of informal enterprise show a different type of restructuring—informal employment concentrated in commerce with only 25 percent in manufacturing (Pérez Sáinz and Menjívar Larín 1991). In all cities surveyed, the informal sector was socially and economically heterogeneous with large differences in income between the owners of small-scale enterprise, their employees, and the self-employed. The poor concentrated in the informal sector, though in all the cities, including San José, Costa Rica, a substantial minority of formal workers also earned incomes that placed them below the poverty line. Case studies of a sample of self-employed and owners of small-scale enterprises indicated that self-employment was a household survival strategy in the face of unemployment and declining real wages. Only entrepreneurs earned a wage significantly above the minimum, and as in Mexico, this sector showed little sign of potential for economic growth or expanding employment.

Supply Side Factors

Wage work among women was a major factor in the growth of the labor market just prior to and during the recession. Of all developing regions, Latin America showed the highest female economic participation rates in the 1970s (Anker and Hein 1987). The increases in female participation rates were due to diverse factors—change in human capital, decline in men's wages, industrial restructuring, and modifications in the social and spatial division of labor. On the supply side, increasing educational levels delayed the age of entry into the labor force and lowered fertility, more educated women sought work outside the household, lower fertility facilitated female labor force participation.[14]

This concentration of women in certain types of work exacerbated gender segregation in the labor market, not merely as a result of competition in the labor market, but as a result of factors such as the potential for combining domestic and extradomestic work and social norms that defined certain occupations as suitable for women (Jelin 1978; De Barbieri 1984). In Mexico there was a marked expansion in female employment even during the recession of the 1980s, with an increase of 6.5 percent per year in the female participation rate between 1979–1987, compared with 3.5 percent annually between 1970–1979 (García and Oliveira 1990; Pedrero Nieto 1990). Brazil showed a similar trend—an annual increase of 7.6 percent in female participation between 1980–1985, compared to 4.6 percent between 1970–1980 (Bruschini 1989).

Social norms, domestic responsibilities, higher education, and lowered fertility were not the only factors influencing women's participation in the 1980s. For instance, in Mexico economic recession led to the mobilization by households of a potential or reserve supply of labor; this included adult women (35–49 years) of low levels of education, and married women with young children. Partly as a result, young, single women (aged 20–34), with middle or high levels of education, showed lower *relative* participation in the labor market. This contrast also was associated with the contraction in nonmanual formal employment opportunities and the increase in certain types of informal work opportunities attractive to women (García and Oliveira 1990).

The Brazilian data indicate a similar tendency by educational level and age of the female labor force. Women with low levels of education increased participation rates by 56.3 percent between 1980 and 1985, whereas women with five or more years of study showed more modest increases. Women aged 30–49 had higher increases in participation than younger women (Bruschini 1989). The studies of informal workers in Central American cities in this period showed they were disproportionately drawn from among women, migrants, and those with low levels of education.

The changes in the age and educational characteristics of women entering the labor market occurred in conjunction with transformations in the form of their insertion. Again, the case of Mexico illustrates these patterns. The percentage of nonmanual workers (professionals, technicians, and clerical workers) in the female economically active population decreased and only the most qualified workers succeeded in obtaining the few nonmanual jobs that were created. Among female manual workers in Mexico City women with low levels of education showed a clear drop in their participation, while those with middle levels of education increased their participation (García and Oliveira 1990).

García and Oliveira (1990) also found domestic servants and manufacturing workers became a significantly smaller proportion of the economically active female population in Mexico City. Self-employed women increased their share of employment, especially women with low educational levels, living in common-law unions, with young children. The increase in self-employment occurred not only in the tertiary sector, where women were concentrated but in manufacturing. This expansion of self-employment represents a survival strategy on the part of poor families, but also was due to the restructuring of manufacturing activity in Mexico City through sub-contracting[15] to workshops and domestic out-workers (Escobar 1986; Tokman 1987b; Benería and Roldán 1987; Marshall 1987; Arias 1988; García 1988; Portes, Castells, and Benton 1989).

The nature of household strategies during the crisis provides further insight into supply side pressures for change in the relative importance of formal and informal employment. In general, households in Mexico and other countries had more of their members in the labor market by the late 1980s than was the case in earlier periods. In the Selby, Murphy, and Lorenzen (1990) resurvey of the city of Oaxaca in central Mexico, the average number of workers per household had increased from 1.4 to 1.85. This increase was sharpest among the poorest families (1.4 to 1.9), but even the 40 percent of families earning the highest incomes increased from 1.3 to 1.6 workers. For the poorest families the result was to soften the impact of the potential decline in real household income between 1977 and 1987.

A similar finding was obtained for Guadalajara by González de la Rocha (1988) for a longitudinal study of 100 families. She reports the largest increases in labor market participation from 1982–1985 among women over 15 years of age and males under 15—mainly informal employment. For instance, among female household heads—whose participation increased by 20 percent—five out of nine new jobs concentrated in informal services, one in an informal workshop, and three in formal enterprises.

In summary, the evidence suggests that the supply of labor in the urban labor market had, in recession years, become orientated to informal work and this orientation was reinforced by (a) the concentration of available jobs in a service sector characterized by intense competition and low wages and (b) the reduction in real wages. The recession made it unlikely that male heads of households could earn a wage sufficient to maintain the family, creating pressures on other previously inactive members (including children of school age) to supplement household income.[16]

The increasing importance of multiple worker households is likely to have a negative impact on the educational levels of members of poor families. Poor families are unlikely to educate their children sufficiently to obtain jobs in the best sectors of formal employment. This would increase segmentation in future labor markets.[17]

The increase in informal employment during economic crisis and the entry of new household members in the labor force are not indicators of the informal sector's potential for growth or the attraction of its work conditions. The levels of income reported in various studies bear out a picture of a depressed sector. Over 40 percent of both the self-employed and employees in the Mexico City survey of informal enterprises claimed to earn less than the minimum salary, at a time when the minimum had declined in real value by approximately 50 percent from 1980 levels (INEGI 1989b). Evidence from Guadalajara shows that workers in informal workshops in the shoe and garment trades had the most severe drop in real incomes between 1982–1987 (50–60 percent) compared with 45–55 percent experienced by workers in a large-scale shoe factory and 15 percent in a successful exporting steel mill (Escobar and Roberts 1989). In Mexico City, only owners of small enterprises had earnings greater on average than the minimum salary, with some earning four or more times the minimum.

In other Latin American countries, levels of pay in the early 1980s were lower in real terms than those obtained in the early 1970s, with the exception of wages in manufacturing, which remained higher than 1970 levels (PREALC 1983). In light of lower real incomes and increasing unemployment, even the low salaries of the young and women were necessary to sustain the household, and this has been the major factor increasing female labor force participation in the poorest households (De Barbieri and Oliveira 1987; González de la Rocha 1987; Cartaya, this volume). The characteristics of workers combine with domestic responsibilities to encourage informal employment.

It must be remembered, however, that the context of informal employment changes again as some Latin American countries emerge from recession and their economies expand under the stimulus of export-oriented industrialization. In Mexico, particularly in the cities of the northern border, informal employment—particularly self-employment and owners of microenterprises—tends to concentrate among heads of household, both male and female, and formal employment among their dependent children (Roberts 1993). Also, the average wage of the self-employed in these locations is higher than that of those employed in large-scale enterprises. The *maquiladora* (in-bond) plants of the northern border pay low wages to a work force composed mainly of unmarried men and women. Turnover is high and prospects for internal promotion are few. In these dynamic border economies, small-scale enterprise and self-employment often offer the best opportunities to increase income in face of wage controls, especially for household heads who can use unpaid family labor. In these circumstances, *informal sector* is not synonymous with poverty.

Conclusion

The increasing importance of informal employment entails a shift from individual to household characteristics in determining the labor market participation of both individuals and their families. Because the informally employed usually receive low incomes, they are often part of a forced household strategy of diversifying work roles to maximize income, increasing the numbers of household members who work for pay. Under these conditions, the type of job that an individual does is a less significant determinant of life chances than other factors such as household composition and cycle, gender and age. Furthermore, the increase in informal sector employment reinforces the local dimension of labor markets and makes people unusually dependent on community ties for finding paid work and meeting their economic needs. Though the informal sector may reinforce community ties as a result, it also puts a strain on relations within households and neighborhoods. There are, moreover, growing numbers of single parent and single person households in the cities of Latin America, and social isolation may be a problem for such households when they depend on informal sector employment and cannot draw on the workplace relations and social security provided by the formal sector.

The discussion of the informal sector and its policy implications in the developing world must take into account the heterogeneous nature of informal work and the socioeconomic context within which it has evolved (see Márquez, this volume). Informals include, as noted previously, small-scale entrepreneurs, some workers in medium- and large-scale enterprises, workers in small-scale enterprises, the self-employed, family labor, servants, and domestic out-working. These categories of worker often differ in their social characteristics, especially gender, have different levels of income, and depending on the employment profile of the households of which they are members, vary in their access to state provided welfare.

Much of the disagreement in the literature about the contribution that the informal sector makes to economic growth is due to the fact that research focuses on different aspects of informal employment, confuses its role in different time periods, and seldom distinguishes between supply side and demand side factors. For instance, the small-scale entrepreneurs of the informal sector have been viewed as possible sources of entrepreneurship and wealth creation whose potential for growth is hampered by excessive government regulation and lack of access to credit and training (de Soto 1986). Policy recommendations include providing small-scale entrepreneurs with access to credit and suitable technology and reducing red tape or any form of intervention in the market that restricts competition, whether by state regulation or private monopolies. Facilitating small-scale entrepreneurship may contribute to overall economic growth, but this is likely to occur only when urban economies enter an economic upswing. Furthermore, unless policy for the informal sector is properly targeted, aid for the small-scale entrepreneur, particularly owners of workshops or small businesses, may also intensify the exploitation of other informal sector workers, particularly women. More important, at least in urban Mexico, entrepreneurs cite high levels of competition, not regulation or state intervention, as their greatest problem.

In the current economic situation of urban Latin America, major problems of the informal sector include, as Márquez (1988) and the STPS (1974) argue, very low wages and lack of access to social welfare systems (Mesa-Lago 1983, 1986, 1978). Thus, at a broad level, the problems of informal employment are due to *the ineffective nature of state intervention*. Historically, but especially during the recession of the 1980s, informal employment has been a substitute for an inadequate state welfare system, and it has grown due to the pressures of an urban poverty made worse by the failure of both the state and the market to provide adequate housing, social services, and other urban amenities. The remedies must include more appropriate government interventions, such as raising the minimum wage, enforcing social security obligations and labor laws (e.g., day care centers, equal pay for equal work) for *all* workers (including out-workers), generalizing welfare benefits for women with young children, and stimulating, through state purchasing and credit policies, the goods and services produced in the "informal" sector.

NOTES

1. These estimates of the sector were derived from national censuses of six Latin American countries by summing the self-employed, small-scale entrepreneurs and workers, and domestic servants. Data have been adjusted because population censuses alone are not accurate sources of estimates of informal employment; most do not record enterprise size nor whether workers receive legally required benefits or pay relevant taxes. In following sections, definitions will vary somewhat because multiple data sources and variations in measurement were used by various authors. Therefore, the term *informal sector* refers, interchangeably, to small-scale firms (fewer than five workers) and employment not legally protected (by standard contract or social security coverage) (Roberts 1990).

2. The self-employed individual and domestic servant offer goods and services to a market made up of middle-class households (Tokman 1987a).

3. Small-scale enterprises are less likely than large-scale enterprises to observe the relevant labor legislation. But large-scale enterprises, particularly in the private sector, may employ workers informally by not providing social security coverage, legal contracts, and so on.

4. Producer services are such business related services as finance, insurance, real estate, advertising, accounting, and so on.

5. Calculated from the 1970 and 1980 population census of Brazil. Business services, electricity, and water start from a low percentage base.

6. Though domestic service declined as a proportion of urban employment in these years, demand contributed to rising real incomes of servants in countries like Mexico (Gregory 1985).

7. This figure for informal employment is calculated as the total of self-employed and employees not paying social security, excepting professionals and domestics (Telles 1988, Table 2.1). Owners of small businesses are not included. Full-time protected employees—equivalent to the formal working class—ranged from a high of 60.5 percent in Sao Paulo to a low of 39.9 percent in Fortaleza.

8. Many factors were involved in these increases in workers' rights: labor union organization, mobilization of certain workers by populist governments as a political base of support, and pressure exerted by international agencies such as the International Labour Office.

9. In Peru, keeping below a certain size enabled firms to avoid the "risk" of some worker protection measures, such as unionization. MacEwen Scott's (1991) data support Tokman's (1991) contention that full compliance with legal regulation was a continuum rather than a sharp break. Even small-scale enterprises observe one or more of their legal obligations, though only a small minority observe all of them.

10. Censuses and surveys often undercount female economic activity, not only because women's domestic labor and its economic value are left out, but because women are unlikely to report activities such as helping in a family business or work for pay done at home. MacEwen Scott (1991) shows how surveys, even of the same women, can report different levels of female economic activity depending on the way questions were phrased and the length of the interview.

11. State employees experienced sharp declines in their real wages; for example, by 1985, public sector workers in Uruguay earned 56 percent of their 1975 wage (ILO 1989).

12. Estimates are based on household surveys in the various cities. The "informally employed" included only the self-employed, unpaid family workers, and workers and owners of firms with fewer than five workers.

13. The automobile unions had been successful in the 1960s and 1970s in winning advantageous collective contracts, giving workers average salaries several times higher than the minimum. This reflected the compromises of the import-substitution period between state, labor and employers. Subsequently, the urgency to obtain foreign exchange eroded these compromises, leading the government and unions to accept what amounts to deregulation of the conditions of work in a new formal sector.

14. Female participation rates historically have been highest in the large metropolitan areas of Latin America. The occupational structures of these cities were conducive to female employment: domestic and other personal services, commerce, public services, and office work. From 1970 on, women's job opportunities expanded both in "middle" class occupations such as teacher or skilled secretary, and informal employment as personal service workers or as domestic out-workers (for example, in apparel).

15. Different samples provide contradictory evidence of the growth of subcontracting in Mexico City. Studies of workshops and domestic out-workers (especially in traditional industries) report an increase in subcontracting whereas studies of registered firms did not. The general consensus is that subcontracting increased throughout Latin America because of a shift to export-oriented production and the recession.

16. In Guadalajara, a survey of male heads of household found they actually contributed a minority of household income in 1985 (González de la Rocha 1988).

17. Among women factory workers in Guadalajara the best paid, protected female workers had a *minimum* of secondary schooling (Gabayet 1989).

Part II

Macro Level Policy Issues

The Impact of Government Policies on Microenterprise Development: Conclusions from Empirical Studies

Carl Liedholm

Introduction

This chapter examines how governmental policies affect microenterprises in developing countries. Because such firms dominate the landscape in most of these countries, it is important to understand how policies can facilitate, or at least not impede, the contribution made by these enterprises to a potentially more efficient and equitable growth process. The chapter draws heavily on the empirical evidence generated from a set of surveys, conducted jointly by Michigan State Uni-

This chapter reports on work supported by Employment and Enterprise Policy analysis Project contract DAN-5426-C-00-4098 at Harvard Institute for International Development, subcontracted with Development Alternatives, Inc., and Michigan State University as well as by the Growth and Equity Through Microenterprise Investments and Institutions (GEMINI) Project, contract DHR-5448-C-00-9080-00, at Development Alternatives, Inc., subcontracted with Michigan State University. These contracts are funded by the U.S. Agency for International Development (Small, Micro and Informal Enterprise Development Division, Bureau for Private Enterprise).

versity and local scholars, that were designed to examine the magnitude, the anatomy, and the constraints (including policy) of microenterprises in over a dozen developing countries.[1] To generate the necessary data from such enterprises, the majority of which keep no records and are invisible from the road, an initial census was usually first conducted, followed by weekly interviews of a sample of these firms for a period of one year; this approach was needed to keep the measurement errors relating from the proprietors' limited memory recall within reasonable bounds. Although the term *microenterprise* is not as yet consistently defined, it will refer for the purposes of this chapter to those enterprises with ten workers or less. Consequently, it includes most of the same enterprises that would be classified as falling within the "informal sector" and with those characteristics associated with it.

The chapter is divided into four substantive sections. The first outlines the array of policies affecting microenterprises and their points of impact. The second section reviews those policies that affect primarily the demand side of the microenterprise (usually via the product market, where their goods and services are sold), and the next section reviews the evidence on those that affect primarily the supply side (usually via the input market, where the enterprise's labor, raw materials and other resources are obtained) of the enterprise. The fourth section moves beyond the standard focus on the enterprise at one point in time and provides new evidence on how these policies influence the expansion of existing microenterprises.

Policies and Points of Impact

A surprisingly wide panoply of policies affect microenterprises in developing countries. Although conceived in isolation from one another to achieve specific objectives (e.g., to protect local enterprises from foreign competition), these policies—labor market, interest rate, trade, and agricultural policies to name a few—cumulate and interact to form a system of incentives and disincentives to which entrepreneurs respond. Table 5.1 furnishes an inventory of policies according to standard, functional categories. Table 5.2 shows how these policies influence output (i.e., the demand side) and input (i.e. the supply side) markets. Perhaps the most striking conclusion to be drawn from Table 5.2 is how wide a range of policies come into play to influence the price of capital, the price of labor, prices of material inputs, the profitability of various categories of production, and the structure of demand for the goods and services generated by microenterprises.

Table 5.1   Inventory of Policies by Functional Groupings

1. Trade Policy
   a. Import tariffs
   b. Import quotas
   c. Export taxes or subsidies
   d. Foreign exchange rates
   e. Foreign exchange controls

2. Monetary Policy
   a. Money supply
   b. Interest rate
   c. Banking regulations

3. Fiscal Policy
   a. Government expenditure
       Infrastructure
       Direct investment in production, marketing, or service
       enterprises
       Government provision of services
       Transfers

   b. Taxes
       Corporate income
       Personal income
       Payroll
       Property
       Sales

4. Labor Policies
   a. Minimum wage laws
   b. Legislation with regard to working conditions, fringe benefits, etc.
   c. Social security
   d. Public sector wage policy

5. Output Prices
   a. Consumer prices
   b. Producer prices

6. Direct Regulatory Controls
   a. Enterprise licensing and registration
   b. Monopoly privileges
   c. Land allocation and tenure
   d. Zoning
   e. Health

Table 5.2 Factor and Product Markets: Points of Policy Intervention for Production, Employment, and Size Distribution of Firms

FACTOR AND OTHER INPUT MARKETS	OUTPUT MARKETS
Policies Affecting the Price and Availability of Capital	Policies Affecting Demand for Domestic Products Through the Price of Competitive Traded Goods
Interest rates and credit availability [2]	Effective rates of protection (import duties on inputs and outputs) [1a, 1b]
Import duties and quotas [1a, 1b]	Exchange rates [1d, 1e]
Exchange rate and controls [1d, 1e]	Export taxation [1c]
Capital-based taxes (i.e., accelerated depreciation) [3b]	
	Policies Affecting Demand Through Sectoral Income Distribution (Agriculture versus Industry; Rural versus Urban)
Policies Affecting the Price of Labor	
Minimum wage laws [4a]	Differential structure of protection [1a, 1b]
Labor legislation [4b, 4c]	Differential export taxation [1c]
Public sector wages [4d]	Differential foreign exchange rates and access [1d,1e]
Policies towards unions [4]	Differential expenditure on services and infrastructure [3a]
Labor-based taxes [3b]	Differential taxation [3b]
	Differential output pricing [3a, 3b]
Policies Affecting the Availability and Price of Other Inputs	
	Policies Affecting Demand Through Vertical Income Distribution
Import duties [1a]	
Exchange rates and controls [1d, 1e]	Fiscal policy, transfers and taxation [3a, 3b]
Price controls [5b]	Preceding section
Regulatory Policies Affecting the Relative Profitability of Different Producers and Production Techniques	Price Controls for Finished Products [5a]
Zoning [6d]	
Licensing and registration [6a]	
Monopoly privileges [6b]	

Note: Numbers in brackets refer to policies in Table 5.1.

On the demand (product market) side, a range of trade policies affect the demand for domestic products, either through the price of competing imports or the price at which exports can be sold. An even wider array of trade, fiscal, and price policies affect the distribution of income. Numerous empirical studies (see Haggblade, Hazell, and Brown 1989 and references) have shown that increased agricultural income, increased rural income, increased export production, and increased income for the poor will all increase the demand for more labor intensive products, often produced by smaller enterprises. This implies that a great range of demand side policies can play a potentially significant role in influencing aggregate employment in an economy.

On the supply (factor markets) side, exchange rates, tariffs, import duties, and interest rates affect the price of capital faced by firms of different size in the economy. Minimum wage laws and other types of labor legislation, government salary structures, and policies governing union activities all affect the price of labor. Tariff rates, exchange rates, and price controls affect the price of material inputs. Regulatory policies such as zoning and licensing laws affect the relative profitability of different enterprise groups as well as different commodities. The evidence on the effects of general policies operating respectively, through the demand for and supply of microenterprise activities must now be examined in somewhat more depth.

Demand Side Policy Issues

Lack of demand (i.e., customers willing to buy the product) is typically one of the most severe problems facing microenterprises in developing countries (Liedholm and Mead 1987). Policies can have an important impact on the ability of microenterprises to overcome this constraint—especially agricultural and trade policies.

Agricultural policies can and do have a strong influence on microenterprises, particularly those located in the rural areas of low income countries. Agriculture is typically not only the largest employer, but also the major source of income for rural households, who themselves are among the primary demanders of the products of microenterprises. Numerous empirical studies have demonstrated the strong, positive income and production linkages (i.e., increases in income and production will lead to increases in the demand for microenterprise goods and services) between rural households and these microenterprises, particularly those located in rural areas (Liedholm and Kilby 1989). There is some recent evidence that these linkages may vary geographically; for example, they may be somewhat stronger in Asia than in Africa, because of the higher levels of irrigation and mechanization in the former area (Haggblade, Hazell, and Brown 1989). Policies designed to increase agricultural production will typically have important, positive indirect effects on the demand for microenterprise activities, effects often overlooked.

The nature and composition of these agricultural policies must also be considered, because they can vary substantially in their effects on the demand for the products of microenterprises. Recent studies have indicated that the overall linkages from policies focusing on large, estate farmers are lower than from those focusing on small- and medium-scale farmers (Haggblade, Hazell, and Brown 1989). Differential effects on microenterprises must be recognized when crafting agricultural policies.

Trade policies also play an important role in influencing the demand for microenterprise activities. The significance of trade looms particularly large for those developing countries with small or stagnant domestic markets. Growing exports can constitute a key way of overcoming small national markets, but microenterprises are frequently thwarted by overvalued exchange rates or non-size-neutral export incentives in the developing countries themselves (Haggblade, Liedholm, and Mead 1986). An overvalued exchange rate, for example, makes the developing country's exports more expensive for foreign buyers and foreign products unduly cheap domestically (i.e., in developing countries). Moreover, tariff protection for domestic enterprises (to compensate partially for overvalued exchange rates) tends to be highest in those product lines in which the largest and frequently most inefficient enterprises dominate (Liedholm and Mead 1987). Consequently, a refocused trade policy could lead to improved import substitution through an expansion of efficient microenterprises. The possibility of microenterprises gaining customers by displacing inefficient and import-dependent larger enterprises, increasing the share of microenterprises in existing markets, becomes particularly crucial in countries where overall domestic demand is weak.

Supply Side Policy Issues

Policies to strengthen the ability of microenterprises to respond to market opportunities also are important in developing countries. Policies working directly through capital and labor markets are of central interest, although one must not overlook those that influence other input markets or strengthen the infrastructure (such as road and power), education, regulatory, and institutional environment.

Capital

A wide array of policies influence the price and availability of capital to microenterprises. The most important of these include the following.

1. *Subsidized credit.* Such a policy makes it possible for those firms, usually only the larger ones, able to obtain it to undertake capital investments at below market costs. This provides incentives for firms that benefit from such subsidized credit to adopt more capital-intensive production technologies than they might otherwise.

2. *Interest rate ceilings.* These are often aimed at protecting the borrower from unscrupulous lenders. Yet, because loan administration chores tend to remain the same regardless of loan size, the costs of lending to microenterprises typically involves higher administrative cost per dollar lent than to larger firms. In such situations, interest ceilings may make it not feasible for financial institutions to lend at all to microenterprises. As a result, microenterprises are typically forced to turn to informal sources of finance, at rates that are often two or more times those offered by the formal financial institutions

3. *Import duties, quotas, and exchange rates.* A system of balance of payments regulations based on an overvalued exchange rate combined with tariffs and quotas on particular import categories has the effect of making nonrestricted imports cheaper than they would be in the absence of such interventions. This is the typical pattern in many developing countries. Capital goods are almost always among the products that can be freely imported with minimal duties, thereby reducing their cost to the investor, usually the larger enterprises.

4. *Tax incentives.* A number of countries have adopted capital-based tax benefits, designed to provide tax incentives to encourage investment. Examples include accelerated depreciation schedules and tax holidays based on amount invested.

All of these well-intentioned policies—aimed at encouraging investment—have the effect of making capital cheaper for firms that benefit from them. Subsidized credit could conceivably be made available to selected microenterprises. The bulk of microenterprises, however, lack access to such special lines of credit and must rely on family or informal sources of credit, at rates much higher than those in the formal credit channels that serve the larger firms (Liedholm 1989). Similarly, large firms are likely to be importing larger pieces of capital equipment, which would be recognized as such in the tariff code. Microenterprises, on the other hand, often find that their capital inputs are mistakenly classified as consumer goods and taxed at much higher rates. Sewing machines for small tailors and outboard motors for small fisherman are examples of capital goods that are often taxed at the same rates as luxury consumer goods (Chuta and Liedholm 1985), whereas larger firms are often able, under government investment incentive schemes, to import their capital equipment free of any tax at all. All of this means that the policy environment tends to make capital substantially cheaper for larger producers than for their smaller competitors.

Labor

Governments also intervene in the labor market in various ways, usually with the result that price of labor is pushed up relative to a situation with less government involvement. The major labor policy instruments include the following.

1. *Minimum wage legislation.* Such legislation, which is designed to put a floor under the wage rate, particularly affects the wages of unskilled labor. It is most frequently found in Africa and Latin America.

2. *Mandated fringe benefits, work rules, and other labor regulations.* These instruments tend to be employed more frequently in Latin America than in Africa or Asia. In the same vein, governments may reinforce the power of trade unions to demand benefits for their members.

3. *Public sector wage policy.* In many developing countries, the government, often by default, is the largest single employer of paid labor; its policies can set the pattern for many others, particularly for the larger public firms.

These interventions all have a tendency to raise the market wage rates above the levels that would obtain in the absence of policy intervention. As in the case of the capital market, they primarily affect only larger producers, leaving microenterprises relatively untouched. Minimum wage and other similar labor legislation generally either exempts microenterprises explicitly or else is enforced in such a way that the microenterprises escape the effects (Haggblade, Liedholm, and Mead 1986). Although there is some interaction between all parts of the labor market, this is generally much closer between the public sector and the larger private firms than between either of these and microenterprises, which often operate in more isolated and rural areas. The result, then, is that the policy package pushes up wage cost primarily in the larger firms, leaving the labor costs of microenterprises relatively untouched.

What has been the magnitude of these policy-induced distortions in the capital and labor markets of developing countries? Haggblade, Liedholm, and Mead (1986) have estimated the distortions by firm size for seven countries where sufficient data were available. This evidence, which is summarized in Table 5.3 (p. 84), indicates that the total effect of these capital and labor distortions has been quite sizeable in most of these countries. The labor market, trade regime, and domestic capital market factor have tended to induce higher labor cost and lower capital costs for larger enterprises when compared with their microenterprise counterparts, all leading in the direction of higher capital/labor ratios for the larger firms. Taxes operated in the opposite direction, but served only partially to offset these other factors. Although each of these sources of pricing disparity between large and microenterprises by itself can be important, operating together their effects are generally magnified. In most instances, the net overall impact has been to subsidize the larger firms and penalize the microenterprises. Consequently, attempts to introduce a more size-neutral policy environment can have an important salutary effect on the economic viability of microenterprises.

Other Inputs

Expansion of infrastructure, particularly in rural towns is another potent policy intervention that should not be overlooked. Given the dispersed settlement patterns in most rural areas, the emergence of rural towns as a focal point enables policy makers to provide the needed infrastructure for microenterprises at relatively lower costs. Infrastructural support includes roads or railroads, electricity, and water, but also needed improvements in the institutional infrastructure such as the development of legal and information systems. The related need for investment in human capital (i.e., education) should also not be overlooked and is of crucial importance in facilitating the future evolution of microenterprises. These various results demonstrate that in reviewing the general policy environment for microenter-

Table 5.3 Policy-Induced Factor Price Distortions, Large Firms and Microenterprises, Expressed as Percent Difference in Large Firms' Costs Relative to Microenterprise Costs

Country	Period	Percent Difference in Labor Costs	PERCENT DIFFERENCE IN CAPITAL COSTS[a] OWING TO				Percent Difference in Wage/Capital Rental Rate
			Trade Regime	Interest Rate	Taxes	Total Capital	
Asia							
Hong Kong	1973	0	0	0	0	0	0
Pakistan	1961–1964	0	-38	-44	+22	-60	+150
South Korea	1973	0	-5	-35	+10	-30	+43
Africa							
Ghana	1972	+25	-25	-42	+26	-41	+112
Sierra Leone	1976	+20	-25	-60	+20	-65	+243
Tunisia	1972	+20	-30	-33	NA[b]	NA	NA
Latin America							
Brazil	1968	+27	0	-33	NA	NA	NA

Source: Haggblade, Liedholm, and Mead, 1986.

[a] All capital related figures have been converted into the annual rental value of a unit of capital (or user costs) using a modification of capital recovery formula.

[b] NA = data not available.

prises it is necessary to focus not only on industrial policy, but also include agriculture, trade, foreign exchange, and other related policies as well.

Much of the policy analysis to date, however, has concentrated on the current status of enterprises. It is also necessary to view these policies in a dynamic framework, in which the expansion of firms are explicitly considered.

Policy Effects on Expansion of Microenterprises

What about the influence of general policies on the expansion of existing microenterprises? Helping the enterprises among this *existing* group to expand and evolve, for example, may provide a less risky and more equitable path to development than one focusing mainly on the formation of "new," larger firms. Yet, even the growth of existing micro firms can often prove to be difficult, particularly when it involves not just their marginal expansion within the microenterprise size category but rather their graduation or transformation into more complex small- or medium-scale enterprises (see Boomgard 1989; Liedholm and Parker 1989).

A key policy issue is what effect government policies have on the expansion of these microenterprises. A recent study has revealed that the majority of modern small and medium firms did not graduate from the micro "seedbed" but rather originated as larger firms (Liedholm 1990). Were policies primarily responsible for this meager micro "graduation" rate and the "missing middle" in the size distribution of firms found in much of the developing world?

It is frequently argued (see Little et al 1987; Biggs and Oppenheim 1986) that most government taxes and regulations, such as those governing minimum wage, working conditions, registration, and zoning, fail to reach the micro firms in most developing countries. As firms increase in size, however, they also more visible and become subject to these various governmental policies. Consequently, there is a disincentive for them to evolve into modern small- and medium-sized firms. Empirical support for this view is provided by an Indian study that discovered an unusually large number of firms just below the size required for registration as a factory (Timberg 1978; Mead, Bolnick, and Young 1989).

To what extent does government policy act as a significant constraint to the expansion of microenterprises? The empirical evidence is rather meager, but one can use several well-documented cases from Nigeria and Ghana to illuminate this issue. In Chuta's study of Northern Nigerian enterprises (1989), government policies and regulations were the most frequently cited of the difficulties encountered by micro and small firms during the period of their most rapid expansion. Overall, it was mentioned as a constraint by over 50 percent of these firms. Yet, in Ghana (Steel and Webster 1990) such policies were not generally perceived to be a significant constraint for expanding firms of this size. Only 15 percent of the microenterprises, for example, cited taxes or regulations as one of the top four problems for expansion.

In general, policy difficulties appear to vary by firm size at the time of the growth spurt. Only 30 percent of the Northern Nigerian firms with one or two workers during the growth spurt, for example, mentioned policy difficulties, but this percentage increased to over two-thirds for firms with over ten workers. Therefore, although policy and regulatory constraints were important for firms of all sizes, these became relatively more significant the larger the firm at the time of the growth spurt and larger firms were likely to become "visible" to government authorities as they expanded.

Which of the government policies and regulations have the largest negative impact on microenterprise expansion? A wide array of government intervention can negatively affect this process, ranging from labor laws, taxes (both national and local), and business regulations to foreign trade and exchange restrictions. Many of these policies and regulations may formally or legally (de jure) apply to microenterprises, but may not be enforced or, if so, are applied unevenly, subjecting these enterprises to harassment or pressures for bribes. Therefore, it is important to determine the extent to which these government interventions actually reach the individual firms (de facto).

Although empirical evidence is again rather sparse, the Northern Nigeria case (Chuta 1989) provides some initial glimmerings of the perceived (de facto) relative importance of various government policies and regulation on firm expansion. The greatest perceived negative policy impact in that country was the income tax (37 percent), followed by licensing and registration *regulations* (22 percent), and foreign exchange restrictions (10 percent), which together accounted for 69 percent of the perceived policy difficulties. Other possible policy constraints, like other national taxes (such as sales or excise), local taxes (such as license and registration fees), and labor laws (such as minimum wage or social security), were infrequently mentioned.

Did the relative importance of these various government policies and regulations vary by the firm's size at the time of its growth spurt? The Northern Nigeria study (Chuta 1989) found that the ranking of negative policies did not vary significantly by size. More studies of this type will be needed to enhance our understanding of this issue.

Some government policies, however, can also have a potentially positive affect on microenterprise growth. As a firm expands, it may now have improved access to finance or subsidized credit, government purchases, technical assistance, foreign exchange, and tax incentives; and these may offset some of the more negative effects of other governmental policies. Chuta's (1989) study again provides the first glimpse of this aspect of governmental policy. Substantially fewer enterprises (only 39 percent of those firms who reported negative policy effects) indicated that governmental policies also had some positive impact on their expansion. A larger percentage of small scale firms (47 percent of total reporting negative policy effects) reported positive effects than did microenterprises (37 percent). The one beneficial policy cited by the majority of responding firms of all size classes was government purchases (51 percent), followed by marketing assistance (14 percent) and *access* to finance (13 percent). Tax incentives, subsidized finance, and technical assistance were rarely at all mentioned by these microenterprises and reflects the worldwide finding that relatively few governmental programs, even credit ones, reach the vast majority of microenterprises (Liedholm and Mead 1987).

A final, but important dynamic policy issue is whether or not these governmental policies, both negative and positive, arise primarily all at once when a firm reaches a certain "visible" size, or alternatively, do they phase in gradually, perhaps in discrete steps, as a firm grows. The only explicit evidence on this issue, Chuta's (1989) Northern Nigeria study, indicates that these individual policies affect firms at different points in their life cycles. In response to the question "did these policies begin to affect your business at the same time?" 90 percent answered no. It is also evident from more episodic and anecdotal information from other countries that these policies do not all affect the firm at the same time as, for example, when the firm reaches the "visible" size. Even the smallest micro firm cannot avoid the effects of import duties, quotas, or an overvalued currency. As the firm grows, however, it may become subject to additional taxes, rules, and regulations. Many of these are in the nature of lump sum levies, such as the *patente* tax (see Ngirabatware, Murembya, and Mead 1988) and licensing and registration fees (Chuta and Liedholm 1985), all of which per unit of output fall heavily on microenterprises. There is thus a strong discontinuity when the firm reaches this size (becomes "visible" or must register), as its marginal tax rate jumps precipitously and regulatory and legal constraints become more serious. If other negative policies also came into effect together, this growth disincentive would be even stronger. These various regulations and taxes, however, are typically imposed by different governmental units so it is unlikely that they would all be applied at the same size level. However, careful attention needs to be paid to identifying and avoiding sharply net negative policy discontinuities that would act as a disincentive to firm expansion. These policy disincentives overall are likely to be similar in Africa, Asia, or Latin America.

Conclusion

This chapter examined the influence of general policies on microenterprises in developing countries, finding that a wide array of policies influence microenterprises. Many policies operated through either the output market (demand side) or the input market (supply side) facing the microenterprises.

On the demand side, agricultural and trade policies were shown to be potent forces that can affect microenterprises. Strong income and production linkages between agriculture and microenterprises make it imperative to consider the effect of agricultural policies on the demand for microenterprise activities. Trade policies typically protect the markets of the larger producers and also can influence demand.

On the supply side, capital and labor market policies were found to be distorting. Subsidized credit, interest rate ceilings, import duties, quotas, and exchange rates have tended to make capital substantially cheaper for larger producers than for their microenterprise competitors. Conversely, minimum wage legislation, mandated fringe benefits, and public sector wage policies have tended to make labor relatively more expensive for the larger producers. In most instances, the empirical evidence indicated that the net overall impact has been to subsidize the larger firms and penalize the microenterprises.

The effects of policy on the expansion of individual firms appears to vary somewhat by country. Nevertheless some preliminary patterns have begun to emerge. The policy and regulatory constraints appeared to be more significant the larger is the microenterprise at the time of its growth. There is also evidence that individual regulations and policies, both positive and negative, did not appear at the same time, but rather are introduced at different points in the firm's life cycle. Yet, careful attention must be still be paid to avoiding sharply negative policy discontinuities that would act as a disincentive to firm expansion. More studies are needed to ascertain exactly how these policies influence, both de jure and de facto, the evolution of microenterprises in developing countries.

NOTES

1. Detailed, in-depth studies were conducted in Jamaica, Honduras, Sierra Leone, Thailand, Egypt, and Bangladesh. Somewhat less detailed surveys were conducted in Dominican Republic, Haiti, Zambia, Burkina Faso, Kenya, Botswana, South Africa, Swaziland, Lesotho, Zimbabwe, Malawi, Rwanda, Indonesia, and the Philippines. In these surveys, enterprises (primarily in manufacturing) with up to fifty workers were included. The vast majority of the enterprises discovered, however, were in the micro-size category. For more details, see Liedholm and Mead 1987.

❑ Chapter 6

Macroeconomic Policy and the Informal Sector

Jeffrey R. Franks

Introduction

The suggestion that economic planners design macroeconomic policy without consideration of (or deliberately omitting) the agricultural sector or the public sector would be greeted with hoots of derision by any economist. Yet throughout the Third World, a sector of comparable size and importance is regularly excluded from policy planning: the informal sector. This chapter argues that the informal sector should be incorporated into macroeconomic policy planning for at least five reasons:

1. Its sheer size makes it absurd to ignore.

2. Its behavioral response to macroeconomic policies is often so different from that of the formal economy that excluding it exposes policy to undermining by large unanticipated effects.

3. Contrary to popular belief, the informal sector can be managed (promoted and controlled) by government economic policies.

4. The existence of a large informal sector can bring economic benefits (as well as well-known social and economic costs).

5. The balance of costs and benefits from informal sector promotion is such that there could exist an "optimal" level of infor-

91

mality which should be acknowledged as a macroeconomic policy target.

Since 1972, when the ILO World Employment Programme missions began to suggest the incorporation of informal sector policies into national employment strategies, some critics argued that informality was something to be eliminated, while others contended that governments would never promote the sector, because it undercut their own power and revenue base. The evolution of thinking and policy toward the sector have belied those early predictions.[1]

A similar evolution of views has begun on the subject of the informal sector and macroeconomic policy. In the 1980s, many studies of the informal sector concentrated on the micro level characteristics of the microentrepreneur, with little attention paid to the interaction between the informal sector and macroeconomic policies. As a result, there is little evidence on the effects of the sector on macroeconomic policies. As governments and international organizations increase awareness of the role of the informal sector, stabilization policies and structural adjustment lending may incorporate the informal sector into analyses. Then, it may be found that ignoring the informal sector for policy making in the 1980s accounts in part for the dismal success rate of stabilization policies (Franks 1987).

Finally, this chapter contends that many developing countries have suboptimal levels of informality. That is, some countries could increase social welfare by actively "informalizing" their economies (up to a point). In other countries, promoting informal sector growth on a macro level could be an important component of overall economic development strategy. Even in countries where this is not true—where the sector is large and should be reduced in size—only by understanding of the macro-micro link can reduction be achieved without undermining the well-being of informal firms and workers or the effectiveness of macroeconomic policies.

Macroeconomic Policy and the Informal Sector

Since the concept of the informal sector was coined by Keith Hart (1973), the idea has invaded the discourse of development studies. Between 1972 and 1990, more than 400 scholarly articles and books about the informal sector were published, along with countless popular reports in both the First and Third World press. Though many different research and political agendas cohabit under the appellation of *informality*, it is clear that the existence of a huge informal economy of microenterprises and sub rosa production and commerce is a major part of the urban reality of most less developed countries around the world. From a macroeconomic perspective, this chapter adopts a working definition of *informality* as "economic activity which escapes traditional national income accounting" (i.e., is "unobserved" officially). This definition excludes illegal activities (crime, gambling, drug dealing, etc.).[2]

The informal sector is neither small nor economically insignificant in any developing country. Though measurement methods and definitions vary widely, all yield informal sectors of large size and macroeconomic importance (de Oliveira and Roberts, this volume). Franks (1989) compiled thirty-seven different estimates of the size of the sector in twenty-nine countries, finding an average of 41 percent of the urban economically active population employed in the informal sector.[3] Employment in the informal sector in many rural settings is second only to agriculture in importance. In more urbanized areas, the informal sector may well constitute the largest single economic sector.[4]

Among both academics and politicians in the Third World there is a growing realization that an intimate interrelationship exists between the informal sector and the formal economy. Liedholm (this volume) makes it clear that government economic policy affects the informal sector, and sometimes does so in indirect ways with results that are significantly different from those the same policy might have on the formal sector. This is of supreme importance to the microentrepreneur and—by extension—to the donor community that works with the sector. The macro question is, Is the response of the informal sector to national economic policy important to that policy? If the informal sector were a small, insulated enclave in the macroeconomic picture, then it would not merit the attention of planning ministries and central bankers. The reality is that the informal sector is neither small nor isolated from the macroeconomy and so should be of paramount importance to national development policy.

Effects of the Informal Sector on Macroeconomic Policy

There are several specific areas where macroeconomic effects of informality can be pinpointed. In monetary terms, the informal sector can affect the exchange rate through its impact on foreign currency markets. It also can have an impact on overall monetary policy and—through monetary policy—on the inflation rate. In "real" terms, informality affects fiscal and taxation policies and employment. Spanning both real and monetary effects, the informal sector also has impacts upon capital markets, affecting investment and the interest rate. Furthermore, the informal sector induces a problem of "omitted variable bias" into all aspects of economic policy making.

Omitted Variable Bias.   The large size of the informal sector alone would not make it a problem for economic policy making were it not for the fact that it responds uniquely to some policy measures. Results of economic models give skewed predictions when not all relevant parameters are included in the analysis. This is why, excluding the informal sector from economic planning leads to a severe "omitted variable bias" in estimates of the policies' effects.[5] Because of omitted variable bias, *any* behavioral differences between the informal sector and the rest of the economy introduce biases not only into macroeconomic models, but also into the policies designed relying upon these models. Omitting the informal sector can lead economic policy makers to devise policies that are inappropriate for the economy as a whole and lead to suboptimal outcomes. After a detailed econometric analysis of the problem of excluding the informal sector from macroeconomic models, J. J. Thomas (1986) concludes that "the effects of ignoring the informal economy are rather serious" (p. 32) and that "there is a need to develop macroeconomic models with appropriate microeconomic foundations that incorporate the main features of informal economic activity" (p. 36). (The appendix to this chapter presents a simplified mathematical illustration of the biasing effects of excluding the informal sector from policy planning.)

Currency Markets and Foreign Exchange.   The informal sector affects government exchange rate policies in two crucial areas. First, currency traders who provide the parallel markets for foreign exchange are part of the informal sector, hence markets have profound implications for government exchange rate policy. Second, informal sector use of imported inputs shows a different intensity than formal sector use, affecting demand for foreign exchange.

Informal markets in foreign currency are a permanent feature of many (if not most) developing countries. Street traders in dollars are not a major part of the informal sector in terms of employment or income, but they can have disproportionate effects on exchange rate policies.

One effect is upon the allocation of resources and on the sustainability of exchange rate controls. The existence of an alternative market in foreign exchange places restrictions on a government's ability to maintain overvalued exchange rates and multiple rates or to enforce strict quantitative controls on foreign exchange (for instance to control capital flight). Because informal currency markets have been shown to be more efficient than their regulated formal counterparts in developing countries (Culbertson 1989), they also help to improve the allocation of resources.

Another effect is that of the link between informal currency markets and illegal activities that either generate or consume large amounts of foreign exchange. In several countries, drug exports or smuggling provide one of the largest sources of foreign exchange. Colombia, Bolivia, and Peru certainly fall into this category due to their cocaine production; Pakistan and Afghanistan have similar effects as a result of the heroin trade; still others, like The Gambia and Paraguay, generate large revenues from serving as a way station in the international smuggling of consumer goods (Junguito and Caballero 1982; Hurtado and Coulson 1988). Although it is important to emphasize that drug trafficking and smuggling—though "unobserved"—do *not* fall within the usual definitions of "informal" economic activity, they are important because they serve as a source of foreign exchange and of products commercialized in the informal sector. Blanes Jiménez (1989) finds in the case of Bolivia that illegal drug money drives the parallel market for foreign exchange and indirectly provides many of the imported consumer goods sold in the commercial branch of the informal sector. These effects tend to depress the parallel market exchange rate while providing cheap imports to compete with domestic industry.

The second area of informal sector impact on foreign exchange policy is a result of the sector's productive patterns. Although informals tend to use fewer imported inputs than formal firms producing similar goods, they are far from isolated from the international economy. Foreign inputs are used by some, and where foreign exchange is rationed, the informal producers are forced into the black market to get the dollars needed to sustain their production process.[6] As a result, an overvalued exchange rate (making imported inputs cheap) can have the paradoxical effect of making imported inputs *more* expensive for the informal sector.

Even when foreign inputs are not regularly employed, often both input and output prices are linked to the external sector because they are tradable goods. Many informal sector products are import substituting, so demand is closely tied to the tariff and exchange rate policies of the government. For example, the prices of most informal manufactures, such as textiles, leather goods, and replacement parts for vehicles and machinery, are substitutes for imported products, and as such their prices are linked to the international economy. Even the demand for some informal services, such as repairs, are linked to international prices for new products through exchange rate and tariff policies.

Monetary Policy and Inflation.   There are two possible ways in which the informal sector could affect government monetary policy. The first is through informal credit markets (Acharya 1983; Acharya and Madhur 1984). This is so because of the feedback effects between the interest rates in the formal and informal markets. For example, a contractionary monetary policy can be offset partially by increased lending in informal markets. Shahin (1990) demonstrates that such standard monetary policy instruments as changes in the reserve requirements and the discount rate in formal credit markets can affect the price and quantity of informal loans and, through them, the over- all money supply. As a result, a typical contractionary monetary policy, such as an increase in (formal) reserve requirements, may be overly contractionary unless the effect on the informal sector is taken into account.

A second channel tying the informal sector and monetary policy is that of the different pattern of use of monetary instruments in the informal sector. Most monetary approaches to the informal sector use these differences. First, the informal sector uses cash more than the for- mal economy. Second, in some countries (particularly in Latin America) the sector may use foreign currency (dollars) for transactions (Franks 1989). Both of these factors can undermine monetary policy by generat- ing unexpected responses to money emission and credit controls.

Fiscal Policy and Taxation.   Fiscal policy plays a preponderant role in determining the size of the informal sector. The tax structure and bureaucratic red tape may be deciding factors in the decision between formality and informality for many microentrepreneurs (de Soto 1986). Some theoretical and empirical studies suggest that higher tax rates lead to increased efforts at evasion, increasing the size of the informal sector (ILD 1987).[7] In some countries, formal firms participate indi- rectly in the informal economy through subcontracting arrangements with microenterprises and domestic out-workers (Portes, Castells, and Benton 1989). Thus, higher tax rates can, ironically, lead to lower tax revenues because of the shift toward informalization.

By reducing the tax base, the existence of a large informal sector can have inflationary consequences. In the face of inadequate tax col- lections, many developing countries rely heavily on monetizing fiscal deficits, generating high inflation and monetary instability. Ironically, then the informal sector often bears a disproportionate burden of the resulting "inflation tax" through its heavy use of cash and its limited access to subsidized credit.[8]

The level of government spending can influence the level of infor- mal economic activity. Bental, Ben-Zion, and Wenig (1985) find that under certain conditions, government consumption is related to the overall size of the informal sector. An increase in government spending can have the counterintuitive effect of *reducing* the size of the informal sector by lowering private sector demand for informal sector products. Because the government consumes fewer informal sector products than private citizens, increasing taxes to finance higher government spending reduces private demand for informal sector products without a compensating increase in informal demand from the government. This effect is different than the informalizing nature of taxes mentioned previously. Increased taxes drive suppliers from formal to informal activities, but those same taxes also might reduce informal sector demand (Bental, Ben-Zion, and Wenig 1985). If supply increases and demand falls, wages within the informal sector will fall; so a Keynesian attempt to boost economic activity by shifting spending from the private to public sector will depress income in the informal sector.

Capital Markets. Control over interest rates and banking are ubiquitous in the Third World. The tendency to set interest rates below their market-clearing levels combines with institutional barriers to prevent access to capital for informals. This produces severe distortions in the price of capital both in the informal sector and in the formal economy. "Contrary to a popular but untested view, official monetary credit policy has a significant effect on the interest rate in the informal credit market ... " (Acharya and Madhur 1984, p. 1593). Informals pay extremely high rates for capital, while favored formal firms receive credit and capital goods at artificially low prices (Haggblade, Liedholm, and Mead 1986; Carbonetto and Carazo de Cabellos 1986). The economy suffers through low productivity, low growth or involution among informal firms, and impoverishment.

More important, under government-controlled credit systems, the existence of an informal credit market distorts capital market policies. In a sophisticated theoretical study, Sweder Van Wijnbergen (1983) concludes that "ignoring this effect [feedback through the informal credit markets] when analyzing restrictive credit policy leads to underestimates of inflation and overestimation of output and current account improvements (from contractionary monetary policy)." In other words, the restrictive credit policies that are standard ingredients in IMF-style stabilization policies can result in higher inflation and greater reductions in output than anticipated because of their effects on informal credit markets. A review of IMF stabilization policies confirms that they often fail to meet their GDP targets and overshoot their inflation projections, just as Van Wijnbergen's analysis predicts.

Employment Policy. The informal sector can have profound effects on macroeconomic policy in employment and unemployment. Employment in the informal sector is extremely complicated because of the segmented nature of labor markets in many developing countries. Structural barriers often inhibit the smooth functioning of market forces in the demand for labor (Cain 1976; Mezzera 1987). On the supply side, informality serves as the employer of last resort for many workers who would otherwise be unemployed in the formal sector, and it often constitutes an entry point into the urban work force for the young or new migrants from the countryside. Many government policies in the formal labor market have opposite effects in the informal labor market. Avoidance of wage, social security, and workplace regulations is often the raison d'être of informal production, especially when it is linked to the formal sector through subcontracting arrangements (Fortuna and Prates 1989; Lanzetta de Pardo, Murillo Castaño, and Triana Soto 1989; Reichmuth 1978). As a result, any of these policies has an inverse effect on wages and labor supply in the informal sector. An increase in the official minimum wage will boost average wages in the formal sector as employers are forced to comply with the legal requirements. But at higher wages employers will reduce their demand for labor, and formal employment will fall. Also, often businesses respond to regulation by actively informalizing their activities. Workers thus expelled from formal jobs will flood the informal sector, and this higher informal labor supply depresses wages there (ILD 1987). The same thing holds for workplace rules. Stricter health and safety regulations in the formal sector will push employment down there. Workers will then shift to informal activities, where conditions are likely to be even worse.

From a macroeconomic perspective, these effects of government policies on informal employment can have dramatic results. Not only can wage rates and wage taxation policies induce opposite effects on the formal and informal sectors, but so can traditional Keynesian aggregate demand boosting measures. Furthermore, under certain conditions, the negative impacts on the informal sector of an employment-boosting policy can actually swamp the positive results in the formal economy! Ginsburgh, Michel, Padoa Schioppa and Pestieau (1985) demonstrate this point. They found that traditional employment boosting measures are effective: "if and only if the observed and the overall situations coincide. . . . Otherwise, the policy instruments chosen in view of the observed regime of unemployment are either useless or even perverse in terms of the overall economy" (p. 214). Thus, if there is a situation of high unemployment in the formal economy, but low unemployment in the informal sector, then government spending policies designed to create formal jobs may actually reduce overall employment.[9]

Costs and Benefits of Macroeconomic Policies for the Informal Sector

The preceding arguments make clear that macroeconomic policies have significant effects on both the overall size and productive characteristics of the informal sector. It is also apparent that the informal sector can have a profound impact on macroeconomic policies and performance. Consequently, it seems sensible to design macroeconomic policies that take the informal sector into account.

The linkages are even more complex. Incorporation of the informal sector into macroeconomic policy planning will affect the macroeconomy, but it will also affect the informal sector. Macroeconomic policies could be designed deliberately to adjust the size and prosperity of the informal sector in order to enhance economic performance. This section examines some reasons why governments might, in some circumstances, want to encourage not the decline of the informal sector (as advocated by Marquez, this volume), but rather its growth through macroeconomic policies.

Disadvantages of Increasing Informality

The existence of a large informal sector represents a challenge to the state because of the degree of autonomy the sector enjoys and its ability to evade many government controls. On a purely political level, the sector poses multiple challenges. First, the existence of a sector outside direct government control may undercut the legitimacy of government authority, as other political actors see the impunity with which informals operate. Second, the very existence of the informal sector is a constant reminder of the government's inability to generate sufficient employment to meet its citizens' needs. Finally, the size of the sector renders it a strong potential force in democratic politics. It constitutes a large bloc of voters potentially mobilized by political leaders. The informal sector as a significant political force manifested itself strikingly in Peru (Cameron 1989a; Annis and Franks 1989; Dietz 1991) and is on the rise in many parts of the developing world.

In the realm of public policy, perhaps the most disadvantageous aspect of the sector for the state is its ability to evade taxes. Any policy to encourage the informal sector runs the risk of eroding the tax base and the efficiency of government revenue collection to the point of impeding its ability to provide important public services. It might also contribute to undercutting structural adjustment policies, which often include boosting the tax base as a key measure.

Although libertarians and other political conservatives might applaud this decline in the meddlesome influence of the state, it clearly has potentially important social disadvantages. Among these are the loss of government control over urban planning and zoning, the lack of health, safety, and environmental regulations in the informal sector, and the lack of protection in the sector for wages, job security, and trade unionization. Anyone who has spent time in the urban centers of the Third World will recognize that these concerns are not luxury issues that poor countries cannot afford to address; they cut to the heart of the "quality of life" problem.

There are also possible economic disadvantages from informal sector promotion. The sector has low labor productivity and correspondingly low wages. The goods produced are often of inferior quality vis-à-vis products on the world market and so may have little potential for export and generating foreign exchange. (There is no complete agreement on this issue.) These two features combine to restrict the market for informal sector goods, depress the incomes they can produce and the eventual growth or survival of small firms. Finally, a strategy of informal sector promotion runs the risk of increasing informality at the expense of formal output rather than as a complement. Such a shift from formal to informal production may do nothing to increase the overall welfare of a country's citizens (it may well do the reverse by further lowering productivity, beneficial regulation, and product quality). Only if informality produces additional advantages could a reallocation of production from the formal to the informal be justified.

Benefits from Promoting the Sector

Advantages of microenterprise promotion have long been recognized by private voluntary organizations and some donor agencies. From a macroeconomic perspective advantages could be summarized as appropriate technology, foreign exchange, poverty alleviation and income distribution, efficiency, and dynamism.

Appropriate Technology. Because the informal sector is generally marginalized from formal capital markets and from imported high technology, the production techniques used are much different from those of modern firms in the same industry. Despite generally low labor productivity in the informal sector, the severe shortage of capital has fostered an admirable efficiency in use of plant, machinery, and equipment (Stewart 1978, 1987). Capital productivity is much higher in the informal sector. Due to overvalued exchange rates, differential tariffs, and subsidized interest rates in the formal sector, capital use is often almost profligate in formal industry. Yet the severe shortage of capital afflicting virtually all Third World countries since the onset of the debt crisis in the 1980s makes efficient use of capital an important ingredient of a long-term development strategy. In this respect the informal sector represents an appropriate technology alternative. The "free market" nature of prices in informal industry causes capital to be valued closer to its true "shadow" price and promotes its efficient use.

Foreign Exchange. So-called macro price distortions also affect the market for foreign exchange (Timmer 1980). As mentioned, because the informal sector generally lacks special access to foreign currency, it faces a much higher price of imports in regimes with currency or exchange rate controls. The well-known result is that informal sector production uses a much lower level of foreign inputs for a given output level than does the formal sector. A low imported input coefficient helps improve the balance of payments, while the high real price paid by the informal sector for foreign currency promotes a more efficient use of this scarce resource.

Poverty Alleviation and Income Distribution. Virtually all empirical studies of informality around the world confirm that the sector contains a disproportionate number of the urban poor. As a result, macroeconomic policies supporting assistance to informal firms and workers could be used to alleviate poverty and improve urban income distributions. This is plausible considering the disproportionate representation in the informal sector of vulnerable groups disadvantaged in the labor market—the old, the young, women, recent migrants. Thus, use of the informal sector as a mechanism for indirectly channeling economic assistance may well provide an effective and efficient means of directing aid to the poor and disadvantaged (Otero, this volume; BRI 1990; Yunus 1989).

Efficiency. At least three aspects of the informal sector may have positive efficiency effects for the national economy. There is an undeniably beneficial effect in employing people who, in the absence of informality, would be unemployed. Informal sector work not only creates productive jobs much more rapidly and at lower resource cost than either the formal private sector or the government, there is some empirical evidence that it provides training opportunities (Nihan and

Jourdain 1978; de Oliveira and Roberts, this volume). This means that participation in the informal sector can increase the productivity of workers over time; many of these workers will transfer to the formal sector. Thus informal employment can subsidize training for formal employment.

The flexibility of the informal sector is well-documented in the empirical literature (Portes, Castells, and Benton 1989). The size, output, and employment in the sector seem to adjust with astonishing rapidity to changes in the macroeconomic environment and in response to changing profit-making opportunities. At the individual and family levels this flexibility may mean large, undesirable variations in income opportunities—informal employment is often much more precarious and incomes fluctuate (up and down) more than employment in a formal job. From the macroeconomic perspective, however, these fluctuations translate into more rapid structural adjustment and more efficient adaptation to shifting economic circumstances. Although debate on the optimal speed of macroeconomic adjustment is an unsettled issue, it is undeniable that many developing countries lack the resources with which to adopt a leisurely pace in conforming to the dictates of the changing world economic environment.[13]

The informal sector has a great efficiency advantage over the formal economy in many developing countries by virtue of the fact that it is forced to "get prices right." Without the coddling of an intrusive government, firms are directly exposed to the signals of a free pricing system that more fully reflects the social costs and benefits of alternative investments (de Soto 1986). This is more true for the informal sector than for a neo-classical model economy because the very process of informal production and consumption contains its own "poverty weighting," that is, consumption and production needs of the poor are more fully reflected in the free market prices of this sector than in the classical economist's ideal market system.

Dynamism.   Short-term disadvantages and advantages aside, the ultimate issue in macroeconomic policy should always be to create an environment conducive to long-term investment and growth. How does the informal sector fare on this score? This is a subject largely neglected by empirical studies. Nevertheless, there are three strong reasons to believe that informal sector promotion may lead to efficient growth.

First, the sparse empirical evidence available suggests that considerable growth dynamic potential exists within the sector. Some studies of micro level informal sector promotion projects demonstrate that real incomes and employment can simultaneously increase in the sector. Two of the largest microenterprise credit projects in the world illustrate this point. Together, the BRI project in Indonesia and the Grameen Bank in Bangladesh have over 2 million informal sector participants in their credit programs. One evaluation of the Grameen Bank reported an average increase in real per capita incomes of 53 percent over three years (Yunus 1989). The BRI–KUPEDES project showed microenterprise profits climbing by an average of 94.5 percent over three years (BRI 1990), with family incomes climbing by over 75 percent. There is no reason to believe that this microeconomic success could not be extended into the macroeconomic sphere. In fact, a rough calculation of the impact of the BRI project on Indonesia's economy suggests that these informal entrepreneurs may have contributed as much as 12 percent of Indonesia's economic growth between 1986 and 1989![14] Though macroeconomic studies on the subject are nonexistent, the data do suggest that under certain conditions growth in the size of the informal sector can coexist with rising per capita incomes.

Second, economic theory suggests that by producing and investing according to prices that reflect social opportunity costs, microentrepreneurs behave in a way that is conducive to efficient growth. All of the static efficiency arguments discussed previously, when applied to investment decisions, imply that the informal sector is capable of producing more economic growth for a given amount of investment than the protected formal sector would.

The conclusion is that, despite well-known disadvantages to informality, on a macroeconomic level there are reasons to believe that an economic strategy building on the advantages of the sector and promoting its dynamic potential might have much to commend it.

Macroeconomic Adjustment and the Informal Sector

The decade of the 1980s has been called the lost decade in terms of the economic development of the Third World, particularly in reference to Africa and Latin America. The litany of causes for prolonged economic crisis are well-known—a combination of world recession and high interest rates toppled countries into debt crisis. These external effects combined with internal imbalances (especially in fiscal deficits and monetary policy) to create circumstances in which economic growth became almost impossible.

The prescription for this malady peddled by international organizations and consultants (particularly the World Bank and International Monetary Fund) has been "stabilization and structural adjustment."[15] Although there has been a ferocious debate over the content and severity of the standard IMF-World Bank adjustment package, the need for adjustment has been recognized almost universally, prompting the design of alternative strategies such as "heterodox" stabilization and "adjustment with a human face" among others (Bruno et al. 1991; Jolly and Van der Hoeven 1991).

Coincident with the economic crises of the 1980s has been an increase in the size of the informal sector. In part, this reflects the importance of the informal sector as a survival strategy in response to economic hardship (Lanzeta de Pardo, Murillo Castaño, and Triana Soto 1989; Carbonetto and Carazo de Cabellos 1986; Portes, Castells, and Benton 1989). The rise of the informal sector has profound implications for the formation of economic stabilization policy itself. Some economic stabilization policies could have been more successful had they incorporated the informal sector into the policy planning process. A threefold argument supports this contention.

First, theoretical studies suggest that stabilization policies based solely on economic analysis of the formal sector may be overly contractionary. Therefore, the gains from structural adjustment are overstated by conventional analysis in these cases. Consider a typical "orthodox" adjustment package. Among its most prominent features are exchange rate devaluation, reduction in the money supply and credit, and a contractionary fiscal policy with higher taxes and lower spending. The accompanying structural adjustment package would feature liberalization of foreign currency and credit markets, along with other liberalization and efficiency-improving measures. An earlier section of this chapter shows that the existence of an informal sector affects each of these key policies.

Black markets in foreign currency both the size of devaluation needed to restore exchange equilibrium and reduce the economic gains of devaluing. With respect to contractionary monetary and credit policies, Van Wijnbergen (1983) demonstrates that contractionary credit policy has a "possibly quite strong stagflationary bias." In other words, standard policies tend to be more contractionary than intended and may induce more inflation than anticipated.

Fiscal contraction is also affected by the informal sector. Increased tax rates may not achieve the desired reduction in fiscal deficits because of the displacement of some economic activity from the formal to informal sectors (see the appendix to this chapter).

The liberalization measures of structural adjustment are also affected by the informal sector. A general equilibrium analysis by Devarajan, Jones, and Roemer (1989) concludes that the existence of parallel informal markets reduces the net gains from market liberalization, because they partially ameliorate the efficiency costs of price and other market controls.

Second, the flexibility of the informal sector makes it ideally suited for incorporation in stabilization and structural adjustment policies. Killick (1989) argues that the key to successful structural adjustment (and to development in general) rests on the existence of what he calls *the adaptive economy*, an economy in which "ends and means are readily adjusted to changing constraints and opportunities" (p. 31). This adaptability depends upon efficient information and incentive systems and the responsiveness of economic agents to these stimuli (see Uzzell, this volume). Furthermore, Killick looks at structural adjustment as a process of "induced adaptation." As a result, the adaptive economy can undergo structural adjustment more quickly and with less cost.

The informal sector is the epitome of the "adaptive economy" and as such could contribute greatly to easing the burdens of stabilization and structural adjustment. It has a price system unfettered by government constraints, so it fully reflects the economic information available. Because of its small scale and many agents, the sector is capable of responding rapidly to changing economic conditions.

The third argument supporting an important role for the informal sector in stabilization is empirical. Some preliminary evidence on the role of the informal sector point to it playing a crucial role in cushioning against the economic shock of draconian stabilization policies in several countries. Two Latin American examples illustrate this point: Bolivia's orthodox stabilization in 1985, and Peru's failed heterodox program that same year (Doria Medina 1986; Toledo 1991).

Bolivia in 1985 underwent a demanding austerity program in an attempt to stop hyperinflation (running at over 10,000 percent per year) and reverse a complete economic collapse. Interest rates were freed, and the exchange rate stabilized through tight monetary policy. Public spending was slashed, thousands of government employees were sacked, public enterprises were brought under tight controls— the state-owned mining firm, for example, cut employment by 75 percent. The package proved to be a macroeconomic success. Inflation virtually disappeared, capital flowed into the country, and within a year GDP decline had halted.

In terms of well-being, however, stabilization exacted a heavy price from many Bolivians. Joblessness rose, poverty climbed, and prospects for real growth in living standard seemed remote. Recent studies of the impact of stabilization on the informal sector (Franks 1991; Escobar de Pabón 1990) demonstrate two important points. First, the informal sector did suffer from economic stabilization. Second, the sector did play a crucial role in mitigating the effects of stabilization. Employment in the sector grew from 51.7 percent of urban jobs in 1985, to 57.8 percent in 1989, while public sector employment fell from 22.7 percent to only 16.8 percent. Incomes fell in the informal sector, partly due to the heavy influx of dislocated miners and other public sector employees. Nevertheless, the evidence suggests that the economic decline experienced by Bolivia would have been more severe had it not been for the existence and adjustment of a large informal sector.

Peru in 1985 was the scene of the only stabilization package that attempted to incorporate the informal sector directly into its policies. The sector proved to be a crucial factor in economic reactivation. Franks (1987) argues that the early success of Alan García's heterodox stabilization policy in Peru in 1985 was due substantially to the fact that it explicitly used macro measures to promote the informal sector. García's policy initiated a growth spurt of over 17 percent in GDP in two years, with informal sector growth leading the way. The fact that the heterodox approach collapsed during 1988–1990 was due to policy failures unrelated to the informal sector—a lack of fiscal and monetary control after achieving initial growth and inflation reduction. The Peruvian example shows how incorporating the informal sector into macroeconomic policy planning can move beyond the "informal-sector-as-safety-net" mentality, and use the sector as a source of economic growth.

An Optimal Level of Informality?

The litany of possible pluses and minuses in promotion of the informal sector just recited is incomplete without a recognition that the balance between costs and benefits certainly changes with the level of informality. Although there might be a great advantage in having at least *some* informal sector to absorb the unemployed and provide dynamism that could boost the whole economy, if the informal sector became too large it would undercut the government's ability to regulate the economy and provide public goods. It also seems likely that as the level of informality grows, the degree to which informal activity is complementary rather than substitutable for similar formal enterprises declines. At low levels of informality, microenterprises concentrate largely on supplying goods and services to low income consumers in peripheral areas, while high levels of informality often imply direct competition with formal firms for markets among middle and upper class consumers. Thus, as the level in informality increases, the two sectors move from a mainly complementary relationship to a more competitive one.

Historical evidence on informality in industrialized countries suggests that the relative importance of these costs and benefits might well change with the level of development. As the income levels rise, the optimal level of informality may decline. This may be a result of a fall in the relative importance of efficiency gains from the free market compared to the need for government provision of public goods and control of market failures. It may also reflect a change in the nature of structural barriers to economic progress faced by the underclass.

Following the cost-benefit reasoning just presented, one could postulate a social welfare function,[16] assigning welfare values to alternative levels of informality in an economy. That is, other things equal, as the level of informality changes in a country, the aggregate well-being of its citizens also varies. As informality increases from a very low level, overall economic well-being would likely increase because of the benefits of informality. After a certain point, increasing the level of informality further would begin to decrease welfare, because the costs of informality increase while the benefits become relatively less important as the informal sector absorbs a larger portion of the economy. This relative structure of costs and benefits leads to the logical conclusion that there may be an "optimal" level of informality at which the marginal benefits and costs of informality exactly cancel.

This simple conceptualization can provide some insight into the impact of macroeconomic policies on the informal sector and, conversely, the informal sector on the macroeconomy. Macro policy measures will have an effect on the level of informality of the economy that will be reflected in a change in social welfare. A stabilization package that depresses the informal sector, for example, might produce a reduction in the dynamism of the economy and greater unemployment if the sector is already below its optimal level. On the other hand, the same policy package might have net positive effects if the informal sector has a superoptimal size. Thus, reducing informality is *not* always a sound economic policy goal. Economic performance may actually be enhanced by policies that increase the informal sector.

Neither the optimal level of informality nor the social welfare function described here could be precisely calculated in practice. That does not mean that it is without practical importance. It would be relatively simple for a government to arrive at a rough, "back-of-the-envelope" idea as to what side of the optimal level a country finds itself. This idea, combined with an understanding of the manifold interactions of the formal and informal economies, would permit the design of macroeconomic policies that would both function as intended (rather than being undercut by unanticipated informal sector effects) and move the economy's level of informality in the right direction for improving social welfare.

Conclusion

The informal sector plays an important role in the economies of the majority of developing countries both as a result of its size and because of its particular characteristics. Neglect of the role of the informal sector in macroeconomic policy planning can lead to measures that are overly contractionary, or that have the opposite effects of those intended. Consequently, it should be included in economic models, policy planning, and empirical macroeconomic research.

In addition to its capacity to boost or frustrate macroeconomic policies, the sector possesses the potential to contribute substantially to the development process. This is particularly true as regards to macroeconomic stabilization and structural adjustment policies. Though the subject is little studied, evidence suggests that the informal sector is more than just a safety valve absorbing workers displaced by economic adjustment. The existence of the informal sector changes the way adjustment policies work (and may help explain why they often do not work). Furthermore, the sector shows signs of a dynamic potential that could be tapped to restore economies languishing in the aftermath of the decade-long debt crisis.

More study is needed on the role of the informal sector on macroeconomic policy and long-term economic development. Particularly important is the need for additional empirical studies on the interaction between the informal sector and economic stabilization and structural adjustment. This research agenda requires the collaboration of economists, anthropologists, and sociologists in developing a coherent picture of the economic behavior of informal sector workers both as individuals and in the aggregate, and incorporating this picture into a more complete portrait of the macroeconomy. The evidence already available suggests that the informal sector is economically more important than previously thought and that economic planners' ignorance of it can impose great costs on the countries of the Third World.

Appendix: A Simple Model of Policy Bias from Omitting the Informal Sector

To illustrate the problem of policy bias for an informal sector, consider the following simple model. Suppose the true economy is modeled by

$$y = \beta t + \phi t^2 + \text{(other variables)} \qquad (1)$$

where y is the GDP level and t is the tax level.

Assume that $\beta > 0$ and $\phi < 0$ so that as the tax level increases the negative effects on the GDP begin to swamp the positive effects. This produces a standard Laffer curve phenomenon. A planner who wishes to choose t to maximize y, will do so based upon observation of the formal economy, F, (ignoring other variables):

$$\max F = \beta_1 + \phi_1 t^2$$

where β_1, ϕ_1 are the coefficients of tax effects on the formal sector. This yields the first-order condition:

$$\partial / \partial t = \beta_1 + 2\phi_1 t = 0$$

$$\Rightarrow t^* = \frac{-\beta_1}{2\phi_1} \tag{2}$$

t^* is positive because ϕ is negative. Note that the planner has ignored the fact that $y = F+I$ (where I is the informal sector). A correct maximization of GDP would look like this:

$$\max Y = F + I = (\beta_1 + \beta_2)\, t + (\phi_1 + \phi_2)\, t^2$$

where β_2 and ϕ_2 are the coefficients for the informal sector. This first-order condition of the true model yields:

$$t^* = \frac{-(\beta_1 + \beta_2)}{2(\phi_1 + \phi_2)} \tag{3}$$

If the coefficients for the informal sectors are the same as those for the formal sector, then equations (2) and (3) yield an identical optimal tax rate. If, however, the negative effects of taxes on GDP are exaggerated in the formal sector due to spill over into informality, then $\beta_1 < \beta_2$ and $\phi_1 < \phi_2$. As a result, it is easy to see that t^* in the true model will be higher than in the planner's formal sector model. How much the optimal results differ will depend upon how large the informal sector is in comparison to the formal sector and on how different the responses are, but common estimates of the size of the sector, combined with the possibility that the coefficients of government policy might not only have different magnitudes but even different signs, inspire the conclusion that ignoring the informal sector might lead to radically different optimal policy calculations.

NOTES

1. These critics contended that, because the informal sector existed outside the state's power to tax and regulate, government leaders would never promote the sector, because they would be increasing the number and prosperity of people beyond their control. Mosley (1978) argued that "'government aid to the informal sector,' as proposed by the ILO report, appears to be a contradiction in terms." Times have changed, as evidence by the fact that in recent years, government economic programs for the informal sector have been widespread (Annis and Franks 1989).

2. This definition employs the criterion of "observability" because, from the vantage point of macroeconomic policy, the main problem with the sector is that it is not taken into account. The overlap between unobservability and other definitions of the informal sector is high, especially the correlation with firm size. Most microenterprises (whether legally registered or not) often fall through the cracks in national income accounting; hence, "unobserved" for purposes of macroeconomic policy making. The exceptions to this rule are illegal activities such as drug trafficking, gambling, smuggling, and other criminal activities.

3. Levels of productivity (and unobservability) generally depress estimates of contribution to GDP.

4. Comparison of the size of the informal sector with other urban activities is difficult not only because they are ignored by national account statistics, but because they are subsumed in labor force data under the "industry," "commerce," and "services" rubrics.

5. Omitted variable bias is also known as *specification bias*. Intermediate level econometrics texts discuss this problem (see Maddala 1977, pp. 155–157).

6. Evidence for this pattern comes from interviews with microentrepreneurs conducted in Lima, Peru, June–August 1988.

7. Tax structure is often used to determine the size of the informal sector (see Frey 1984; Frey and Weck 1983; Tanzi 1982; Smith 1981).

8. The term *inflation tax* is commonly used to refer to the decline in the value of currency held in the hands of the public. The government prints money to finance its fiscal deficit, and the income this monetary emission produces is known as *seignorage*. This additional money in circulation produces inflation. Hence, inflation is a type of "tax" on cash balances, and the seignorage revenue to the government are the proceeds from this tax. In some high inflation economies (e.g., Argentina, Bolivia, Brazil, Peru), seignorage has been a major source of government revenues (Bruno et al. 1991).

9. This is not as paradoxical as it might first appear. In many developing countries, the official unemployment figures have little correlation with the true picture, because to be unemployed is a "luxury" in countries with no

social safety nets. When government policies target reducing formal unemployment, resources may be indirectly siphoned away from informal sector activity into government spending. Increased government spending will increase employment in government and related activities, but because the cost of creating formal jobs is much higher than for informal jobs, a shift of expenditure from the informal sector to the formal sector could eliminate more informal sector jobs than it creates in the formal economy.

10. Carbonetto and Carazo de Cabellos (1986) found for several Latin American countries that the average capital per worker in the formal sector was twenty-five times the level in the informal sector.

11. "Shadow" prices are money prices adjusted to take into account true resource costs. They differ from nominal prices whenever there are distortions in the economy. For example, suppose a formal sector firm borrows money to import capital goods. The firm pays for the goods at the official exchange rate with the money it borrows at the bank rate of interest. Now suppose that foreign exchange and credit are rationed due to shortages at the official prices, that is, the nominal prices do not reflect the true resource costs. Economists can calculate a "shadow" price incorporating the exchange rate and interest rate that would prevail if the markets functioned freely. This implies that the true "shadow" cost of imported capital goods is much higher than what the formal firm actually pays (Sen 1975).

12. *Macro prices* refer to the interest rate, the exchange rate, and the terms of trade (the chief prices used in macroeconomic policy).

13. Given the limited external financing available to finance slow adjustment schemes, the lack of a social safety net to support families suffering prolonged unemployment, and the efficiency costs of slow adjustment, flexibility in structural adjustment is a clear macroeconomic asset. For a discussion of the issue of appropriate speed of adjustment in a liberalizing context, see Mussa (1984).

14. The calculation is as follows: roughly 1.1 million families participated in the BRI project from 1986–1989. Average family income increased by 2.2 million Rupiahs per family per year in real terms. This yields a total growth of 2443 billion Rupiahs among BRI families. Total GDP growth (in real terms) was 19,654 billion Rupiahs over the same period. Thus 12.4 percent of total economic growth came from families involved in the BRI project. (Some of these families engaged in both formal and informal sector activities, especially agriculture.) Non-family members also benefitted from increased employment and wages in the informal enterprises, which is not included in this rough calculation.

15. *Adjustment* is defined as a "comprehensive set of economic measures designed to achieve broad macroeconomic goals, such as an improvement in the balance of payments, a better utilization of productive potential, and an increase in the long-term rate of economic growth" (IMF 1987). The *World*

Development Report 1988 (p. 59) distinguishes between stabilization and structural adjustment: "Stabilization addresses short-term problems that need to be
dealt with urgently: inflation, loss of foreign exchange reserves, capital flight,
and large current account deficits. Structural adjustment addresses obstacles to
longer-term growth: distortions in the incentives for production . . . ; controls
on prices, interest rates, and credit; burdensome tariffs and import restrictions;
and excessive taxes and subsidies."

16. The term *social welfare function* is used in its economic sense—a function that aggregates the individual well-being of each member of a society into
an aggregate index of social preference (Arrow 1963; Sen 1982). This is *not* welfare in the sense of a poverty ameliorating net of social services.

❏ Chapter 7

When More Can Be Less:
Labor Standards, Development,
and the Informal Economy

Alejandro Portes

Introduction

This chapter explores some aspects of the relationship between so-
called fair labor standards, the informal economy, and national development. Although the argument has been made in different ways, it is
by now generally accepted that a relationship exists between the
absence or relative weakness of legally enacted labor standards and
the onset of successful export-led development. A low-wage and pliant labor force is not the only factor contributing to the growth of
export-oriented industry, but its absence makes such development difficult in the Third World today. It is also generally accepted that the
counterpart of the success of this type of strategy in developing coun-

This chapter was prepared as a paper for a symposium on Labor Standards
and Development, cosponsored by the Bureau of International Labor Affairs
of the Department of Labor and the Overseas Development Council. It
appeared in an edited volume of papers emerging from that symposium, titled
Labor Standards and Development in the Global Economy, ed. Stephen Herzenberg
and Jorge F. Pérez-López (Washington, D.C.: Bureau of International Labor
Affairs, U.S. Department of Labor, 1990). Many thanks to the U.S. Department
of Labor for permission to use the paper in this volume.

tries is increasing pressure on existing labor standards in advanced nations, as manufacturers in the latter are forced to compete with goods produced in the former by minimally paid and easily replaceable hands (Sassen-Koob 1984; Walton 1985; Fernández-Kelly and García 1988).

This debate centers on whether or not interfering with the free play of market forces would undercut the possibilities for authentic Third World development and introduce inefficiencies in world trade. Those who support this contention, led by neo-classical economists, allowing the seemingly perverse initial phases of export-oriented industrialization to play themselves out, would lead to long-term benign consequences in terms of higher employment, greater efficiency, and lower consumer costs. The premature introduction of labor standards in developing countries would undermine the process by depriving them of their sole competitive advantage in world markets; namely, an abundant and unprotected labor supply (Fields and Wan 1986; Lim 1988).

On the other side of the debate are trade unionists and neo-institutionalist economists, who see unrestricted global competition leading to a downward spiral of wages and work conditions. Threatened producers in the advanced countries seek to lower labor costs to stay competitive and Third World exporters counteract by further slashing the already paltry compensation of their workers. The result is not only widespread poverty and income inequality, but rising class consciousness and political strife. In addition, unrestricted competition contains the seeds of its own destruction, as the aggregate demand of the laboring masses fails to keep pace with ever-expanding production. Therefore, a "floor" of labor standards under international trade is in the long-term interest not only of workers, but also of their employers and the respective governments (Kochan and Nordlund 1988; Castells and Portes 1989).

Arguments for and against the application of global labor standards are by now familiar. Stripped of their academic garb, the antistandards position tends to be favored by employers and the pro-standards thesis by organized labor. Beyond this predictable cleavage, there is another configuration of forces in which both employers and workers of the advanced countries are pitted against those in developing nations seeking free access for their export goods. In an ironic twist of fate, neo-classical laissez-faire becomes the ideological banner of much of the Third World while a form of protectionism—anathema to generations of Western European and North American economists—finds increasing receptivity in the developed world.

The core of this debate focuses on the consequences of absence of fair labor standards among major Third World producers on the advanced societies. This is not too surprising since the latter are the ones most threatened by the new forms of international trade competition and the focus of academic and institutional resources bearing on the debate. The remainder of this chapter will not address this central issue, but a tangential one so far neglected in the literature. Proponents and opponents of global labor standards tend to assume that their application would have consequences in the newly industrializing countries similar to those they had in the developed West. Put differently, implementation of legislation to facilitate trade union organizing, enforce a minimum wage, and maintain certain protections in the workplace would lead to similar constraints on employers' practices anywhere.

The empirical literature that has examined the issue tells us a different story. Its lessons are worth noticing because they bear on the ultimate success or failure of different labor policies. In the following sections, results of recent empirical work are discussed to the extent that they address two broad questions:

1. What are the consequences of enactment of "advanced" labor standards in labor-surplus economies?

2. What are the characteristics and potential of activities that take place outside the pall of state regulation?

Labor Standards in the Third World

Global Diffusion of Values

Many Third World nations have implemented labor regulations that, on paper at least, have little to envy those of the most advanced countries. In Colombia, Peru, and Mexico it is more difficult to fire a worker with some minimum tenure on the job than in the United States. Similarly, accident protection, unemployment insurance, old age pensions, rights to unionization, and grievance procedures have been legislated in minute detail (Malloy 1979; Mesa-Lago 1986; Jatobá 1988).

Working-class mobilization and struggles have undoubtedly provided the main impetus for the enactment of such legislation, as they have done elsewhere. However, protective regulations in much of the Third World do not simply reflect workers' needs, but are influenced as well by ideas, values, and practices diffused from abroad.

One of the principal features of a situation of "underdevelopment" is that it is defined by reference to those situations that transcend it. From the developed world come not only machines, technology, and capital but also ideas and institutional forms (Thomas and Mayer 1984; Sassen-Koob 1983). Just as technological solutions are imported from the advanced countries, social solutions are often copied from them even when the problems they are called to address are not the same.

The influence of European and North American labor legislation on the development of social security and other protective codes in the Third World is difficult to exaggerate (Mesa-Lago 1986; Malloy 1979). This process of diffusion accounts for the paradox of working classes that still depend on direct subsistence production for survival and the parallel enactment of elaborate labor laws complete with ministries, courts, and magistrates to enforce them. These laws and bureaucracies do have effects on social reality but, as will be seen, they are different from what the rosy legal preambles would lead us to believe.

Consequences for Firms

The fundamental weakness in the application of protective legislation in Third World nations is the existence of a large mass of surplus labor, not all of it unskilled. Modern firms confront the dilemma between observing all regulations and thus being saddled with costly and inflexible labor arrangements or trying to bypass them. Competitive pressures generally lead enterprises to settle for a combination of both practices. Manufacturers producing for the domestic market, for example, face a kind of prisoner's dilemma in which full observance of the law by everyone leads to stabilization of competition at high-cost levels, but also offers a golden opportunity for surplus profits by those who bypass the rules. Once one or more firms do so, others must follow suit to stay competitive. The situation tends to stabilize in a mixed-mode labor arrangement in which firms observe legal regulations to the minimum necessary to avoid state sanctions or public denunciations (Benería 1989; Bromley 1978b).

The obverse of labor legislation imported from the developed countries is the rise of an informal economy. Contrary to its usual characterization in the popular literature, informal activities in the Third World are not limited to isolated subsistence production but encompass a vast gamut of enterprises closely articulated with those in the modern sector. The fact that modern firms in less developed countries promote and make use of unprotected labor may come as a surprise to those who rely on official statistics for analysis of these economies.

Recent field studies have given us a better grasp on the character of such arrangements. For the most part, they rely on the unregistered direct use of casual labor in the plants or on various forms of subcontracting. Figure 7.1 portrays some of the forms that this formal-informal articulation takes, as documented by studies in several Latin American cities.

An informal marketing chain is portrayed in Figure 7.1, part A. It has been found in urban retailing of such products as food stuffs, cigarettes, and papers and magazines. By making use of informal distribu-

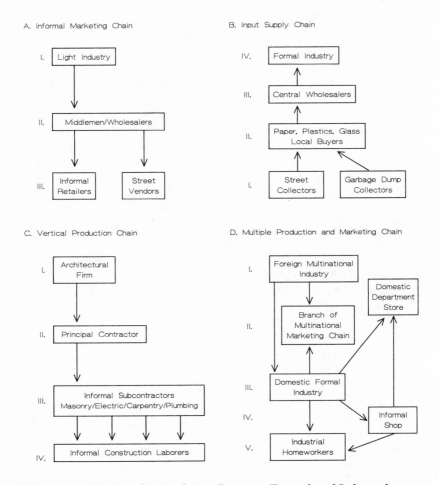

Figure 7.1 Modes of Articulation Between Formal and Informal Sectors in Latin America

Source: Portes and Sassen-Koob 1987

tion networks, industries eliminate the substantial costs of maintaining a permanent sales force (Möller 1979; Bromley 1978b; Duarte 1978). Case studies that illustrate this relationship in a number of cities suggest that the activities of an apparently disorganized mass of street vendors and merchants, a familiar sight in Third World cities, are actually being well coordinated by a group of middlemen dependent on formal firms.

A second type of linkage is portrayed in Figure 7.1, part B, which summarizes research among the most marginal workers such as those who collect trash from garbage dumps and the streets at night. In every case it was found that these apparently self-employed workers supply large formal industries with significant quantities of substitutes for raw materials at a fraction of market costs (Birkbeck 1979; Fortuna and Prates 1989). The collectors are, in effect, industrial outworkers who labor under the illusion of self-employment but who actually work for the large firms.

Figure 7.1, part C portrays subcontracting in the construction industry, as described in studies of several cities. Construction firms seldom have a stable wage-earning work force. Instead, contracts are assigned to firm engineers who activate their informal networks to supply the requisite labor. Lomnitz (1978) cites the example of a subcontractor in Mexico City who commanded an informal organization of 300–400 laborers in periods of peak activity and earned more than the engineers in charge of the job. His own workers were paid less than minimum wage.

More complex subcontracting chains, found in manufacturing, are illustrated in the last diagram of Figure 7.1. In this case, industrial and retail multinationals, such as Bata-Canada, General Electric, and Sears Roebuck, subcontract the more labor-intensive parts to informal sweatshops employing two to ten workers and situated, for the most part, in the shantytowns. When demand exceeds the modest capacity of their own installations, informal sweatshop owners turn to industrial homeworkers, mostly women who produce the same component on a piece-rate basis that is below the legal minimum. These arrangements have been found in studies of the footwear industry in Colombia (Peattie 1981) and of the electrical appliances industry in Mexico (Benería 1984).

Firms producing for export in regulated contexts face the added pressure of external competition. When the good in question is labor intensive, there is every incentive to bypass cumbersome and costly legislation. As will be seen later, governments bent on an export-oriented strategy of development often support the process by failing to enforce their own laws. It is not the case that only the unskilled aspects of production are subcontracted to informal shops. Studies in Mexico,

Peru, Uruguay, and other countries indicate that skilled operations can also be informalized. In Uruguay, for example, the rise of an export footwear and leather industry in the mid-1970s was based on a labor arrangement that kept inside the factories the most unskilled and less costly aspects of production and put out the rest to skilled artisans working for a piece rate (Fortuna and Prates 1989).

Consequences for Workers

The counterpart of informalization in response to imported labor standards is segmentation of the domestic working class. The most common, although not exclusive situation is a division between a fully protected and relatively high-paid minority and a mass of unprotected workers employed in manifold informal arrangements. The conventional view, expressed by international organizations such as ILO and PREALC, is that the labor absorption capacity of the modern sector has not been sufficient to employ all workers and that many are therefore relegated to "traditional" activities. There is reason to believe, however, that this "absorptive capacity" of modern firms is greater than what is generally assumed, but that it is implemented through arrangements that escape official record keeping (Portes and Benton 1984). These subcontracting arrangements are only a sample of those that have been reported in different Third World countries. This evidence suggests that a high proportion of the informal labor force is in reality composed of "disguised" wage workers, who toil for modern firms, but are not formally employed by them (Birkbeck 1979; Möller 1979; Benería 1989).

The character of the formal-informal articulation has been conventionally described in the literature as one between a "modern" sector and a "backward" sector, when actually a good part of the interaction is between modern-type activities situated on either side of the protected-labor divide. This particular configuration may help explain why, contrary to the predictions of both orthodox and Marxist economists, the informal sector has not shrunk with increasing industrialization in many countries but has actually represented a constant, if not increasing share of their labor force. Latin America is a particularly appropriate example because it is a region that experienced rapid and sustained industrial development from the post-Second World War period up to 1980. Table 7.1 summarizes the relevant empirical evidence for the seven largest Latin American countries, three metropolitan areas, and the region as a whole. Although these data suffer from limitations, the pattern they illustrate is unmistakable.

Table 7.1 Segmentation of the Economically Active Population
(EAP), 1950–1980

	YEAR	GNP[a]	INFORMAL WORKERS, URBAN EAP[b] (%)	INFORMAL WORKERS, TOTAL EAP[b] (%)	SELF-EMPLOYED[c] (%)
Argentina	1950	12.9	21.1	22.8	7.8
	1980	31.3	23.0	25.7	16.7
Brazil	1950	10.0	27.3	48.3	28.6
	1980	59.2	27.2	44.5	33.7
Chile	1950	3.4	35.1	31.0	22.4
	1980	7.7	27.1	28.9	18.6
Colombia	1950	2.5	39.0	48.3	23.4
	1980	9.5	34.4	41.0	18.9
Mexico	1950	10.0	37.4	56.9	37.4
	1980	44.2	35.8	40.4	23.2
Peru	1950	2.2	46.9	56.3	—
	1980	8.3	40.5	55.8	40.2
Venezuela	1950	2.4	32.1	38.9	28.8
	1980	8.3	20.8	31.5	31.8
Bogotá	1975		33.0 (60.5)[d]	—	—
	1984		34.2 (59.7)	—	—
Montevideo	1968		12.5	—	—
	1983		16.2 (19.3)[e]	—	—
Sao Paulo	1976		29.7[f]	—	—
	1982		34.4	—	—
Latin America	1950	51.8	30.8	46.5	27.3
	1980	190.9	30.3	42.2 (60.3)[g]	28.3

[a]Gross national product in billions of 1970 dollars, 1950–1976.
[b]Country figures and those for Latin America are the sum of unpaid family workers, domestic servants, and the self-employed minus professionals and technicians.
[c]When 1980 figures are unavailable, 1970 figures are used.
[d]Column figures are based on the definition given under [b]. Figures in parentheses are percentage of workers not registered with the national social security system.
[e]Column figures are the sum of unpaid family workers and the self-employed minus professionals and technicians. The figure in parentheses includes these categories plus wage workers without social security protection for a sample

representative of approximately 65.4 percent of the city's population.
[f]Figures are percentages of "irregular" workers, defined as those receiving
less than the legal minimum wage per labor hour.
[g]Figure in parentheses is the sum of the three occupational categories listed in
[b], plus the estimated proportion of informal wage workers.

Source: Portes and Sassen-Koob 1987.

Between 1950 and 1980, Latin American economies grew at a
weighted average of 5.5 percent. As shown in Table 7.1, the regional
gross national product (GNP) quadrupled during this period. Without
exception, individual countries more than doubled their national products, although rates of growth were much higher in such countries as
Colombia, Mexico, and Brazil. Because of rapid population growth,
GNP per capita did not grow as fast, but, in 1980, it stood at approximately 200 percent of the 1950 figure. The most dynamic element in the
growth of this region was, without doubt, the industrial sector. Industry's share of gross domestic product (GDP) registered an unweighted
average annual increase of 6 percent between 1950 and 1975, with
much higher increases in Brazil, Mexico, Peru, and other countries.

The response of labor markets to this accelerated process of
industrialization was not what neo-liberal and Marxist theories would
have predicted. As shown in Table 7.1, informal employment, as
defined by the United Nations' Regional Employment Program for
Latin America (PREALC), declined only from 46 percent to 42 percent
of the Latin American labor force. In 1950, informal activities occupied
30 percent of the urban economically active population; in 1980, with
an industrial plant four times larger, informal employment still stood
at 30 percent. Contrary to its course in the advanced countries, self-
employment did not decline with industrialization but remained
essentially constant during this thirty-year period.[1] Furthermore, there
is reason to believe that declines in informal employment, minimal for
the region as a whole but significant for a few countries like Mexico
and Venezuela, reflect an over-optimistic assessment of actual trends.
The international agencies that are the source of these data define *informal employment* as the sum of the self-employed—excluding professionals and technicians—plus unremunerated family workers and
domestic servants. Excluded are informal wage workers; that is, those
who are hired casually and lack social security protection. According
to this definition, therefore, all wage workers are part of the formal sector. In Latin America, with the exception of Argentina and Uruguay,
this assumption leads to a gross underestimate of informal employment because a large proportion of wage laborers are employed in

small enterprises that are either legally exempted from the existing labor legislation or simply do not observe it.

Table 7.1 presents figures that indicate the likely size of this underestimate. In Bogotá, informal workers, as defined by PREALC, represented about one-third of the urban labor force in 1984, the figure being essentially the same as ten years earlier. An alternative and more appropriate definition, based on exclusion of labor from social security coverage, increases these estimates drastically to about two-thirds of the urban EAP in both years. In general, whenever unprotected wage workers are added to what has been defined as the informal sector, the relative size of the latter increases significantly. As shown in Table 7.1, this corrected definition leads to a revised estimate of total informal employment in Latin America that exceeds the PREALC figure by approximately 20 points. Regardless of how the informal sector is operationally defined, however, it is clear that the predicted secular trend toward its disappearance with the advance of capitalist industrialization has not materialized in any country of the region.

Consequences for Governments

High labor standards in the model of the advanced countries and the resulting labor market dualism can be sustained when the strategy for development revolves around import-substitution industrialization and protection of domestic industry. When economic growth is predicated on expansion of the domestic market, there is an incentive to create and sustain a relatively high-wage segment of the labor force. The model requires, however, that domestic industry operate behind high tariff barriers (Fishlow 1986; Felix 1986; Balassa, Bueno, Kuczynski, and Simonsen 1986).

The situation changes when the model shifts to export-led growth. In this situation, it is possible for modern firms to bypass legal requirements with the connivance of governments, as done by the Uruguayan leather industry, but the arrangements are cumbersome and subject to public challenge. Although the experience of labor struggles and labor regulation varies widely in the Third World, a common thread is that benefits, once granted, are difficult to take back. Constituencies are created around each right that prove highly resilient in the face of opposition. The recent history of countries like Turkey, Argentina, and Chile where military regimes put all their might into breaking the power of unions and other working-class organizations and failed attests to the futility of such efforts (Hartlyn and Morley 1986; Waisman 1987; Cagatay 1988).

One alternative is to attempt to increase productivity in the modern sector through technological innovation. Countries like Brazil and Mexico have made strides in this direction during recent years, as they shifted development strategies. This approach can be hampered, however, by technological limitations and the existing labor codes that obstruct the implementation of more flexible arrangements (Balassa et al. 1986; Schydlowsky 1986; Malloy 1979). For this reason, the governments of heavily regulated countries attempting to break into export markets have adopted the strategy of establishing special production zones (SPZ) in remote areas away from the centers of union strength. What is "special" about these zones is precisely that provisions of the existing tax and labor legislation do not apply to them and that they are generally "union free." In this manner, nations informalize themselves vis-à-vis their own laws just as individual firms attempt to do and for the same reason: the search for international competitiveness (Castells and Portes 1989).

Some authors contend that the mass production system in industry necessarily leads to the observance of certain labor standards, absent under more primitive sweatshop conditions. The reason is that employers need to ensure the efficient use of the heavy capital outlays invested in large plants that entails, in turn, a modicum of attention to the situation and needs of workers (Piore 1988). Conditions in large plants in the SPZs tend to contradict this benign prediction. As documented by eyewitness and participant observer studies, the combination of sweatshop practices (such as piece rates) with mass production practices (such as speed-ups and specialization in minute tasks) is common. The result is high levels of labor exploitation without the minimal compensation of casual face-to-face relationships common in the more traditional informal shops (Fernández-Kelly 1983; Deyo 1987).

The configuration of labor market situations in Third World countries with extensive labor standards may be usefully contrasted with those in the Asian NICS (newly industrializing countries), particularly South Korea, during their periods of expansion. In the latter, little mention is made of an informal sector because the absence of state-enforced protective regulation rendered the formal-informal distinction meaningless. Instead, there emerged, in Castells' (1975) phrase a "nineteenth century proletariat with twentieth century technology." Significant wage gains were made as a result of growing scarcity of labor, but the right to organize, independent unions, collective bargaining, and other measures of working-class autonomy were vigorously resisted by governments bent on maintaining their competitiveness in world markets (Deyo 1987; Gereffi 1987; You 1988).

In Mexico, Brazil, Peru, and other Third World countries, on the other hand, powerful independent unions represent the protected sector of the working class. Although their rhetoric is populist and even radical, the fact is that they tend to represent only the better-paid and more stable fraction of the working class. Alongside, there toils a vast unprotected proletariat employed by sweatshops and other informal enterprises and linked, in ways hidden from public view, with modern sector firms. Finally, sweatshop-style conditions also prevail under the new mass production for export organized in a belated imitation of the NICS. As in the latter, pliant segments of the working population, especially young women, tend to be the preferred source of labor for "special" export production.

Alternative Policies

From the viewpoint of North American and European trade unions, the extension of advanced labor standards to the entire Third World would be ideal. Unfortunately, this is not a realistic goal because, as seen, premature importation of such standards leads full circle to a situation where countries end up by informalizing themselves vis-à-vis their own regulations. It is therefore necessary to ask what labor standards can be applied that combine effective protection for the greatest number with the implementation of successful plans for national development. The question already suggests part of the answer; namely, the need to fine tune the application of labor standards to local conditions, rather than opt for either their wholesale rejection or acceptance.

Table 7.2 presents a breakdown of items commonly included under labor standards as a heuristic device to guide the following discussion. Those labeled *basic rights* include standards where a global consensus seems to have been attained and that are therefore amenable to international monitoring. The final category, civic rights, encompasses standards that have also come to be accepted as consensual by democratic nations. Although agreement on the latter is less broad, it is sufficiently widespread to justify requiring governments, especially those that claim to be democratic, to observe them.

The intermediate categories (survival and security rights) depend for their implementation on local conditions and do not lend themselves readily to fixed international standards. They are best left to bargaining between workers, employers, and governments, once basic and civic rights have been fully implemented. Negative consequences associated with premature importation of labor standards have involved primarily these intermediate categories and not those

Table 7.2   Minimum Labor Standards

TYPE	EXAMPLES
Basic Rights	Right against use of child labor Right against involuntary servitude Right against physical coercion
Survival Rights	Right to a living wage Right to accident compensation Right to a limited work week
Security Rights	Right against arbitrary dismissal Right to retirement compensation Right to survivors' compensation
Civic Rights	Right to free association Right to collective representation Right to free expression of grievances

that could plausibly form part of an internationally accepted package of labor rights. Of the two middle categories, the implementation of extensive job security, rather than the existence of a minimum wage or other survival rights, has created the greater rigidities. Studies in several Latin American countries indicate that the drive to informalize by modern firms is motivated primarily by the desire to avoid adding to a regular plant of workers that, once hired, can seldom be let go (López Castaño 1984; Portes and Benton 1984; Roberts 1989a).

Hence, apart from basic and civic rights that may become amenable to internationally enforced standards, the implementation of others also requires fine tuning, lest they act as a brake on economic development or on the extension of minimal protection to greater numbers. There is reason to doubt the popular dictum that Third World economies function best when wages are allowed to sink to their "natural" levels (Lim 1988). Firms relying on very cheap labor lack incentive to innovate technologically; their workers lack motive to remain with a particular firm or collaborate with management in increasing its efficiency; their paltry wages also add insignificantly to domestic demand (Benton 1989; Sabot 1988; Standing 1986).

The Latin American studies cited previously indicate that it is not high wages per se, but rather high wages to an immobile labor force regardless of business conditions, that constitute the main incentive for widespread informalization. Following this logic, the preservation of enough flexibility of employment would go a long way toward avoiding the pattern of labor market dualism characteristic of countries with premature labor standards.

What to Do with the Informal Sector?

The Maximum Flexibility Argument

Previous statements in favor of flexibility in the use of labor can be confused with a second argument making the rounds of international development circles. Backed by research conducted in Lima, Peru by the "Institute for Freedom and Democracy," the argument advocates not only greater flexibility of employment but removal of all state restrictions from the operation of the economy (see Bromley, this volume). Part of this antistatist argument is the familiar laissez-faire doctrine and requires no additional comment. Another part, however, is more novel, because it argues that the removal of constraints created by tax and labor legislation on the informal economy would allow it to mushroom into a true engine of growth (de Soto 1986). According to this view, informal enterprise—which already employs the majority of the labor force—is hampered by efforts of the state to suppress it or increase control of it. If such restrictions were removed, the extraordinary ingenuity and energy demonstrated by grassroots entrepreneurs would be allowed to flourish, leading to development on the basis of small firms and with the full utilization of labor.

The argument of de Soto and his followers seems to blend well with the descriptions by Piore and Sabel (1984) of the advantages of "flexible specialization," as implemented by cooperatives of microenterprises in central Italy. This mutual reinforcement and the apparent simplicity of de Soto's prescription may well account for its sudden popularity in development circles: remove state interference from the informal sector and the dynamism of the market place plus the entrepreneurial abilities of common people would lead to self-sustaining growth. What could be easier?

Types of Informality and Development

A review of the research literature indicates that informal economies of growth—those that move from semi-clandestine shops to become viable networks of small enterprises—represent the exception and not the rule. Central Italy is the most commonly cited and sometimes seemingly the only example (Brusco 1982; Capecchi 1989). Others have been identified, however, including the complex organization of informal producers for export in Hong Kong (Castells 1986) and the impressive growth of urban ethnic economies in the United States—in particular in Los Angeles and Miami (Light and Bonacich 1988; Stepick 1989). All these instances are found in relatively developed regions. In the Third World, small-scale informal activities are restricted to (1) direct subsistence production and (2) sweatshop-style production and casual trade subordinated to firms in the modern sector. Studies of the informal economy in Latin America, for example, have been unable to uncover a single case of a network of small-scale enterprises bearing even an incipient resemblance to the phenomenon to Central Italy or Hong Kong (Portes and Benton 1984).

These findings give pause to optimistic predictions about what grassroots enterprise can accomplish when liberated from state intervention. The growth of small business is by no means automatic, and the obvious reason is that, except in very exceptional circumstances, informal entrepreneurs lack the capital, technological know-how, and organizational resources to implement anything beyond sweatshop or homework production. Further, the experience of central Italy and others in the literature indicate that it is not the absence of state intervention, but its sustained presence and aid that have been necessary to lead experiments of "flexible specialization" to success. State assistance need not come from central governments, but can be more effectively provided by local agencies. It involves, at a minimum, training assistance, flexible access to credit, transportation facilities, and support of cooperative efforts by microenterprises (Capecchi 1989; Benton 1989).

Hence, the transformation of informal economies of survival into informal economies of growth does not depend on getting the state "out of the economy," but "into it," albeit in new and unorthodox ways. So far, national development plans in the Third World have been almost obsessively concerned with the implementation of grand industrialization schemes, based on large projects and plants. Such plans, which also reflect the imitative orientation toward the advanced world, have created a number of unexpected bottlenecks and difficulties, not the least of which is the pattern of labor market dualism noted earlier. Active state involvement in promoting small enterprise represents not only an important, yet neglected, element of development planning, but also a means to improve labor standards for the majority of labor.

This causal linkage is a corollary of the basic difficulty in enforcing protective labor legislation noted at the start; namely, the existence of a mass of surplus workers at the bottom of the labor market. Even after implementation of flexible hiring rules to encourage modern firms to absorb more labor directly, it is unlikely that the informal sector will be totally drained of workers. To the extent that informal enterprise remains a low-tech, low-wage appendage of the modern sector, it will continue to undermine labor standards no matter how actively enforced. The transformation of such enterprises into technologically advanced small producers also reinforces existing rules by weakening their dependence on exploitable labor.

The research literature supports the point made by de Soto and his associates concerning the entrepreneurial ingenuity of common people and the ability of informal businesses to overcome large obstacles (Lomnitz 1978; Peattie 1981; Roberts 1989; Fortuna and Prates 1989). However, in the absence of specialized training, access to technology, access to credit, and other support facilities that only the state can provide, the informal sector will remain confined to the role of reservoir of vulnerable labor for large firms atop Third World economies.

Summary

In this chapter, I have taken an approach that departs from both dominant positions in the debate on labor standards for newly industrializing countries. These standards are commonly portrayed as a holistic set of rules, to be adopted or discarded in toto. Instead, I propose their separation into discrete categories amenable to different levels of implementation and international monitoring. For those who advocate a full set of advanced regulations for implementation in all countries, I offer the example of those less developed nations that attempted to do so and failed. Their sophisticated legal codes tended not so much to reflect labor market realities as the influence and prestige of things foreign. A common result was an acute labor market dualism protecting a privileged segment of the labor force at the expense of the majority. Firms and states alike subsequently sought to bypass this protected sector in their quest for international competitiveness.

For advocates of the opposite solution—removal of all state regulation to let popular entrepreneurial energies flourish—I offer the contrast between the exceptional experiences of self-sustained communities of flexible producers and the reality of sweatshop conditions dominant throughout the Third World. Removal of state regulations would certainly benefit large firms in the short run by increasing flexibility and reducing costs, but it would not by itself transform the informal economy of most countries into anything more than what it already is.

There is no alternative to state intervention in the labor market, but it should not consist of enacting unrealistic laws and then erratically enforcing them. Instead, basic rights that have become consensually accepted throughout the civilized world should be implemented and enforced, followed by others as local conditions permit. Of these, survival rights come first, with rights to job tenure a definite second. Flexible implementation of labor rules should be accompanied by strong support for the development of a dynamic small-scale sector (Otero, Márquez, this volume). This bias for grassroots capitalism is not justified by populist ideology, but by growing evidence that networks of high-tech small producers can prove more efficient in certain areas and more adept at coping with market uncertainties than large plants.

The development of technologically advanced small enterprise and a transition from sweatshop production to this higher form will strengthen labor standards in three ways. First, downward pressure on wages and work conditions lessens as the viability of firms ceases to depend on vulnerability of labor. Second, workers in new firms will benefit from apprenticeship opportunities and a chance to launch their own businesses in the future. Third, the development of communities of small producers gives workers in larger industries the opportunity to shift into this sector. The existence of this option strengthens the workers' position vis-à-vis managerial power. Thus, state-supported transformation of the informal sector can represent an efficient means to promote labor standards, not by enforcement of unrealistic rules but by giving workers an opportunity to make independent use of their energy and ingenuity.

NOTES

1. Between 1900 and 1930, the percentage of self-employed in the United States declined from 34 percent to 23 percent of the civilian labor force (Lebergott 1964).

❏ Chapter 8

Informality, de Soto Style: From Concept to Policy

Ray Bromley

Introduction

Hernando de Soto's concept of *informality* is clear, simple, and directly linked to an interpretation of history and a set of policy prescriptions. This chapter summarizes his concept, explains his central argument, and reviews the ways in which he has used them to formulate policies. The concern is not with whether he is "right" or "wrong," with whether his field research conclusions are correct, or with his impact on Peruvian politics—issues that have been amply discussed elsewhere (Bromley 1990; Cueva 1988; Fajardo 1990; Tokman 1987a; Urriola 1988). The focus is on his ideas: how they are structured; their intellectual roots; what they imply in the arena of public policy; and their limitations. The prime sources of information are de Soto's book, *The Other Path* (1986, 1989),[1] my various periods of field research in Peru, and extensive coverage of the Peruvian press.[2] Because *The Other Path* has few citations, it was often necessary to "read between the lines" to assess how ideas were expressed and tested, and to search out their sources.[3]

My introduction to informal sector debates came in the mid-1970s, a decade before de Soto emerged as a major contributor to the field. My background and intellectual inclinations can be characterized as Euro-Socialist, heavily influenced by Keynesian thinking, Orwell's internationalism, and 1970s debates about the applicability of

Marxist and neo-Marxist ideas to the Third World. With extensive research on Ecuadorian and Colombian street and market traders to bolster me, I enthusiastically joined the wave of research and debate that followed the publication of the ILO's inspirational Kenya Report (ILO 1972; Bromley 1979, 1985; Bromley and Gerry 1979). On first reading reports of de Soto's work and first meeting him in 1984, I had no way of putting his work in context. The first reaction was to view him as an ill-informed intruder into a well-researched arena. Subsequently, however, though still in disagreement with many of his views, I have come to appreciate their roots, their importance, and their internal consistency.

For readers who share a background in Marxian, Keynesian, and ILO informal sector ideas, the most important advice for understanding de Soto is: "Start again!" Go back to the Age of Enlightenment, to the moral philosophy of Adam Ferguson (1767) and the political economy of Adam Smith (1776), and examine pre-Marxian ideas on nations, governments, economies, and human rights. Then, read some of the works of the late Friedrich von Hayek (1899–1992), notably *The Constitution of Liberty* (1960) and the *Law, Legislation and Liberty* trilogy (1973–1979). Finally, read a contemporary conservative rejection of dependency theory, such as Harrison (1985) or Rangel (1986), where blame for poverty and economic stagnation is placed squarely on the shoulders of the governments, elites, and institutions of the poor countries. These will put de Soto in context, helping to frame his work in a tradition of conservative and libertarian scholarship, rather than as dissent from dualist economics (cf. Lewis 1954), the ILO's informal sector (cf. Sethuraman 1976a), or Keynesian or neo-Marxist explanations of development and underdevelopment.

The Concept

De Soto does not deviate from the ILO or world systems (underground economy) concepts of an informal sector; he develops his own concepts without any reference to those models. In *The Other Path* and numerous interviews, speeches, and short articles, he has defined and elaborated a concept of informality with four fundamental characteristics. First, as pointed out in a preceding chapter, it is sociolegal in character, deriving from the interdisciplinary field of law and economics,[4] rather than from mainstream economics or sociology. Second, it focuses on economic activities and enterprises, rather than on individuals, households, or neighborhoods; it represents a way of doing things, rather than a fixed population or territory. Third, it bridges the gap between production and reproduction, dealing with the totality of income-generating and expenditure-saving activities. Fourth, it is not dualistic, because it does not presuppose that the whole economy is, or should be, divided into two sectors. De Soto sometimes uses the expressions *informal sector* and *informal economy*, but they seem little more than alternative ways of saying "those activities and enterprises that can be deemed informal."

De Soto views informal activity as an intermediate between formal and criminal activity, on the basis of a simple means/ends criterion. Formal activities have legal ends and are conducted by legal means. Informal activities have legal ends, but are conducted illegally because it is difficult for the participants to comply with official regulations. Criminal activities have illegal ends and therefore cannot be conducted any way other than illegally.

Though an intermediate between formal and criminal on the basis of the means-ends criterion, de Soto places informal activities on a par with formal ones in terms of social utility. He sees informal activities, just like formal ones, as essentially moral and law abiding, fulfilling socially useful purposes. He calls participants in informal activities *the informals*, and he continuously emphasizes that they are decent, hard-working and productive individuals. In his view, criminal activities should be persecuted and punished, but informal activities should not be penalized because they are well-intentioned and useful. Thus, to the first definitional criterion for *informality* (activities with illegal means but legal ends), he often adds a second criterion, social utility, that the people involved and the society as a whole are better off if the law on these activities is broken than if it is obeyed. Hence, "an activity is informal when it neither produces a deterioration in the social situation nor an antisocial result when the law and the regulations applicable to it are disobeyed" (Ghersi 1991, p. 46). This second criterion allows de Soto to exclude such morally questionable economic activities as prostitution, gambling, child labor, and begging from the category of informality. It can also be used to exclude such hazardous activities as manufacturing fireworks in residential areas, selling in the middle of busy traffic arteries, and selling contaminated food or drink.

Applying the two criteria (illegal means but legal ends and social utility), de Soto gives numerous examples of informal activities in *The Other Path*, with a particular emphasis on trade, transport, housing, manufacturing and repair. Using extended case studies of Lima's street and market traders, para-transit operators, and squatter settlements (*barriadas*),[5] he shows how the poor struggle to make a living and to feed, house and clothe themselves and their dependents. Although they achieve these objectives, they also contribute to the national economy, provide vital services, and enhance the nation's human resources through the development of craft and entrepreneurial skills and through their increased capacity to educate themselves and their children. In some cases, they help reduce the country's imports and indebtedness by providing goods or services that otherwise would have to be imported.

Despite all their positive contributions, de Soto's informal activities are illegal because they do not comply with official regulations on licensing, location, or form of operation. As a result, at any time the enterprises could be closed down, property could be confiscated, or squatter homes could be demolished. To minimize these risks, the informals are forced to keep their businesses small and to stay away from prime locations so as to remain undetected, or to pay bribes to police and other officials so as to keep on operating. The informals have no access to official credit, subsidies, technical assistance, or duty-free imports because their businesses and homes do not officially exist as authorized activities and establishments.

The Argument

In *The Other Path*, when de Soto argues that informality results directly from the promulgation of unjust regulations by local and national governments, he sees the state as the villain. Government stimulates informality by imposing excessive and inappropriate regulations and by implementing exclusionary policies designed to limit enterprise. He follows the ideas of Thomas Paine (1737–1809) and other Age of Enlightenment philosopher-revolutionaries in making a clear and very sharp distinction between "natural laws" (moral principles that are socially necessary, right, and just) and "formal laws" (the artificial creations of governments). Because governments can be inefficient, repressive, exploitative, over-intrusive, or simply "too big," their formal laws are not necessarily socially useful, right, or just.

In the second part of *The Rights of Man*, written in 1792, Paine (1915, p. 159) sets out this view very clearly:

> Formal Government makes but a small part of civilized life. . . . The more perfect civilization is, the less occasion has it for Government, because the more it does regulate its own affairs, and govern itself; but so contrary is the practice of old Governments to the reason of the case, that the expenses of them increase in the proportion they ought to diminish. It is but few general laws that civilized life requires, and those of such common usefulness, that

whether they are enforced by the forms of government or not, the effect will be nearly the same. . . . All the great laws of society are laws of nature. Those of trade and commerce, whether with respect to the intercourse of individuals or of nations, are laws of mutual and reciprocal interests. They are followed and obeyed, because it is the interest of the parties so to do, and not on account of any formal laws their Governments may impose or interpose. But how often is the natural propensity to society disturbed or destroyed by the operations of Government! When the latter, instead of being ingrafted on the principles of the former, assumes to exist for itself, and acts by partialities of favour and oppression, it becomes the cause of the mischiefs it ought to prevent.

Typically, national constitutions are deeply imbued with Age of Enlightenment conceptions of "natural law," upholding the rights of the individual to life, food, drink, housing, education and health care, and to work, to do business, and to make profits. They also define the responsibility of adults to protect and defend minors, the weak, the disabled and the aged, and they charge the state with the responsibility to provide services, and to maintain law, order and human rights. These are accompanied by pronouncements that the state should uphold liberty and democracy, "protect enterprise," and act "in the public interest."

When the noble and constitutionally enshrined natural laws are contrasted with the maze of petty regulations produced by most governments, it is easy to conclude that the citizen has a right and duty to ignore, disobey, or protest such regulations. This argument, used by Paine to justify the bloody French and American Revolutions, is used by de Soto to justify a peaceful revolution, a grassroots mass civil disobedience of unjust regulations. The original Spanish-language version of *The Other Path* is subtitled "The Informal Revolution," whereas the English language translation is subtitled "The Invisible Revolution." Either way, the basic message is clear. Millions of "informals" in Peru and other Third World countries have joined a grassroots uprising against unjust and excessive regulations by starting their own businesses and developing their properties outside the framework of "formal law."

To underline the distinction between natural and formal, de Soto develops the concept of a "system of extralegal norms" in *The Other Path* (pp. 19–57) to show how rules and procedures are developed in informal economic activities. In Lima's *barriadas*, for example, a great deal of organization and collaboration is needed to lay settlements out, assign lots, and obtain services. The resident households respect each other's property rights, properties can be rented or sold, and community organizations petition the government for utilities, public transport, and garbage collection. The residents even organize their own systems of law enforcement, property registration, and census taking, using these both as mechanisms to preserve order in their neighborhoods and to pressure the government for legalization and support.

Though these systems of extralegal norms provide an atmosphere of order and stability for informal enterprises and housing, investment and profits are still restricted by the absence of formal legal ownership. The businesses and properties are bought and sold in parallel informal markets at prices significantly lower than they would fetch if they had formal legal documentation. Profits are reduced when enterprises must be kept small or located away from the prime sites or when bribes must be paid to the authorities. Informal enterprises and *barriada* houses are not eligible for many forms of government support or subsidies, and they are denied bank loans because they do not have formal titles that can be used as collateral.

Probably the most innovative section of *The Other Path* is Chapter 5, "The Costs and Importance of the Law," where de Soto explores in considerable detail how much time and money is required to legalize businesses and squatter housing in Peru. The cause célèbre, recounted hundreds of times in speeches and articles citing *The Other Path*, was a simulation of the process of legalizing a small garment factory. The simulation was done by staff of the Institute for Liberty and Democracy (ILD), a think tank and research center that de Soto founded in Lima. It took the ILD staff 289 days and the payment of two bribes and numerous fees to complete the process. Including the value of the time lost from work in fulfilling the eleven separate requirements to legalize the business, the whole process cost the equivalent of US$1,036.60 (p. 134). Studies of actual cases of legalization showed the time required to complete various other key legalizations as follows: for a group of families wishing to build legally to be adjudicated a piece of state wasteland, a development permit, and building permits, 83 months; for a household to open a small store in a legally owned building, 43 days (costing US$590.56); for an organized group of market sellers to obtain permission to build their own market, 14.5 years; and to obtain recognition of a minibus route, 26 months.

De Soto goes on to show how, even after laboriously achieving formality, retaining that status also has costs in taxes and ongoing bureaucratic requirements. Thus, petty entrepreneurs and *barriada* dwellers are hard hit either way: by "the costs of informality" or by "the costs of formality and of remaining formal." Whether they opt to formalize or stay informal, long-term improvement and growth potentials are reduced by barriers to legality and the costs of overcoming those barriers.

For de Soto, unjust and excessive regulations are not usually the product of mindless bureaucrats or of megalomaniac dictators, but rather of entrenched vested interest groups, which he labels *mercantilists*. They form powerful coalitions of bureaucrats, legislators, magistrates, financiers, landlords, and business leaders, who benefit by generating regulatory jobs, opportunities for corruption, and protected markets for the goods and services they provide. In the short term, he sees the mercantilists as building and preserving their wealth and power, but in the long term, they damage their own interests as well as everyone else's by slowing their country's economic growth. The informals act as peaceful revolutionaries by engaging in socially beneficial forms of popular resistance to mercantilist regulations.

In *The Other Path*, de Soto portrays the poor as hard working and entrepreneurial, struggling to make a living and provide much-needed services in the face of stifling regulations. They are forced into "self-help" employment and housing by exclusionary market structures that deny them access to formality. Their effort and dynamism ensure that most of them work, but their incomes and entrepreneurial potential are drastically reduced by their informality. They do not have legal title to most of their property; they have no collateral to obtain low-interest credit; and they are continuously subject to the threat of fines, arrest, or the confiscation or destruction of their property. Official harassment reduces the profitability of informal enterprises and deters many potential entrepreneurs from starting business.

De Soto's portrayal of "mercantilists" and "informals" is linked to a highly simplified interpretation of world history, explaining the wealth of the rich countries in terms of a process of enlightenment to the values of the free market. He sees the rich countries as rich because their mercantilist elites came to realize the error of their ways, removed the barriers to free enterprise, and allowed a market economy to flourish. As a result, their own enterprises flourished, informal enterprises formalized, and numerous new enterprises were founded. Most of these enterprises prospered because the total market expanded rapidly through a process of circular and cumulative causation. Just as the wealth of the rich countries is explained by a process of enlightenment and a transition from mercantilism to a free market economy, the contemporary poverty of most of Latin America, Asia, and Africa is explained by their lack of enlightenment and consequent stagnation in mercantilism.

Despite their current poverty, de Soto sees great potential for enlightenment in poor countries because their mercantilist elites can learn from historical counterparts in the rich countries and unleash the market economy through a combination of three types of measures to reduce the impact of the state: deregulation, debureaucratization and privatization. By promoting deregulation, debureaucratization, and privatization—henceforth known as DDP, de Soto argues that the size of the state apparatus can be reduced, the quality of life of every citizen improved, and the nation's vast entrepreneurial potential unleashed. *The Other Path* means to promote this transformation by providing an explanation of how rich countries became rich, how the natural dynamism of the peoples of poor countries is restrained by mercantilism, and how poor countries can achieve economic growth by unleashing their potential. He avoids even the slightest implication that violence, austerity, or suffering may be necessary to trigger change and instead advocates a peaceful revolution that is strongly populist and libertarian in character. He promises the long-term benefits of economic development and enhanced social mobility to both elites and masses, conditioned only on the abandonment of mercantilist policies that are essentially short term, selfish, and against the public interest. He leads the reader to believe that all poor countries can "take off" into self-sustaining economic growth—a take-off triggered by DDP rather than by Rostow's (1960) prescription of sharp increases in savings and corporate and public investment.

De Soto's analysis and prescriptions have considerable appeal. They promise a peaceful and essentially painless process of economic development for the poor countries, and they remove any burden of guilt the rich countries may have borne because of their dominant role in colonialism and imperialism. The blame for poverty and economic stagnation is fixed on the mercantilist elites of the poor countries, and growth can be achieved through their enlightenment. The human resources of the poor countries are emphasized, and the poor are depicted as full of energy, initiative, and entrepreneurial dynamism. *The Other Path* has no discussion of natural resource constraints to economic development or environmental limits to growth, and there is little discussion of topics like dictatorship, militarism, racism, crime, and speculative profiteering.

The mercantilists are portrayed as coming from both the left and right wings of the political spectrum, a coalition of monopolists and statists who conspire to achieve short-term gains by blocking the long-term growth potential of free markets and entrepreneurship. [6] By criticizing those he labels *the mercantilists of the left and right*, de Soto appears to take a moderate and centrist position, sidestepping the conventional ideological dimensions of political debate. Most of the text of *The Other Path* has a conservative tone, scrupulously avoiding class analysis or any reference to exploitation, dominance, and dependency in the world system or the social relations of production. De Soto even avoids the term *capitalism*, preferring to speak of free market economies. *The Other Path*'s dedication (p. v), however, goes out of its way to set a populist, radical, and libertarian tone and to heal potential rifts with the Left: "To Latin America's competitive workers and entrepreneurs, formal and informal, who through their efforts are tracing the other path. And, of course, to my left-wing friends, whose ideals I share, in the hope that we might also agree on ways to achieve them."

In many senses, Hernando de Soto is a late twentieth century exponent of "rags to riches" parables—a Horatio Alger or Samuel Smiles who both tells the story of poor peoples' entrepreneurship and also exemplifies entrepreneurship in his own life. On the jacket of the English edition of *The Other Path*, he describes himself as simply "a Peruvian entrepreneur." His style in public meetings and television interviews is bouncy, optimistic, and charismatic—full of personal dynamism and "can do" spirit. His message was launched on the world scene in the 1980s, during an exceptionally favorable period for such views, with the ascendancy of the new Right under the Reagan-Bush-Quayle and Thatcher-Major administrations, and with the collapse of the former Soviet Bloc. He has played a small but significant role in establishing DDP as the conventional wisdom for economic restructuring and growth and in building a worldwide vision of enterprise and prosperity.[7]

The Policies

De Soto's career can be divided into three main phases: pre-1980, his formative period as a businessman and public administrator, oscillating between Peru and Switzerland; 1980–1986, in which he established the ILD in Lima, built an international network of support, and directed the research for *The Other Path* (see Schuck and Litan 1986); and post-1986, in which he and the ILD have worked intermittently with different Peruvian political movements and with the governments of Alan García (1985–1990) and Alberto Fujimori (1990-).

The ILD was launched in 1980, the same year as *Sendero Luminoso*, "the Shining Path" (henceforth, *Sendero*), emerged as a guerrilla movement in opposition to the Peruvian governmental system. The choice of *The Other Path* as a book title by de Soto was a conscious play on words, making his prescriptions a nonviolent alternative to *Sendero*'s apocalyptic prescriptions of national purification through blood and fire (PCP 1989; Tarazona-Sevillano 1990, pp. 29–54). On the jacket of his book, de Soto argues that "Peru is already undergoing a revolutionary and irreversible process of transformation." He assumes that millions engage in creative civil disobedience by finding informal solutions to the shortage of jobs, housing, and services, and that public awareness is rapidly growing that mercantilism is the fundamental obstacle to development.

Since the mid-1970s, the economic and social conditions in Peru have deteriorated dramatically. De Soto's optimism was not exceptional in the early 1980s, a period in which many Peruvians and foreign observers, including myself, sincerely believed that the decline could be reversed and the national economy could be revived. But by 1993 it seemed decidedly unusual. The country has experienced a massive deterioration in living standards between 1987 and 1992; law, order, and human rights came under severe pressure; and the government lost control of substantial parts of the national territory. Drug trafficking, repression by the "security forces," guerrilla violence, hoarding, contraband, corruption, and capital flight were all rampant; and politics is pervaded by bickering and resentment rather than by any sense of mobilization for national unity. Though hyperinflation was brought under control in the early 1990s, the long-term prospects for the economy remain problematic because local elites and international big business are frightened to invest in the country and seek every opportunity to remove their assets. The course of events seems to parallel *Sendero's* vision of gradually accentuating contradictions, and growing repression and impoverishment, rather than de Soto's peaceful enlightenment.

So far at least, and despite the worsening national crisis, de Soto's research, writing and policy prescriptions have focused primarily on Peru, his country of birth, citizenship, and current residence. *The Other Path* is overwhelmingly focused on Lima's petty traders, transporters, and self-help housing. It is a book written for foreigners and local elites, describing how upper- and middle-class researchers went out into the poor neighborhoods and workplaces of Lima between 1982 and 1985, and discovered how the poor manage to survive. The poor are renamed *informals*, squatter houses are renamed *igloos*, and the information gathered is focused around de Soto's concepts and arguments. In most senses, however, the basic description of how most of Lima's poor obtain income and housing has many similarities to the earlier writings of Turner (1967, 1968), Mangin (1967), Matos Mar (1984) and numerous other social scientists who are not cited in *The Other Path* (MacEwen Scott 1979; Andreas 1985; Grompone 1985, among others).

Peru's deteriorating economic, social, and political situation is profoundly negative for most of the country's population, who must struggle to survive in a seemingly never-ending spiral of national collapse. To say the least, de Soto's interpretation of informality as an "invisible revolution" against mercantilism and a sort of collective disobedience against regulatory excess is highly controversial. Most of the phenomena he describes in *The Other Path* have been going on for decades, and it is easier to attribute recent growth to increasing desperation than to any form of popular awakening. The informals are not necessarily doing what they want to do, but rather doing whatever they must do to survive. ILD research focuses overwhelmingly on the immediate rationale for specific behavior, rather than on the broader systemic forces governing the markets for labor, land, housing, and services.

In policy terms, *The Other Path* prescribes DDP as the solutions for street and market trading, public passenger transport, housing, and other sectors of the national economy. The book suggests that national and local governments should withdraw from the provision of public market buildings, public transport systems, and public housing and transfer the existing facilities to their occupants and workers. Instead, the authorities should concentrate on providing law and order, public utilities, and a clear, simple, and highly simplified environment for private enterprise.

More specifically, *The Other Path* advocates the conversion of existing municipal market buildings to trader-managed cooperative markets, and support to organized groups of street traders so as to establish new cooperative markets and "commercial centers" with individual ownership of the stalls inside. It also advocates drastically simplified property registration procedures, both for small enterprises and self-help housing, and the removal or simplification of most building codes and planning and zoning controls. In general, it recommends the conversion of de facto status for informal enterprises and properties to de jure status, thus effectively formalizing them. De Soto's desired future is not a massive informal sector, but rather the absorption of currently informal enterprises into the formal economy through the removal of rules and procedures that exclude the informals from the benefits of formality. The final results of such a process would be the virtual disappearance of informal activity, a massive growth in formal activity, and if de Soto's assertions are correct, rapid, self-sustaining national economic growth.

Since the late 1980s, through agreements signed during the last two years of García's presidency, de Soto and the ILD have been aiding the Peruvian government with three major sociolegal projects: a simplified property registration process developed for, and applied to, urban squatter settlements; individual land title registration in rural areas, most notably in the cooperative and collective farms (CAPs and SAIS) established during the Velasquista agrarian reforms (1968–1975); and administrative simplification, a euphemism for debureaucratization (see Amaro 1988), chosen because it sounds less critical of Peru's bureaucrats. The registration of urban properties and rural smallholdings is a simple de jure recognition of a de facto situation, making it easier for the property holders to obtain formal titles, to petition for the installation of utilities, and to use their property as collateral to obtain improvement loans. The administrative simplification legislation short-cuts official procedures for the ordinary citizen by reducing the number of steps to be followed and the number of documents that must be presented (ILD 1989b). It has significantly reduced the time and expense required for most Peruvians to register births, marriages, and deaths; to obtain property titles, identification papers, and passports; and to get replacements for lost documents.

Few Peruvians doubt the value of property and land title registration and of administrative simplification, and many consider them to be the most useful, or even the only useful initiatives launched during García's presidency. To achieve their full potential, however, they require many supports, some of which have never existed in Peru and others that have been absent for at least a decade: an efficient, adequately remunerated bureaucracy to do the necessary paperwork; the absence of strikes, power cuts, bomb scares and other impediments to efficient bureaucratic work; an efficient public transport, phone, and postal service to facilitate easy communication; a climate of law and order, with honest, efficient police and swift justice; spatially deconcentrated government agencies, so that most official procedures can be completed locally in every subregion of the national territory; continuing economic growth in per capita terms; and, a strong, stable national currency with a low inflation rate, so that lenders, borrowers, and entrepreneurs can effectively manage their cash flow, assess potentials, and gauge risks. Peru is so far from most of these prerequisites that many of the benefits of title registration and administrative simplification cannot be achieved in the foreseeable future. The same policies, implemented in other Latin American countries that are not in such dramatic crisis situations, would have a much greater impact.

The gravity of Peru's problems and their impact on DDP reforms is all too evident in the *barriadas* of Lima, squatter settlements that, even without DDP, won an international reputation in the 1960s and 1970s for self-help and successful upgrading (Turner 1967, 1968). As the city has extended further and further outward at relatively low densities, the problem of transportation to and from the peripheral *barriadas* and the problem of extending the road and utility networks to reach these areas have become more acute. During the 1980s, the process of improvement in many neighborhoods ground to a halt because most households lacked the purchasing power to pay for construction materials or to hire skilled workers. Now, in the 1990s, even where utilities have been installed, drinking water and electricity supplies are highly irregular. The cholera epidemic of 1991–1993 is dramatic proof of the deterioration in hygiene, nutrition, and health care. *Sendero* is targeting community leaders for assassination, and the *barriadas* are alternately visited by armed bands of terrorists, police, and soldiers. Torture and disappearances have become commonplace, and many of the communal soup kitchens and other informal institutions have ceased to operate.

Though bureaucratic procedures for property registration have been dramatically simplified by the reforms promoted by de Soto and the ILD, many *barriada* property owners have failed to take advantage of them. Public offices are often closed because of strikes and power cuts, and even the cost of bus fares and photocopies are painful now that purchasing power has fallen to such a low level. Furthermore, even when properties are registered, most banks are unwilling to lend to *barriada* property holders because of the generalized "climate of insecurity"—the breakdown of law, order, and economic confidence associated with guerrilla violence, official repression and corruption, and the heritage of hyperinflation. Using the language of economic anthropology, Peruvian markets are so far from perfect—atomistic, open, free, and rational—that, even for the most fervent believers in the power of the marketplace, increased reliance on market forces offers no easy passage to mass prosperity.

Since their relatively successful and popular involvement in title registration and administrative simplification, de Soto and the ILD have become officially involved in three other attempts to reform Peruvian public policies: "democratization of decision-making," "pardons," and "opening free-market alternatives to coca production." Each of these efforts goes beyond the case studies and policies discussed in *The Other Path*, but it fits the general DDP thrust of the book. In each case, however, the ILD's actions have been intermittent and, so far at least, relatively ineffective. No long-term and definitive change in Peruvian public policy has been achieved, and the democratization of decision making was further postponed by President Fujimori's assumption of dictatorial powers in April 1992.

The democratization of decision-making idea, officially embraced by President Fujimori in his inaugural speech in July 1990, calls for mandatory procedures to encourage public discussion of potential legislation, limiting the capacity of the executive to legislate by decree, and forcing the legislature to publish and publicly discuss its proposed laws before voting on them (see Schuck and Litan 1986, pp. 65–66; ILD 1990a). The idea has great potential and inherent attraction as a means to limit the number of overlapping and contradictory laws, to increase popular involvement in the governmental system, and to develop a more structured system for consultation and lobbying. Regrettably, however, it runs against the obvious need for speed and secrecy in developing measures to stabilize and revive the economy, to refinance the national debt, to combat terrorism, and to punish repressive and revolutionary elements within the armed forces.[8]

"Pardons" was another ILD project that achieved a momentary official recognition under Fujimori late in 1990, but that is now indefinitely postponed.[9] The project resulted from the recognition that the Peruvian judicial system is very slow and inefficient, that most prisoners in the country's jails have never been tried, and that many have never been formally charged with any crime. Peruvians are often arbitrarily arrested, and unless they have influential friends and relatives who petition for their release, they may be held for months or even years without being formally charged. These horrific abuses stem from the viciously authoritarian traditions of the police and military, an obsession with "national security" accentuated by the emergence of *Sendero*, and the hopeless bureaucratic inefficiency and corruption of the judicial system. In the last three months of 1990, several hundred long-term residents of Peru's jails who had never been convicted or sentenced and who may well have been falsely accused and arrested were released by a high-level judicial commission. Regrettably, however, this very welcome presidential initiative, advised and supported by ILD staff members, was quickly dropped by the Fujimori administration. Arguments about the constitutionality and legality of the procedures blew out of control, and the security forces reaffirmed their claim to do whatever they feel appropriate in a seemingly never ending state of "emergency."

In 1990 and 1991, de Soto played an important role as a senior advisor to the newly elected President Fujimori, developing a network of high-level contacts in Washington and New York, helping him to reach agreements with the international banking community, and serving as his "chief advisor on narcotics policy." De Soto refused to accept the role of prime minister or any official title, but for most of the first eighteen months of the Fujimori administration he was viewed by his friends as "the power behind the throne" and by his enemies as "Fujimori's Rasputin." During this period, he focused his efforts on Peru's role as the world's largest coca producer and the raw material source for the global cocaine traffic. He traveled to Washington on numerous occasions to argue Peru's case for more favorable treatment by the U.S. government, and to develop a joint Peruvian–U.S. strategy for the "War on Drugs."

De Soto's (1992) position on narcotics, backed by various ILD working papers, has acquired the semi-official name of "the Fujimori Doctrine" and has been forcefully presented as the Peruvian governmental position in the international "drug summits" held in Cartagena in 1991 and in San Antonio, Texas, in 1992. It recognizes that around a quarter of a million coca producers are living and working in isolated areas on the eastern fringes of the Peruvian Andes and that they are generally poor farmers who grow coca because it is the only viable cash crop for that region. All other potential cash crops are ruled out because of low average prices, high bulk, perishability, unreliable and costly transport, and the lack of agroindustries in the region. Some, like rice, coffee, and corn, are made even more problematical by the actions of government marketing boards, the imposition of international production quotas, or the "dumping" of foreign food aid. De Soto very reasonably argues that the coca producers have no desire to break the law or contribute to an international trafficking network, but they currently have no viable alternative means of making an income in the remote areas where they live. He views coca production as an "informal" survival strategy, imposed on local farmers by market failures resulting from decades of inappropriate government policies.

Though de Soto takes a sympathetic position toward the coca producers, he condemns the international cocaine traffickers as criminals who should be subjected to the full force of the law. Since the early 1980s, however, the coca producing areas have been subjected to increasing penetration by the Peruvian military and U.S. military advisors and also by *Sendero* and MRTA[10] guerrillas. Coca producers have been attacked by ground and air forces, and there has been widespread use of crop defoliants and herbicides. Thousands of coca farmers and their families have been killed, wounded, tortured, or have "disappeared."

De Soto's basic objective for the coca producing areas is "crop substitution." He believes that this can be achieved through four major policies: immediately halting all military attacks on coca farmers and their crops; granting land titles to the coca farmers, so that they can use their property as collateral to obtain credit; removing all price controls, marketing boards, production quotas, subsidies, and foreign dumping of alternative crops; and offering stimuli to international agribusiness to start buying alternative crops in the regions that currently produce coca. Though he presents these policies as new and highly innovative, they are rather similar to ideas that circulated in AID/Peru circles in the early 1980s.[11] "Crop substitution" has long been one of the alternative strategies in the U.S. government's narcotics portfolio, with a heavy emphasis on agricultural extension, farmer credit, and agroindustries. Recently, however, at the highest levels this strategy has been viewed as too slow, long term, and impractical.[12] The growing strength of *Sendero* and the MRTA in the coca-producing areas, combined with the U.S. military's concern since the end of the Cold War and the collapse of the Soviet Union to justify its budgets by getting more involved in a "War on Drugs," have led to increasing U.S. emphasis on military solutions.

Although superficially attractive, de Soto's recommended drugs strategy faces great obstacles: a world trade system in agricultural products that is massively distorted by quotas, subsidies, dumping, and "food aid" and the de facto occupation of the coca-producing areas by *Sendero* and MRTA guerrillas, international drug cartels, elements of the Peruvian military and police (many of them corrupt and viciously repressive), and substantial numbers of U.S. "advisors." However virtuous free markets may be, they are not likely to be the prime concern for local farmers when most visitors come with machine guns! De Soto himself recognized the near impossibility of the situation in early 1992, when he renounced his role as the Fujimori administration's unofficial narcotics policy advisor, citing police and army corruption and widespread human rights abuses in the coca-producing areas.

Conclusion

Though clear and simple, de Soto's concept of informality is far from unambiguous. The means-ends definitional criterion can be problematical when some means are legal and others are illegal. If an enterprise is required to have six official permits, for example, but has only five, should it still be considered informal even when the sixth derives from a moribund regulation that most entrepreneurs ignore? Formality and informality are really the opposite poles of a continuum with many intermediate and mixed cases. Extralegal norms often acquire a quasi-legality that adds further ambiguity to our definitions. Even more problematic is the social utility criterion, which relies very heavily on the investigator's judgment. How do we deal with enterprises involving gambling, child labor, or prostitution, for example, or street enterprises that provide useful services but significantly increase the possibility of traffic accidents? De Soto's position on the informality of coca production and the criminality of cocaine traffic involves even more complex value judgments, with both the means-ends and the social utility criteria in question. Coca has been grown for thousands of years on the eastern slopes of the Andes. Most contemporary coca producers, however, have migrated voluntarily into the region, and many have arrived since coca became the chief cash crop. Almost all the coca producers know that the leaves they sell are destined for the international cocaine market.

The Other Path focuses mainly on commercial, transport, and manufacturing enterprises and on the development of Lima's *barriadas*. It does not discuss the "informal" procedures of national and transnational big business, where laws are broken very frequently, yet "the gentlemen" involved assume that they will not be treated as criminals. It is very common, for example, for government contracts and permits to be obtained through false promises, lavish hospitality, or outright bribery and for "creative" accountants to use international transfers of profits as means to avoid paying taxes. *The Other Path* is also remarkably silent about the wage labor relationships that prevail in such sectors as domestic service and construction. These are crucial areas of the labor market for the employment of poor migrants to major cities like Lima, and the employers involved use numerous mechanisms to avoid complying with labor legislation (MacEwen Scott 1979). Domestic servants in Lima, for example, often start their careers as minors "indentured" by their parents to city families, and most "employers" do not pay the wages and social security contributions or give the rest and vacation periods mandated by Peruvian law (Rutte 1976, p. 160).

Despite these notable ambiguities and omissions, there are certainly fewer problems in applying de Soto's two-criterion definition of informality than in applying the ILO's (1972) seven-criterion definition of the informal sector or Sethuraman's (1976b) labyrinthine extension of the ILO position. Nevertheless, it is obvious that the reader should view with great skepticism anything more than highly approximate measurements of the extent of informality or the size of the informal sector. Precise figures, as cited in *The Other Path*, developed more fully in some of the associated ILD studies (ILD 1989a, 1990b), and criticized by Rossini and Thomas (1990), give a spurious accuracy and precision to a very complex area of judgment. They fall into the dualist trap that de Soto's original concept of informality so neatly sidesteps. The statement on the jacket of *The Other Path*, for example, that "informals represent 60 percent of the Peruvian economy," raises dozens of questions: now or when? plus or minus "X" percent? including or excluding big-business "informality"? which legal ends–illegal means activities were not deemed socially useful? including or excluding subsistence production? with or without narcotics production and money laundering from the narcotics traffic and contraband? how did they find out the turnover of all those enterprises when few entrepreneurs seem willing to honestly state their turnover? how were all those values interrelated under hyperinflation? how did they get data on the enterprises in zones controlled by *Sendero*? and so on.

De Soto's concept of informality is not a magic solution to overcome the problems of applying the ILO or world systems (underground) concepts of the informal sector. Nor is it a substitute for the ILO and world systems perspectives. Each concept and perspective was established for specific reasons.[14] In de Soto's case, the main reasons are obvious: as a means to advance a policy agenda of deregulation, debureaucratization, and privatization, and on a broader scale, to promote free-market policies emphasizing grassroots entrepreneurship and community self-help.

Though he is just one of many distinguished advocates of DDP on the world stage, de Soto has a distinctive brand of libertarian populism that emphasizes the sociolegal obstacles to entrepreneurship and economic growth. His work reminds us that a dynamic private sector and vibrant small enterprises are important elements in economic growth and that government can be overintrusive, can overextend itself, and can stifle popular initiatives through excessive bureaucracy. Every country in the world could benefit from in-depth research on "the costs and importance of the law," and de Soto's studies and simulations of the costs of formality and informality should be replicated in many different contexts.

Though innovative and potentially important, de Soto's sociolegal focus has great limitations. It is based on a very simple interpretation of world economic history, and it covers a relatively limited section of the policy arena. It cannot work to any great extent in Peru because national security concerns, international relations, ideological and class conflicts, and the macroeconomic environment all impede the conduct and impact of DDP. De Soto, like thousands of libertarian scholars before him, falls into the classic paradox: only a strong state can comprehensively reform the policy environment, and no strong state apparatus ever dramatically reduces its own powers and roles. His most important role, so far, has been to stimulate debate, rather than to bring about dramatic real-world changes.

Beyond his role as a globe-trotting speaker and consultant to promote DDP, de Soto is not a major actor in public policy debates outside Peru. Even a cursory reading of *The Other Path* will show that it is primarily a book about Peru deeply rooted in Latin American realities. The testing ground for de Soto's policy prescriptions has been Peru, and the record of achievement is decidedly checkered. In July 1992 the excesses of de Soto's optimism for a peaceful revolution were savagely underlined when *Sendero* bombed the ILD offices, killing three persons, wounding twenty, and destroying much of the structure.[15]

It is unfortunate that de Soto has developed his ideas in Peru since 1980. However good and useful his ideas are, they seem like rearranging the deck chairs on the Titanic. Few astute observers of Peru offer optimistic prognoses. Each new turn of events confounds the optimists and most actors in the drama feel impotent to change the course of events. No scenario seems likely to promote self-sustaining economic growth and a flowering of free enterprise and popular entrepreneurship. A transfer to a more favorable context, like Ecuador or Costa Rica, seems best for testing de Soto's research and policy interventions.

NOTES

1. All specific references to *The Other Path* are to the English edition (1989). De Soto wrote the book with two junior coauthors, Enrique Ghersi and Mario Ghibellini. Their contributions are correctly acknowledged on the cover of the Spanish edition, but are limited to a brief mention under "Acknowledgements" in the English edition. For a lively postscript to *The Other Path*, see de Soto (1988) and his numerous contributions to discussions recorded in the same volume.

2. In the 1980s I spent over three years working in Peru as a government advisor and an independent researcher. I had several opportunities on different visits to Peru to meet de Soto, to observe him at public events, and to visit his Institute for Liberty and Democracy (ILD). I also had numerous discussions about his work and the ILD's projects with his colleagues, friends, and critics and with a wide range of astute Peruvian scholars, politicians, and business leaders.

3. The few quotes or citations in *The Other Path* were included to sustain its tone and argument, rather than to indicate the intellectual parentage of its ideas. Most citations are of North American and British writings on economic history and law that concentrate primarily on how rich countries achieved their wealth. The strongest influences seem to be North (1981), North and Thomas (1973), and Olson (1982); note also North (1990). There is hardly any reference to the vast literature of Latin American Studies and development economics, which de Soto sees as full of dismal and ingrained fatalism. The only significant social scientists that receive mention are Collier (1976) on government policies toward Lima's *barriadas* and Sánchez León, Calderón, and Guerrero (1978) on Lima's public transport.

4. For a good introduction to "law and economics," see Axelrod (1984), Coase (1988), Olson (1965), Polinsky (1989), Posner (1986), and Poundstone (1992).

5. Many observers would consider squatter settlements to be criminal rather than informal because squatter homes are built on land that cannot be used by its rightful owner without expulsion of the squatters. Though de Soto does not discuss the issue in *The Other Path*, he views squatters as informals because the landowners were not making good use of the land when it was invaded and because the squatter homes help reduce the housing shortage. This view is easily justified in Lima, a city surrounded by vast expanses of desert—barren land, owned mostly by the state. Lima's situation parallels that of many Latin American cities, where squatter settlements expand onto deserts, swamps, steep hillsides, or saline flats. De Soto's view of squatters as "informals" is more difficult to justify on the rare occasions that they invade farmlands, or easily developable private property. In such cases they directly challenge private property rights and are more likely to engender a violent official response in defense of those rights.

6. In ILD circles, the most frequently mentioned case of such collaboration between right-wing monopolists and left-leaning statists is in Peru's import-substitution industrialization process under the radical military government of President Juan Velasco between 1968 and 1975. During this period, there was a massive expansion of industrial capacity, public investment, and the bureaucracy. Most new industries targeted the domestic market and were established as joint ventures between transnational corporations and the Peruvian state or business elites. They were guaranteed duty-free imports of equipment, raw materials, and components, plus high tariffs to protect them from foreign competition. As virtual monopolies, the new industries had no incentive to increase their efficiency or achieve scale economies. Peru's foreign debts were greatly increased by this industrialization process, and its consumers were forced to pay much more than the going world price for manufactures.

7. As extreme examples of the new faith in entrepreneurship, see Mario Vargas Llosa's Foreword to *The Other Path*, Havel's (1992) vision for Czechoslovakia, and Osborne and Gaebler (1992).

8. It was common in the early 1990s for middle- to upper-class Peruvians to compare the presidencies of Salvador Allende and Augusto Pinochet in neighboring Chile and to argue that discipline, secrecy, and repression are vital elements to ensure government efficacy and achieve national transformation. Initial widespread public support for Fujimori's *autogolpe* was a further sign that many Peruvians feel that the national crisis is so serious that "democracy" is no longer a prime concern.

9. See *Carétas* [Lima] (Sept. 24, 1990), pp. 36–37 and 88, and (Nov. 5, 1990), pp. 30–35; *El Peruano* [Lima], D.S. 017–90–JUS (October 2, 1990), pp. 90300–02.

10. The *Movimiento Revolucionario Túpac Amaru*, a smaller and less ruthless guerrilla movement than *Sendero*, which controls many of the northern coca-producing areas.

11. As a personal services contractor with AID/Peru in 1984–1985, I had ample opportunity to study documents, attend meetings, and see "crop substitution" projects.

12. See *Carétas* [Lima] (March 2, 1992), pp. 19 and 90.

13. In Peru, for example, organized groups of squatters can acquire a "legal personage" and negotiate the legalization of their holdings with the government. In contrast, individual squatters have no rights whatsoever. Similarly, the registration of squatter properties is just a first stage in a process that can lead to the granting of legal titles, yet it is viewed by both the squatters and government as an agreement over the squatters right to stay. Equally, if any state utility agrees to extend its lines to a squatter property, this is viewed by both the squatters and government as a mark of legitimacy, even though the property may not be registered.

14. Bromley (1978a) lists the problems in applying the original ILO (1972) informal sector concept, and Peattie (1987) explains why the concept is still used, even though it is riddled with definitional and conceptual ambiguities.

15. See *New York Times* (July 23, 1992), p. A11.

Chapter 9

Inside Informal Sector Policies in Latin America: An Economist's View

Gustavo Márquez

Introduction

The purpose of this chapter is to discuss the evolution and future of the informal sector as a policy "notion," outlining its changing influence on policies during the decade of the 1980s and suggesting policies for the 1990s. In doing so, the chapter contributes an ample vision of the role played by the informal sector notion in policy making, ranging from social welfare "help-the-poor" policies to macroeconomic policies to microenterprise promotion as a component of a broad package of development and restructuring policies. The word *notion* is used intentionally to evoke the "fuzziness" of the different policy formulations of the informal sector, without negating the fact that something about the notion determined its success and resilience.

The debate on the complexities of the informal sector as a "concept," a clearly delimited theoretical construct, has been covered in

Some portions of this chapter appeared in "Los informales urbanos: ¿Pobres o eficientes?" In *Economía Informal*, ed. Gustavo Márquez and Carmen Portela (Caracas: Ediciones IESA, 1991) pp. 1–42. I would like to thank Cathy Rakowski for a marvelous editing job that contributed in no small measure to clarifying the ideas in the chapter.

preceding chapters by Moser and Rakowski and by Peattie 1987 and Khundker 1988. This chapter, then, presents an overview of changes in the application of the notion to policy formulation and planning, especially economic, as observed by participants in that process of change. A large part of my professional work—as a practitioner, an academic, and a labor-in-development specialist—has included informal sector analyses. Both my own familiarity and the fact that a particular notion of the informal sector evolved and predominates in Latin America limits the scope of my inquiry to that region.

The chapter is divided into three sections. The first section is an insider's exploration of the complex interplay by which the informal sector notion attained its surprising popularity and influence in Latin America. The second section outlines specific policies for the informal sector or that take it into account. The third section critiques policies and suggests a more appropriate policy framework.

Evolution of the Informal Sector Notion Among Latin American Economists

Few ideas have had the lasting influence that the informal sector notion has had in thinking about, designing, and implementing economic policy, although this influence was not without costs in terms of conceptual precision. Yet, the informal sector notion in use in 1993 shares little more than a name with the concept Latin American economists used ten or five years before. This is explained by the diverse uses and meanings assigned to the notion. These, in turn, are related to the Latin American approach to planning and development theory.

During the 1960s and 1970s growing dissatisfaction with traditional, growth-oriented development theory (Lewis 1954) combined with an historic affinity for radical thinking among Latin American scholars and the visibility of social problems. Although Latin American economies grew rapidly and created a phenomenal number of jobs in the 1960s, a significant proportion of the population was believed to suffer from underemployment,[1] evidence that "trickle-down" approaches were not working. In the social sciences this resulted in the widespread popularity of dependency theory and the concept of "marginality"[2] (Quijano 1974), both of which represented elements of a political agenda for social reform "within the system." But dependency theory and its related concepts had limited usefulness for the small group of development economists who staffed national planning offices for three reasons. First, planners were concerned primarily with transforming the economy: substituting "traditional," small-scale activities "marginal to development" (believed to be synonymous with poverty and underemployment) with more "modern" endeavors (believed to be synonymous with improved income, benefits, skills, job security). Second, social science approaches were not easily operationalized or applied to planning. Third, even when planners, primarily economists and technical experts, shifted attention to poverty (and away from technocratic projects), they lacked an understanding of poverty, and this hindered their ability to design policy programs that could address the needs of the poor.

This was not a comfortable situation for policy makers or the planners who advised them. Here is where the macroincarnation of the informal sector notion came to the rescue. First, it "explained" why standard policies of economic expansion based on industrialization failed to improve income distribution and reduce underemployment. Second, it gave a name to the economic activities that occupied a large part of the urban population in Third World cities, activities planners regarded as residues from the past. Third, labeling activities *the informal sector* made them more accessible to policy models and, thus, legitimate subjects of public policy (ILO 1970, 1972; see Moser, this volume).

By the early 1980s, many Latin American economists (including me) were working on models of the labor market that included an informal sector. We were trying to operationalize empirically the notion as it was introduced into the labor market debate a few years earlier by Victor Tokman, P. R. Souza, and the group of economists who formed the core of PREALC, the influential International Labour Office's Regional Employment Program for Latin America and the Caribbean (Tokman and Klein 1979). When we first began analyses of the informal sector, it was conceptualized as a problem of poverty (see Cartaya, this volume) and underemployment, leading to the conclusion that the size of the informal sector must be reduced. Subsequently, we became equally likely to see the informal sector as a potential tool, strategy, or opportunity for development—the informal sector should be supported, not repressed (Otero, Bromley, this volume).

Both Moser and Rakowski (this volume) describe how the informal sector notion was defined alternately as a segment of a labor market, a set of activities, a nonregulatory status, a form of insertion in the labor market, and a type or size of firm (micro). For policy makers, these variations enhanced the usefulness of the concept (Sethuraman 1981). Therefore, despite conceptual problems, the notion was rapidly adopted, especially by economists.

An outcome of our work was the transformation of the informal sector notion from a component in macroeconomic analyses of development (which focused on labor markets) to a microeconomic insight into a particular segment of the economy and the economic units conforming it (typically referred to as microenterprises). The macroeconomic incarnation proposes mostly macroeconomic policy recommendations aimed at reducing the size of the informal sector through the absorption of its labor force into modern sector jobs. The microeconomic incarnation advocates mostly policy prescriptions oriented toward improving the employment potential, income, and productivity of economic units (microenterprises and self-employment).[3]

This transformation did not arise from any empirically based rejection of early hypotheses or predictions. Instead, it took the form of a "gestalt switch" from a macro to a micro oriented vision. At that point, it was not difficult—encouraged by a conservative economic environment and structural adjustment prescriptions in Latin America[4]—to make the shift to a dual policy tract of poverty alleviation and "empowering" the poor. Thus, the informal sector also came to represent the opportunity and means for empowerment (through self-sufficiency), and informal sector policies (at the micro level) focused on access to productive assets with which to help the poor out of poverty. Income transfers or food subsidies would target only the critically poor. This shift to a combined empowerment and poverty alleviation approach led to a necessary shift in informal sector policies from the realm of macroeconomic planning to include the realm of social welfare planning.

The Informal Sector and Labor Market Analysis

Economic development theory had postulated that urban industrial development would draw labor from the backward rural areas up to the point when rural-urban productivity differentials were exhausted (Lewis 1954). But Latin American countries had not experienced the predicted reduction in rural-urban productivity differentials. Instead, the countries that economists like Aníbal Pinto (1965) studied during the 1960s seemed to show two different and separate productive structures, even in the urban areas. One was highly productive, mostly industrial, dominated by large, capital-intensive units operating in oligopolistic or monopolistic markets, and generating high incomes for a small fraction of the total work force. The other was plagued by low productivity and low income, dominated by small, labor-intensive units operating in fiercely competitive markets.

The labor market correlate of structural heterogeneity (economic dualism) was the underemployment of a large part of the work force, which we economists blamed on the failure of labor market mobility to eliminate *real* productivity differentials among workers we *assumed* to have *equal* productive *potential*.[5]

By the mid-1970s, the informal sector notion was firmly entrenched among economic advisors as a description of a heterogeneous labor market. This was encouraged by several factors, including changes in the economic context, improved statistical tools, and the simplicity and elegance of the notion. The informal sector advocates of the 1970s were writing in a period when growth had slowed or stopped and unemployment and underemployment were rising; this got the attention of the policy-making community. Large data bases in the form of household surveys became available in the mid-1070s. Whereas measurement of underemployment required estimation of complex human capital-based wage equations, informal sector advocates used a simple method based on a count of workers who had jobs in units classified as informal. Finally, although underemployment described abstract productivity differentials, the "informal sector" applied to a highly visible segment of the labor force. This did not lead to widespread acceptance among economists. The usefulness and theoretical importance of the informal sector notion are still debated heatedly in economic circles.

The growing use of the notion was directly relevant to policy making, however, and this reinforced its acceptance. Politicians, bureaucrats, and the general public require inputs from economists presented in terms of problems to be solved so policies can be designed as remedies. Problems need to be quantified, and solutions and policies must be evaluated by summary indicators. Whereas standard economic theory rarely leads directly to policy design, the informal sector notion provided a name and means of quantifying the problem that could be understood by almost everyone. Its primary virtue was its usefulness for policy design; therefore "fuzziness" was overlooked or deemphasized. Whatever the criticism regarding the pertinence or accuracy of the notion for economics, it increased the awareness of problems of labor underutilization among politicians and the general public.

Policy Applications of the Informal Sector Notion

The Informal Sector and Macroeconomic Policies

Standard economic development policies have been concerned mainly with industrialization, investment in key sectors, supply bottlenecks, and economic growth. The informal sector notion gradually raised issues of equity and equality by introducing "the poor" into policy formulation, promoting a type of "affirmative action" for the poor and displacing trickle-down theories. That is, policies could no longer promote growth in GNP without concern for distributional issues. They would have to take into account the impact of a planned economy on "spontaneous" (unplanned) activities. There were several obstacles to a policy shift, however.

First, the informal sector had to be described and characterized before it could be applied to policy making. The list of attributes proposed by the ILO reports did not define a clear set of entities or actors, so a first task was to operationalize the concept for study. This was determined, ultimately, by the type of data available (census and survey) and their underlying rationale (e.g., questions were geared to a market, not a subsistence, economy). Useful variables (which fit the ILO attributes) that could be obtained from the standardized household surveys included worker characteristics and firm size. Therefore, surveys became the most commonly used tools for policy making in the 1970s and 1980s. They represented a cost-effective source of data and a feasible way of determining what percentage of the labor force had different types of jobs—different forms of insertion in the labor market. As a result, the *informal sector* came to be defined as all self-employed workers in nonprofessional occupations, owners and workers in private establishments of less than some small number of workers (usually five), domestic servants, and all unpaid family workers. Formal or modern sector workers included self-employed professionals, technicians, and managers; public sector workers; and owners and workers in private establishments of more than five workers. The findings of studies using this method of operationalization suggested the informal sector was large, an important source of jobs, and related to poverty. Such studies also assessed its growth relative to economic cycles and other variables and contributed in great measure to the debate regarding the role of the informal sector in development.

Despite ongoing definitional and theoretical debates (see Moser, this volume), those of us in the policy advising community were in basic agreement about some traits of the informal sector identified through our analyses of survey data and complemented by ethnographic and case studies. We found informal sector workers concentrated in a few sectors (commerce, personal services, repair, furniture making, metal shops), where they developed their activities with much ingenuity and little capital, selling their products in fiercely competitive markets. From studies of growth in the informal sector under diverse macroeconomic conditions, we concluded the sector acted as a buffering, countercyclical device in the labor market, absorbing labor when modern sector employment declines and releasing labor again in the recovery phase. Real incomes in the informal sector showed a pronounced pro-cyclical pattern, falling in a recession and rising in periods of growth, resulting in stable and low overall unemployment rates and stable real wages in the modern sector. This led to policy recommendations to consider selective support for informal activities with promising growth potential.

Politicians and bureaucrats, however, resisted changing the content of *economic* policies. They were not particularly seduced by the more radical and egalitarian aspects of policy advice. They preferred to assume an official "myopia" when it came to the informal sector, which they saw either as a problem outside the realm of policy (after all, were these not "unplanned" activities?) or as evidence of the failure of the state's enormous investment in top-down, growth-oriented development models. This attitude was compounded by some policy advisors who emphasized "do nots" and the reversal of long-standing state policies (do not repress street vendors, do not exclude informal sector producers from government purchases and contracts, do not raze informal squatter housing).

PREALC economists had the lead in formulating employment policies, and they were among the few who also stressed macroeconomic "dos" to affect the informal sector. PREALC's influence helped maintain the policy environment of the 1980s and popularized the informal sector notion in planning offices. These policies were mainly macroeconomic, neo-structuralist, and Keynesian in orientation. Within this approach, the informal sector was one more market imperfection that justified government intervention. For instance, given balance of payment restrictions, these economists supported expansionary macroeconomic policies with strong sectoral and regional emphasis. Expansion has the goal of absorbing informal sector workers into modern jobs at higher real incomes. A complementary policy favored state investment in sectors and regions with important links to informal sector firms and workers (through subcontracting and trade). This latter policy would promote higher incomes and opportunities for firm growth (for eventual graduation to formal status). Such an investment policy would, it was argued, give "more bang for the buck" since informal sector jobs require less capital per job created. Therefore, the macroeconomic policy package emphasized state investment in areas that would (a) expand growth opportunities for informal firms and (b) reduce the levels of competition in the sector by drawing a portion of the labor force into modern jobs.

The Transition to a Micro-Oriented Policy Vision

The emergence of various independent factors encouraged the transformation of the notion of informal sector toward a more microeconomic approach.

Decline in Economic Growth Rates.   The first set of factors was the dramatic decline in growth rates and the external constraints (including contracting markets) faced by Latin American economies. The debt crisis of the 1980s put a brake on the financing of growth and increased the importance of the balance of payment constraint. In this crisis context, macroeconomic expansionary policies (e.g., "reactivating" formal industries to absorb labor from the informal sector) were simply not feasible. Governments were busy trying to keep economies afloat in the midst of a mounting external debt burden, surging fiscal deficits, rising inflation, falling real wages, and expanding poverty. The macroeconomic role left to the informal sector was as a social welfare and unemployment buffer (*colchón contra desempleo*) during economic decline, and the policy shifted to support for low-cost employment generation—from intervening in the demand for labor to intervening in the supply of labor.

Debate over Economic Approaches to Development.   A second development was taking place in social science and economic research on employment. The descriptive approach of informal sector research—well suited to a structuralist, heterodox tradition—was criticized by colleagues favoring a "mainstream" approach to development theory and policy, including analyses of chronic inflation and stagnation problems and human capital theory.[6] In response, some economists (including me) began to apply a labor market segmentation model as a way to test the existence of differential returns to human capital for workers in different sectors whose characteristics predicted similar productivity levels. These studies used the PREALC method of operationalization and confirmed the importance of the informal-modern distinction, now found to be the segmenting line in the labor market.[7] This did not resolve criticism of the informal sector notion. Some criticism arose from widespread rejection of the closely related hypothesis of labor market segmentation (Cain 1976; Gregory 1985). Part was due to an economists' monopoly as planning advisors and the type of theoretically grounded concepts favored by mainstream economics. Despite continued resistance of some mainstream-leaning economists, labor market segmentation studies greatly strengthened the policy relevance of the informal sector notion and called attention to small firms and self-employment. Thus, through the mid-1980s the notion of informal sector alternated between being explored, ignored, and criticized.

The tide of criticism began to turn with the publication of McDonald and Solow's (1985) paper describing a segmented U.S. labor market model and Dickens and Lang's (1985) evaluation of a statistical test of duality in the labor market. Further support came from a

1986 conference where researchers of varied disciplines presented empirical studies showing that the informal sector was also a trait of labor markets in developed economies (Portes, Castells, and Benton 1989). Thus began a period of increasing acceptance and respectability for segmentation as a feature in the functioning of real labor markets and not just an idea in the mind of institutional economists and other social scientists.

Small Firm Studies.   A third factor in the transition to a micro policy were small firm studies, some conducted by official planning offices. Others came from evaluation studies of international donor agencies' microenterprise promotion projects (Bowles 1988), which concluded that informal sector–small enterprise units showed low productivity and paid low wages because of lack of access to credit and inadequate technical and managerial skills.

The Notion of "Entrepreneurs."   The fourth development was the publication of Hernando de Soto's *El Otro Sendero* in 1986 (see Bromley, this volume). Initially, de Soto was ignored by economists (including me) who strongly criticized his "sloppy" methods. His findings contradicted the findings we produced through more methodologically sound studies, and they attacked the very notion of state planning and intervention in development. The deepening of the crisis in the second half of the 1980s and its sequel of unemployment, underemployment, and expanding poverty kept governments too busy to pay attention to de Soto. Furthermore, few had the means or inclination to devise direct policies to address expanding poverty and informality; these seemed beyond the scope of government policies. (Uzzell, this volume, would add that policy makers were busy trying to maintain the status quo for entrenched political interests.)

The support de Soto received in the press and from private business groups gradually encouraged government attention to this newcomer and his contention that the informal sector was the product of mercantilist government policies that granted monopolistic privileges to modern sector firms. More appealing—and in direct contradiction to both modernization and dependency models—was the notion that, far from being the undesirable offspring of capitalist development (or underdevelopment), the informal sector was the form that capitalism and free enterprise took within this mercantilist policy framework, the response of small entrepreneurs lacking power and access to government-granted privileges. Attractive in this period of democratization was his argument of a link between the informal sector and democracy through the empowerment of small entrepreneurs. De Soto, therefore, renewed the equity theme by proposing policies to redress official regulations that hamper the growth of firms forced into the informal sector. Policies included establishing legitimate property rights of informal entrepreneurs and access to credit.

Other secondary actors—nongovernmental organizations (NGOs) and international donor agencies—entered the policy field about this time and tended to reinforce de Soto's messages. This period witnessed an impressive increase in NGOs developing credit and training programs for informal sector–small enterprise promotion in Latin America. Because their success involved matters in the realm of economics (such as financial viability, selection of credit worthy clients, etc.), these NGOs enlarged our (economists') vision of the informal sector. Furthermore, we came to realize that the triple set of objectives typical of such programs echoed the themes of earlier labor market studies: increase employment, raise incomes, and improve worker productivity.

Subsector Debate. Other factors influenced the macro-to-micro policy shift, including a debate among policy-oriented economists regarding whether or not to exclude commerce activities from microenterprise programs. On the one hand, commerce borrowers tend to have a faster turnover (reducing the total capital needed for individual credit and accelerating the financial self-sufficiency of lenders), and were poorer, self-employed individuals (especially women). Credit resulted in a dramatic income rise or stability over time, but employment did not expand and productivity levels did not improve as they did in manufacturing (where more clients graduated to formal status). Yet fewer credits were disbursed to manufacturing firms, amounts were larger, and more time was needed to achieve self-sufficiency because of slow turnover.

International Assistance. Another factor that encouraged economic policy and programs to address the needs of the informal sector was the availability of international assistance (e.g., from the International Monetary Fund and the World Bank) as part of a policy package to cope with the debt crisis and the impoverishment resulting from implementation of structural adjustment programs. Because adjustment programs tend to have high social costs, at least in the short run, they often are accompanied by compensatory policies (direct subsidies, transfers, and special social programs focused on health and nutrition) directed at the most vulnerable groups of the population. The availability of funds represented a strong impetus to create the policies and programs that would attract those funds.

Social Welfare Interests. Structural adjustment and poverty alleviation policies represented a radical change from the earlier approach to social policy and came at a time when the traditional apparatus of social service delivery in heavily indebted nations was in shambles. The cost of creating new services and efficient delivery mechanisms threaten powerful groups entrenched in the traditional social service apparatus (Medici 1989), including militant unions, rich contractors, and political parties that use the provision of social services to gain support from disadvantaged groups. In democracies these groups often form the core of the government party.

Governments, already under heavy fire from the negative social effects of macroeconomic adjustment policies, did not need a new enemy—much less one that could affect their own ranks (see Uzzell, this volume). Therefore, states shifted from more traditional social policies to a focused set of actions delivered through ad-hoc mechanisms (Cartaya and Márquez 1990), including direct subsidies, maternal and child health care, special nutrition programs, and an informal sector–microenterprise program. The logic is clear and dear to the conservative policy environment of the late 1980s and the 1990s: avoid direct subsidies that tend to "spill over" to the nonpoor; build on the consensus that vulnerable groups (pregnant or breast-feeding women, children) should be protected; help the poor to help themselves (through improvements in access to and use of productive assets); avoid a blanket policy approach to the informal sector by supporting different programs for different situations and activities (Mezzera 1991). Ironically, in direct opposition to de Soto's approach, the importance of governments for informal sector programs increased significantly (Otero, this volume) with some organizing their own organizations (GONGOs—government sponsored NGOs) to join private NGOs as the operational nucleus of an informal sector policy.

A final twist was added. Empirical evidence linking poverty and informality, long assumed by economists to be highly correlated, convinced governments that informal sector policy is social policy (poverty alleviation), rather than economic policy (growth oriented). Thus, *informal sector programs were wrested away from economists doing macroeconomic policy and allocated to social welfare ministries.*

Therefore, the late 1980s were characterized by a small revolution in policy and action toward the informal sector. NGOs and international donor agencies promoted aggressive programs to give credit, training, and technical assistance to microenterprises, without much effect on official macroeconomic policies. Government policy makers began to follow suit, turning toward a more microeconomic approach, including microenterprise development as a legitimate subject of state policy (see Otero, this volume). Those uncomfortable with the earlier egalitarian policy recommendations of informal sector advocates could devise a "conservative" action agenda calling for reduced state intervention in the market.

Through the rising popularity of "microenterprise development" and the notion of "informal entrepreneurs" in a competitive market economy, the informal sector became both a theory of labor markets, widely accepted by economists and planners, and the new champion of people-powered development, postulated as a hero from opposing angles of the political spectrum (Biggs, Grindle, and Snodgrass 1988). These include right-wing romantics, conservatives eager to break the influence of labor, and leftist proponents of the "little guy" (Peattie 1987). The second half of the 1980s witnessed such a dramatic change in accepted notions of the functioning and structure of labor markets in developing countries, that Judith Tendler (1988) spoke of "the remarkable convergence of fashion on small enterprises and the informal sector."

With the benefit of hindsight, one can see that, beyond political overtones, the policy recommendations of *El Otro Sendero* and NGOs were not divergent or incompatible with the earlier informal sector approaches. Official hostility toward informal sector activities had been condemned in the Kenya and Colombia ILO reports as early as 1972, and extending access to credit for informal sector producers was compatible with prior observations that one important disadvantage of the informal sector was a lack of capital. Furthermore, access to credit was already firmly entrenched in microenterprise programs funded by USAID and NGOs.

Where Do We Stand and Where Should We Go from Here?

It is not without a certain feeling of hidden pioneer pride that an economist-policy advisor-insider like myself observes the current popularity and policy relevance of a notion believed in years ago. The informal sector notion has finally found its way into mainstream social policies, though still marginalized in economic policies. Government officials proudly announce the number and amount of credits granted to microenterprises. Microentrepreneur organizations find official recognition, and individuals are encouraged to organize into solidarity groups to seek credit and training. Some states have acted to reduce the red tape faced by entrepreneurs, legalize property rights, and create special privileges for production cooperatives.

But, lest pride overcome, it also must be acknowledged that the informal sector notion has undergone so many changes (with much confusion) that the meaning assigned today hardly seems related to that of earlier periods. The fuzziness of the notion, and its original conceptual weakness, made it easy for diverse groups to adopt it for their own causes: economists from international financial organizations find economic units in the informal sector use the "right" factor intensity; Latin American structuralists find an alliance of interests between informal and modern sectors, which are seen as interacting in a virtuous circle of demand expansion; neo-liberals find there the last reserve of entrepreneurship and democracy in the mercantilist Latin American societies. Each group highlights the trait most convenient to its message and focuses on evidence that supports its position. Perhaps pride is not justified if little more than the name remains from the informal sector notion of the 1970s.

At this stage, the informal sector notion of the 1990s may be unavoidable for economists working on labor market problems in developing countries. (Some economists are troubled by the superimposing of segmentation on data, instead of allowing it to emerge from statistical analyses.)[8] For policy makers, the informal sector is heralded as the new promise of development: informal sector policies are expected to increase jobs and incomes for the poor, create more competition, and even lead to a more democratic society. That these hopes are doomed to fail must be obvious to any observer with some historical perspective. I would argue that the rush into informal sector policies by so many different actors with different agendas and different notions obstructs improvement of the informal sector notion.

This contention is supported by an outpouring of information on informal sector characteristics emerging from program evaluations and quantitative studies. Although they confirm some generally accepted ideas about informal sector units (e.g., they concentrate in specific sectors—commerce, some services, and some industries; they operate with little capital; they suffer endemic shortages of fixed and working capital, etc.), they also point to the failure of informal units to comply with official regulations related to urban planning, working conditions, minimum wages, licenses, and permits. And they raise three seldom-discussed issues: the nonhomogeneity of the informal sector due to sectoral heterogeneity; internal social differentiation; and the link between poverty and informality. These warrant consideration because of their support for a reconsideration of the 1990s' emphasis on a micro level social welfare policy approach.

Heterogeneity by Sectors.   The informal sector is visibly heterogeneous but less so than the modern sector. Márquez and Portela (1991) found that more than 70 percent of total informal sector employment in Venezuela concentrates in the four largest industry sectors (services, transport, retail trade, and construction). In sharp contrast, employment in the modern sector or segment concentrates in social services, public administration, retail trade, and construction, which make up 45 percent of the total. Also, differences in incomes and productivity across industry sectors are larger within the informal sector than among their modern sector counterparts (Márquez and Portela 1991). Furthermore, the pattern of industry-wage differentials in manufacturing is highly correlated across different firm sizes, suggesting that *industry sector*, more than firm size, is the underlying determinant of the size and sign of industry-wage differentials. Cartaya's (this volume) finding of a striking pattern of industry sector concentration of low income workers (both informal and modern low income workers tend to be concentrated in the same sectors) also suggests that industry sector, more than firm size, has an important influence on productivity and income levels.

The picture of the informal sector that emerges from such studies is of a pyramid. At the top of the pyramid are economically successful informal sector enterprises that employ wage labor and tend to be relatively stable sources of income and employment. At the base are a large number of economic units, many subsistence operations that could not, under any conceivable economic conditions, become stable sources of income and employment. At the midsection, fluidity is the dominant trait. There are economic units going up from the base pushed by favorable conditions in their particular niche of the market and others coming down from the top crumpled by unfavorable demand and competition. For example, in Venezuela (Márquez and Portela 1991), less than 17 percent of total informal sector employment was generated by enterprises at the top of the pyramid, with the bulk of informal sector employment generated at the base. To what extent can credit and training programs benefit those at the bottom versus those at the top when market demand, level of competition, and industry sector are determinants of growth and profitability?

Internal Social Differentiation. Social differentiation within the informal sector is pervasive, comprising different kinds of work relationships—in sharp contrast to wage relations that dominate the modern sector. Self-employment, family help, firm owners who work alongside wage employees, and subcontracting all characterize informal sector units. Instead of a community of the impoverished (as evoked by the early notion) or a reservoir of entrepreneurs (evoked by de Soto, NGOs, and a neo-liberal vision in general), this informal sector exhibits a deeply differentiated social context where exploitation and unsafe or unhealthy working conditions are widespread.

The Venezuelan studies cited above found that in sectors with higher average incomes, the self-employed and microenterprise (ME) owners had incomes similar to employee wages in the modern sector, but ME employees had much lower incomes. Furthermore, ME employees had similarly low wages independent of the industry sector in which they held a job. This clearly suggests that self-employed and ME owners are able to appropriate some sort of industry-sector-specific rent, while ME employees sell their labor in a competitive market at wages well below the legal minimum. Fragmentary results from firm studies also show that the main comparative advantage of successful MEs that employ wage workers (those firms at the top of the pyramid) lies in their use of cheap labor and their disregard for safe and healthy working conditions (Cartaya 1990; Portes, this volume).[9]

Poverty and the Informal Sector. The more we learn about the relationship between poverty and informality, the more confused the debate becomes. As Cartaya (this volume) points out, informality is a job characteristic and poverty; is a family attribute; poverty is not exclusively correlated with a family member having a job in the informal sector. Therefore, in some cases improving the conditions for inserting family members into the labor market can have a greater impact on reducing poverty than delivering credit to a borderline activity. One such example is the provision of child care facilities to enable women to take jobs outside the informal sector (Uchimura 1991).

Furthermore, most informal sector programs in Latin America deliver credit and support to the less poor among the informal sector workers. This is not the result of social callousness among these organizations, but the implicit outcome of pressures for sustainability. Credit must be repaid. By focusing assistance on more viable activities, lenders increase their chances of becoming financially self-sustaining (and miss targeting the poorest informals).

A Policy Proposal

One conclusion to be drawn from the preceding discussion is that there is no such thing as *the* informal sector, but rather a complex and differentiated set of activities that should be separated to develop a more efficient and focused set of policies. Informal sector advocates have put too much emphasis on common problems of those in the informal sector (e.g., assumed poverty) and paid too little attention to its internal differentiation, both sectoral and social. PREALC's early hope that informal sector policies would be a mechanism for a more egalitarian income distribution has been displaced, because credit and training are directed toward the informal sector "elite." And the emphasis of de Soto and microenterprise promoters on the positive role the informal sector could fulfill in development is somewhat misplaced, because it ignores the well-documented, unacceptable working conditions that informal sector workers often endure in microenterprises (Portes, de Oliveira and Roberts, this volume).[10]

Policy must address the heterogeneity and internal differentiation of the group of economic activities called the *informal sector*. The informal sector notion encompasses too many realities for a blanket approach to policy. It is encouraging to this insider to note that some policies are beginning to differentiate among the various situations within the informal sector. The combination of special employment programs and microenterprise schemes is one example of this process. The problems faced by Latin American economies also are too broad to be encompassed by a focus on the informal sector; they require a broader policy approach.

As a starting point in policy design, I propose that, in the interest of modernization and development, policy should focus initially (as PREALC has always proposed) on reducing the size of the informal sector and that this should be accomplished through two procedures. First, the less viable informal sector activities should be allowed to disappear (or be left to function as survival strategies for the unemployable), and when their characteristics permit, workers should transfer to modern jobs as they open. Second, the more viable informal sector units should receive the necessary assistance to help them graduate into technologically and organizationally modern, albeit still relatively small, enterprises. In this sense, I agree with Biggs, Grindle, and Snodgrass (1988) that the "leveling the playing field" approach of microenterprise promotion programs is an insufficient one. Although governments should actively support the development of small firms—because they are an essential component in economic growth and development—an exclusive reliance on markets hinders small firms' growth, given the structure of market power in developing countries and power differentials in relations between large and small firms.

Poverty alleviation is a daunting task faced by Latin American governments under conditions of recession and crisis. However, policies that focus on turning the ultra poor into self-sufficient poor cannot be more than a transitory goal in a genuine process of modernization and development. Similarly, the importance of social welfare ministries and their large role in informal sector programs produces discomfort. I perceive a wider and more important role for the informal sector in economic development, beyond and above the role these programs can fulfill in poverty alleviation. I argue that poverty will be alleviated permanently only through economic growth and human capital accumulation, both tasks that require articulated economic and social policies, not a "help the poor help themselves" approach.

There is an inherent risk in helping the poor help themselves. Since support is delivered to the poor because they are small and poor, this precludes serious analyses of the potential for efficiency or success. Financial analyses of repayment capacity are not a substitute for a real growth potential analysis to assess whether or not the loan will build up the productive potential of the activities it targets. Suppose a credit program for informal textile firms is so successful that sector production doubles. If demand is stable, or growing less rapidly than supply, prices are going to fall and hurt the economic and financial viability of a good number of the borrowers. As a consequence, they will go out of business, reducing employment and incomes in the sector. The paradox is that such programs are evaluated according to repayment levels and initial increases in productivity. This is but one of the pitfalls of an exclusive reliance on a micro vision of the informal sector.

The question, then, is whether it is possible to develop a policy framework toward an heterogeneous informal sector that can increase its usefulness in the process of economic restructuring. An industry sector approach could be an appropriate tool in this direction. If governments are genuinely interested in poverty alleviation and equity, however, then attention also must be paid to a particular dimension of the problem of social differentiation, that of working conditions in informal sector enterprises.

The Industry Sector Approach.   The notion that the industry affiliation of informal sector units has a bearing on program impact is witnessed by the commerce versus manufacturing debate reported earlier and has implications for the economic restructuring of Latin American countries in the 1990s. Sectoral restructuring is a type of industrial policy that encompasses a broad array of measures oriented to improving productivity and competitive position in the international or domestic market. Measures contain implicit subsidies and support devices that target larger and modern enterprises.

The industry sector (or subsector) approach to informal sector policy design is oriented by analysis of the product chain (Haggblade, Davies, Boomgard, and Mead 1990). This highlights quite efficiently the conditions under which small enterprises contribute to increasing productivity and a more competitive positioning of the product in the market. Because modern and informal enterprises interact quite intensely in parts production, subcontracting, and other production arrangements, a subsectoral approach can enhance the impact of small or informal enterprises' credit programs by evaluating the whole production process. One outcome could be the development of mechanisms like *comercializadoras* (trading houses) as a way to better integrate informal units products into the market. The approach would reintroduce the informal sector as a critical factor in mainstream economic restructuring policy.[11]

Exploitation. The exploitative nature of modern-informal sector enterprise relationships must be addressed. Working capital and technical assistance to improve the quality and reliability of the informal sector firms' production will not address the intrinsic unstable market relationship between the two types of enterprises. Because the rationale of existing market arrangements is that modern enterprises use informal sector production as a buffer to smooth the impact of market fluctuations on its own payroll costs (Piore and Sabel 1984), it is hard to imagine that modern enterprises will develop a new, more stable and cooperative relationship with informal sector firms without some kind of extramarket incentives. This is an area where governments could play an important role by conditioning access to restructuring programs' incentives on the development of "fair" marketing and production arrangements with informal sector firms in industry sectors where subcontracting arrangements exist.

The Working Conditions Problem. Microenterprise promotion policies ended up supporting informal sector enterprises (both independent and subcontracted firms) that do not adhere to legally established labor standards on wages and job security. They risk creating—with the explicit or implicit permission of the state—a double-tiered labor standard system with one for informal sector firms and another for formal or modern firms (see Portes, this volume). This risk can be avoided—and economic growth and development better served—through an approach that supports enterprise growth to potentially fill the "missing middle" and contributes to a more rational size distribution of firms and compliance with labor standards. This approach combines a microeconomic vision of a heterogeneous informal sector—some units with growth potential, others survival strategies—with a macroeconomic vision of the role these units play in development.

Many researchers (Sassen-Koob 1984; Portes, Castells, and Benton 1989) perceive the main common trait of informal activities as down-graded, unprotected labor. Although *workers* cope with the consequences of downgrading and lack of protection, *microenterprises* often find in those traits their main competitive advantage. The question becomes to what extent the state or NGOs should be willing to help enterprises whose main competitive advantage is the violation of accepted labor and wage standards. Government officials and NGOs involved in informal sector programs often naively accept that enforcement of working conditions and wage standards should not be formally required from enterprises enrolled in credit or technical assistance programs. Ironically, this results in governments investing resources in those very enterprises that openly violate public regulations of the labor market. These same governments tend to deny requests by formal firms to change the overall system of labor regulations to allow for more hiring and firing flexibility.[12] Portes (this volume) rightly identifies the danger of governments enforcing a two-tiered system of labor standards, one for modern enterprises and another for the informal sector. Costly regulations create incentives for modern enterprises to informalize, either by fragmenting the production process or by contracting out.[13] If labor standards are inadequate for the relative level of development of Latin American countries, they should be changed overall. But creation of a two-tiered system, with second-class jobs for second-class citizens, is a gross violation of democratic standards that should not be permitted, much less encouraged. The state could learn from informal sector programs which regulations are crucial and which could be changed and enforced for informal sector borrowers. No credit should be forthcoming to violators of labor standards regulations.

Final Comments

Much work is needed to improve our understanding of what the informal sector can become, rather than what it is. Economists find in the Latin American experience clearcut evidence that countries that develop over time a set of regulations granting monopolistic privileges to a few inefficient large enterprises tend to show less rapid growth than economies that have a large sector of small and medium enterprises. At the microeconomic level the reason is that smaller enterprises tend to be more flexible and adaptable to market fluctuation and new product development. They also tend to accumulate less power, thus being less able to influence (and create) distortionary government regulations in their favor. As a result, economies with strong small enterprises tend to be more dynamic and adaptive to the changing world market conditions.

But economists have established the fact that developing countries show a pattern of employment by firm size radically different than that of developed countries (Biggs et al. 1988). For instance, manufacturing firms in developing countries tend to show a bimodal distribution of employment with 40 percent of total employment in micro- and very small enterprises, another 40 percent at big firms, and the remaining 20 percent or less in small to medium-sized enterprises. A closer look is needed at the relative optimal size of firms producing different products for different markets.

For those at the bottom of the informal sector pyramid, the issue is one of poverty alleviation and human capital accumulation. Their numbers and intrinsic disadvantages make it unlikely they can be helped by enterprise development programs. Poverty alleviation programs can provide relief, but expansion of social services could help many accumulate enough human capital to move into modern sector jobs when these became available.

NOTES

1. *Underemployment* is defined as working fewer than 30 hours a week, earning less than a minimum wage, or working at a job that does not utilize the worker's skill and training.

2. Those groups labelled as *marginal* by this approach were engaged in activities that later were labeled as *informal*.

3. This shift from a labor market focus to a focus on firms had an added benefit: it increased awareness of a phenomenon known as the *missing middle*, in which enterprises cluster at either end of the size scale (defined by number of workers) with few of intermediate size.

4. Structural adjustment policies include cutbacks in social welfare budgets, public employment, food subsidies, and protective tariffs as well as privatization of state enterprises and incentives to foreign investment.

5. This could not be tested in the 1960s because neither the large data bases with information on workers and jobs nor the computing equipment needed to analyze them were available at that time.

6. Other social scientists continued to produce in-depth studies of poverty, marginality, grassroots organizing, community development, and survival strategies.

7. Studies estimated independent human capital wage equations for the two segments and concluded that segmentation existed. They showed lower returns to education and experience in the informal sector than in the modern.

The characteristics of firms in each segment led to the conclusion that differences were rooted in different capital/labor ratios for informal or modern firms.

8. To my knowledge, no statistical analysis of labor market data from a Latin American country has been performed to obtain multiple wage equations endogenously (that is, with a selection mechanism that "chooses" which worker belongs to what segment). Replication of the Dickens and Lang (1985) analysis with LDC data would be a useful way to determine the relevance of segmentation as proposed by informal sector advocates. By comparing segmentation endogenously obtained from the data with that obtained by operationalizing the informal sector prior to analysis, would explicitly permit evaluating overlapping results between the (conceptually solid) segmentation hypothesis and measures of the informal sector notion.

9. Cartaya found that for some firms the cost of improving working conditions to comply with minimum regulations and pay mandatory contributions (social security and indirect payments) far surpasses the increase in labor costs from rising wages.

10. Some informal activities may be an inevitable trait of flexibilization processes, even though unfair to the workers forced into those informal sector jobs.

11. Analyses of product chains require more specialized and orthodox techniques than human resources engaged in informal sector programs have. Coordination with industrial policy institutions can provide the needed skills and techniques. But this requires convincing industrial policy institutions that the informal sector can make a significant contribution toward increasing total factor productivity in the product chain. Studies of subcontracting available for specific countries could provide the basic information needed to convince them of this point.

12. It is a standard feature of labor market regulations in Latin America that internal rules for work assignment, time schedules, and working conditions must be approved and can be modified by the Ministry of Labor.

13. The outcome (exploitation, impoverishment) of this process was foretold by the experience of the apparel industry in diverse settings (Puerto Rico, Mexico, Venezuela, Southeast Asia, Northern Africa, etc.).

Part III

Micro Level Intervention Issues

❏ Chapter 10

The Role of Governments and Private Institutions in Addressing the Informal Sector in Latin America

María Otero

Introduction

The growing informal sector in Latin American and Caribbean cities raises important considerations for governments as they enter the decade of the 1990s.[1] In almost every country similar issues and questions related to the sector constitute part of the overall policy and development debate. As the informal sector grows, how should its role in economy and society be perceived by the state? Are there strategies to integrate this sector into the broader economy or is the tendency to restrict its activity? Is the thrust of governmental interest in the informal sector framed by policy, economic, regulatory, or political concerns? Indeed, should a government respond to this population, and if it does, should its role be to design strategies, to formulate policies, to provide direct assistance, or to engage in all three?

This chapter is a substantially revised and updated version of "The Role of Governments in the Informal Sector" published in 1990 in *The Critical Connection: Governments, Private Institutions, and the Informal Sector in Latin America*, ed. Katherine Stearns and María Otero (Cambridge: ACCION International). Many thanks to ACCION for permission to use material from the earlier version.

Nongovernmental organizations (NGOs) have worked directly with the informal sector in the last decade providing financial services, training, or advocacy; this raises additional questions.[2] What level of knowledge exists among policy makers and government officials regarding the successes and failures of assistance? How do experienced nongovernmental organizations view government interest, and to what degree are NGOs versed in the informal sector policies evolving in their own countries? Can nongovernmental organizations operate solely at the micro level or must they now enter the macro level policy arena?

These questions gave rise to a five-day international conference in Quito, Ecuador, in November 1989 convened by ACCION International[3] and the Institute of Socioeconomic and Technological Research (Stearns and Otero 1990).[4] This event was attended by representatives from government entities, donor agencies, and local private development organizations to discuss whether public and private sector organizations can or should collaborate in reaching the informal sector and how to understand, initiate, or improve this intersectoral relationship.

This chapter uses the proceedings from this conference and subsequent writings to address two points: factors that increased government interest in the informal sector in all countries in Latin America since 1985; and the various governmental approaches toward the informal sector. Five factors are identified as important and contrasted with the reasons behind, continued interest in, and role of private organizations in developing informal microenterprises. The discussion of government approaches focuses on how resources are allocated and programs implemented programs, not overall economic strategy or policy formulation process (see Márquez, Franks, this volume). The discussion suggests that private development organizations cannot operate in an isolated manner but must enter into a dialogue with governments, especially in the area of extending services to the informal sector. Various strategies for public and private sector collaboration and interaction are discussed, as are conference recommendations for future government, private, and donor assistance to microenterprise development.

The Government Perspective

Country reports prepared for the conference documented diverse factors that explain government involvement in the informal sector debate—most of which have already been mentioned in preceding chapters. First, the magnitude of the informal sector, its heterogeneity, and its rate of growth have forced state, municipal and local authorities to take it into account. For instance, estimates in Guatemala are as high as 125,500 microproducers in urban areas alone (Marroquín and Rolando 1987). In Bolivia, it is estimated that as many as 5.2 million people or 75 percent of the population depend on income from the informal sector, including subsistence agriculture (PRODEM 1990). A review of 6,500 microentrepreneurs in Paraguay detected more than 1,230 types of activities and eight categories of manufacturing and commerce (Fundación Paraguaya de Cooperación y Desarrollo 1988).

A second set of reasons for increased government interest includes concern over tax evasion, circumvention of the law, and undetected net transfers between formal and informal sectors (de Soto 1989). Yet, in all the countries studied, the government's underlying position in recent years has been to support the informal sector's development rather than to obstruct it (Portes 1989). Conference reports identify this position with diverse factors.

Third, government interest stems from the decade of the 1980s in Latin America, characterized by economic crisis (see de Oliveira and Roberts, Márquez, this volume). Per capita production fell to its lowest levels in over a decade and fixed investment in productive capital fell by over 30 percent between 1980 and 1985. Practices associated with the 1970s such as high commodity prices, cheap external financing, increased public investment, and social welfare programs yielded to reduced international flows, lower commodity prices, high real interest rates, rising poverty, and the overwhelming debt burden of the 1980s. These represent a development setback for the region, and hundreds of millions of people experienced a decline in their standard of living (World Bank 1989a).

Governments of the early 1990s engage in structural adjustment reforms while simultaneously searching for ways to foster growth. Foreign borrowing to finance development is not an attractive option due to high interest rates and levels of foreign debt from the 1970s and 1980s. Large, modern, transnational companies have not led to economic growth. Thus, Latin American governments look internally for ways to create economic growth, identifying the informal sector as having productive potential that must be considered in development plans. Although the informal sector cannot solve the difficult economic situation each country faces, it is one in a broad range of responses to economic problems. (In fact, Franks, this volume, points out that ignoring the informal sector may imperil government macroeconomic policies.)

Fourth, demographic patterns constitute another reason for government interest in the informal sector. Although thirteen of twenty

Latin American countries registered lower annual population growth in the 1980s than the 1960s and 1970s, rates remain high; projected increases for Mexico and Brazil are of 23 million and 37 million respectively, by the year 2000 (World Bank 1989b). Age composition of the population and concentration in large urban centers particularly trouble governments; over 50 percent of the population in most countries currently resides in cities and is composed primarily of semi- or unskilled young people (World Bank 1989b). From a government's perspective, the informal sector creates employment opportunities for this growing population. Job creation requires low investment levels, no foreign exchange, low skill levels, and encourages the production of low-cost goods and services for poor markets (Blayney and Otero 1985).

Fifth, since the late 1980s, nearly a dozen countries in Latin American and the Caribbean have conducted peaceful presidential elections, one of several indicators of a return to democratic structures. Democracy brings with it increased emphasis on development strategies that include the poorer sectors of society, an emphasis reinforced by competition for votes among political parties, who, in turn, pressure the state on behalf of their constituents. Also, because of the informal sector's size and growth in the 1980s, it cannot be ignored by democratic governments. The formation of organizations and associations by the "informals" to represent their interest—inexperienced as they may be—promises to be a significant component of emerging democratic processes. It is ironic that democratization encourages the organization of civilian groups precisely when trade union systems are weakened by the changing nature of the labor force due to the greater relative importance of the informal sector (Cartaya, Rodríguez, and Bernardo 1989; Liedholm, this volume). Finally, writings like de Soto's *The Other Path* (1989) raise complex issues regarding the way policies, laws, and regulatory environment affect government–informal sector interaction and the democratic process.

Sixth, governments are acutely aware of the existence of a rich body of literature on the sector's emergence and its place in social and economic structure. Competing theories and research findings have had differential impacts on the policy debate among governments and NGOs (Cartaya 1987). Four arguments stand out:

1. Governments are most familiar with the approach of the International Labour Office and the Regional Program for Employment in Latin America and the Caribbean (PREALC) that postulate the informal sector results from an excess supply of labor not absorbed by the modern productive system and

from the scarcity of capital for production (Tokman 1987a; Mezzera 1989; Moser, Rakowski, Márquez, this volume).

2. Also influential among Latin American governments are approaches that focus on the productive viability of the informal sector, identifying it as the means to lower production costs by keeping salaries low and avoiding the cost of worker benefits (Moser 1984; Peattie 1987; Portes, this volume). This informal sector subsidizes part of the cost of formal enterprises and reinforces low wages weakening the ability of small firms to accumulate surplus capital. This leads to growing disparities between the formal and informal economies (Bromley 1978a; Annis and Franks 1989).

3. Also influential is the notion that the informal sector is a manifestation of entrepreneurial spirit that absorbs a significant percentage of the labor force, and whose productive potential is sabotaged by excessive regulation that forces extra-legal operations (de Soto 1989). Promoted by the Institute for Liberty and Democracy, this interpretation emphasizes the burden that governments place on this sector and the role that deregulation and improved laws would play in strengthening its production (see Bromley, Márquez, this volume).

4. A promising approach—less well known among academics— uses a model of labor market evolution in developed countries to explain the type of production characterizing the informal sector. [6] Smaller productive units represent a new form of organization that can lower production costs and may respond appropriately to the economic crisis in most developing countries. This approach encourages empirical studies on the nature of micro- and small-scale production in developing countries, and uses these data to analyze returns to labor and capital for purposes of policy formulation (Davies, Mead, and Seale 1990).

These approaches have played an uneven role in the NGO-government debate. They have advanced theoretical analyses of the informal sector, but provide less direction on how to reach the sector. Some call for government action, policy formulation, and allocation of resources to the sector, but do not specify strategies. Hence, governments draw selectively from these schools of thought to buttress their position regarding the informal sector, but look elsewhere for strategies to service the sector.

A seventh factor influencing government interest in the informal sector is the growth in resources and the over fifteen years' experience, especially in credit, of multilateral and bilateral donor organizations that extend services to informal sector producers. Most major U.S. and European donor organizations have a keen interest in financing research and action programs in this field. For instance, the United States Agency for International Development (USAID) received a Congressional mandate to earmark $75 million in microenterprise lending for fiscal year 1990 (U.S. Agency for International Development 1990). That year the Inter-American Development Bank (IDB) initiated its own microenterprise program to assign nearly $500 million in loans over a five year period.[7] The World Bank also has explored the possibility of integrating the informal sector into their broader industrial sector loans. Similarly, smaller foundations, such as the Inter-American Foundation and the Ford Foundation, assist Latin American nongovernmental institutions in initiating pilot programs to expand their outreach. In some cases, donors and governments have collaborated in developing program strategies. Colombia, Ecuador, and Uruguay are examples of countries that negotiated multimillion dollar, countrywide microenterprise programs with the Inter-American Development Bank (which played a major role in negotiating the programs, policies, and terms for their implementation).

In summary, a deteriorating economic situation, growing labor force, increased pressure for democratization, availability of empirical data and economic models of the informal sector, and the disposition of donor agencies to provide resources for programs are the major factors that bring the governments into the arena of the informal sector. To understand which strategies are most appropriate for government intervention in the informal sector, it is first useful to look at the experience of nongovernmental organizations in this area.

The NGO–Private Development Organization Perspective

Myriad private development organizations in Latin America provide assistance, training, credit, and other services to the poor of the informal sector (Farbman 1981). For example, ACCION International maintains a formal affiliation with thirty-three NGOs in twelve countries in Latin America and the Caribbean (ACCION 1989). These NGOs extend working capital loans and training in over sixty-five cities to very small producers and retailers. The impact of these programs in the aggregate is significant. In 1989, they disbursed about US$24 million in small loans with less than 1 percent default (ACCION 1990b). In 1990 total disbursements were about $38 million. Half these loans are extended through solidarity groups[8] and average about US$200 per person. The remaining funds are disbursed to individual microentrepreneurs with loans averaging about $520 per person. These programs have grown considerably since 1975; by 1991, they disbursed the equivalent of US$4.5 million in loans each month and reached tens of thousands of microentrepreneurs. Evaluations of the economic and social impact of their work, measured in terms of income changes and job creation, suggest a positive impact of credit programs on the lives of the poor they reach (Olivares 1990; Gómez and Saladín 1987; Hatch and Gómez 1989).

Although ACCION-affiliated institutions probably represent the bulk of the credit activity in Latin America and the Caribbean, other institutions show substantial portfolios and years of experience in microenterprise development. These include the Carvajal Foundation (Fundación Carvajal) in Colombia which developed a training-based approach to assisting very small producers now used throughout the continent, and literally hundreds of smaller NGOs conduct programs with small target populations (Cartaya, Rodríguez, and Bernardo 1989). Nearly all programs are financed externally through private or bilateral funds.

Approaches and strategies vary among these institutions, and some are more successful than others (McKean, this volume). The most successful are those who aim to reach the poor, have a proven method, and emphasize self-sufficiency.

Reaching the Poor

To reach and assist the poorer sectors of society was the primary objective behind the formation of most private development organizations during the 1960s and early 1970s (Rakowski's Chapter 3, this volume; Korten 1987). At the time, they worked in rural areas developing projects with poor communities previously ignored by broader government programs and large donor supported projects. In the late 1970s and the 1980s, as poor populations migrated to urban centers, NGOs helped create services and infrastructure in poor urban communities— housing improvement, day care, water, health care—and helped neighborhoods organize around these issues. Support for vocational training and income generation programs soon followed.

The emphasis on providing financial resources—capital—to the poorest producers evolved when it became clear that lack of credit, unattainable through the established banking sector, hindered investing in local income generating activities. Specialized institutions evolved with credit and training programs—some of considerable magnitude—geared to the needs of the informal sector poor. Today, these organizations have developed successful techniques for providing credit to the poor and have taken the lead in developing methods and policies to provide financial services throughout the informal sector (Boomgard 1989; World Bank 1990b).

Development of a Successful Technique

Because of their organizational characteristics, NGOs were well suited to test innovative strategies and approaches for effectively extending credit to microentrepreneurs (McKee 1989). In particular, the ACCION experience yielded a methodology for program implementation that is the basis of programs among country-level affiliates. The characteristics of this approach are straightforward—group lending, commercial interest rates, systems for agile loan review and disbursement, incentives for repayment, flexibility, and responsiveness to borrowers' needs—and are the result of many years of experimentation and revised design by affiliates (Otero 1986). The broad application of this approach means that programs can deliver credit to more micro businesses, at a lower cost, while incorporating the poorest individuals, including a large percentage of women.

In the 1990s, many new programs that extend credit to microentrepreneurs are adapting this methodology to their context. Furthermore, older, successful programs experiment with changes to improve this methodology, its reach, and its potential for meeting needs. In Guatemala, for example, two programs have expanded the role of the solidarity group from merely receiving and managing loans to conducting the loan review procedure and assuming other tasks previously held by NGO staff.

Provision of financial services to hundreds and thousands of poor borrowers in an efficient and effective way requires a complex mix of institutional capacity, monitoring structures, information systems, trained staff, promotional activity, and resources. Some NGOs demonstrate great success in reaching the poor.[9]

Creation of Self-Sufficient Programs

The concept of creating and maintaining self-sufficient development programs that reach the poor is a revolutionary feature of successful NGO credit programs (Otero 1988; Boomgard 1989; Rhyne and Otero

1990). All NGO programs begin with an infusion of capital, usually from external sources. Self-sufficiency is achieved when a program generates enough revenue to cover all its operational costs as well as the costs of money the program borrows to onlend, lending activity has reached a considerable size (some suggest a portfolio of US$1 million as a guideline), maintains high repayments, charges interest rates that reflect the costs of lending, and keeps its costs low (Rhyne and Otero 1990). Self-sufficient programs should need added infusions of outside money only when operations expand or exogenous factors such as high levels of inflation make it impossible to maintain the real value of the portfolio.

Some of the more advanced programs demonstrate that it is possible to accomplish a high level of self-sustainability. In 1989 and 1990, ADEMI (Dominican Republic) registered higher income than the total costs of operations during those years (ADEMI 1989; 1990). PRO-DEM's (Bolivia) income covers nearly 100 percent of its costs (50 percent of these costs are for borrowing money to onlend) (PRODEM 1990). As self-sufficiency increases, the reliance on outside donors lessens because organizations are able to combine international grants with their own revenue and loans from the banking sector in their own countries. The combined portfolio of ACCION affiliates shows that these organizations obtain approximately 38 percent of their resources from local commercial sector loans (ACCION 1990a). With this, NGOs graduate to larger operations that function more like the financial system of the country, while still reaching a population with no previous access to that system.

Government Response to the Informal Sector

Government action and policy can be important to these programs and their impact on the informal sector. The findings of the international conference cited earlier and the papers commissioned for it suggest that there are four categories government response to the informal sector: a detached role, passive collaboration, active collaboration, and directive collaboration (Campos 1990; Carrasco 1990; Chávez O'Brian 1990; Revere 1990; Fadul 1990; Díaz 1990).

The Detached Role

This type of government response is characterized by a lack of interest in the informal sector and a tendency to exclude it from planning or policy making. Many governments in Latin America fit into this cate-

gory in the early 1970s. This position was buttressed by a lack of information on the sector and the widely held belief that it was of little economic or social consequence. The only emphasis governments placed
on small-scale production focused on small farmers through subsidized credit programs of newly formed financial institutions (Adams,
Graham, and von Pischke 1984; World Bank 1989b). Today, most governments no longer fit into this category. Growth of the sector, among
other factors, turned most governments into actors.

Passive Collaboration

In this category, a government recognizes the existence of very small
enterprises that operate informally, retains an ambivalent position
regarding its own role toward them, but allows local organizations
and international donors to channel resources and services to them.
There is very little interaction between government entities and local
implementing organizations, which prefer to operate at arm's length
from the government. The goal of these NGOs is to conduct small programs and they do not see their mandate as one of influencing national
level policies or strategies toward the informal sector.

As a passive collaborator, a government does not define relevant
policy or build its own strategy and program, even when research
indicates an important economic role for the informal sector. There
may be an initial call to consider the sector at the national level, but
there is no consensus regarding its relative importance. Honduras is an
example. In 1987, over twenty NGOs were providing services—usually credit and training—to groups within the informal sector, such as
women producers, commercial vendors, and small manufacturers
(Blayney and Clark 1987). These programs operated with outside
funding, primarily from USAID, and maintained no direct link with
any government institution. The government conducted no studies on
the informal sector and had no department or mechanism to interact
with these existing programs or to establish its own.[10]

In the late 1970s and 1980s, many governments displayed some
characteristics of passive collaboration. In the late 1980s, governments
assumed a more active or directed role vis-à-vis the informal sector.

Active Collaboration

Under this category a government begins the process of integrating
responses to the informal sector into its national agenda. It assumes

the role of defining relevant policy and engages in debate with policy makers, academics, practitioners, and donors regarding the relationship between macro policy and microproduction. The state also studies diverse ways to respond to the informal sector, including allocating resources.

In this process, a government can look to NGOs as a means to channel credit and training to microproducers, building on their existing experience. Active collaboration in this sense is defined as the establishment of a favorable climate to enable these institutions to continue and expand their work with support without interference from government entities. Such an environment can include national recognition of the microenterprise sector, possible revisions in the policy or regulatory environment, support for forums to discuss the topic, funds for research. In other cases, it may mean the state provides funds for the scaling up of these programs, becoming an important resource for the NGOs.

Directive Collaboration

In this final category, the government establishes policy toward the informal sector and also constitutes the main implementor of programs directed to informal sector activities. Its role becomes less that of the facilitator or coordinator and more that of the main player in policy and program design and implementation.

Now the role of NGOs becomes more closely controlled by the government. The state involves itself in designing methodologies and creating new departments or institutions to implement its programs. Once functions are combined, funds are assigned for implementation, and the government creates a parallel source of services that operates independently or in competition with existing NGO programs. In some cases, the government seeks to integrate the work of existing NGOs into its program, and to regulate and administer them.

Table 10.1 summarizes the characteristics of each of the four approaches discussed and locates government response of countries under these categories. These categories should not be considered rigid characterizations of government response, but rather descriptions of general tendencies. Because government responses constantly evolve, some countries may exhibit characteristics of two categories, as is the case with Bolivia and Ecuador.

Table 10.1 Government Approaches to Informal Sector Collaboration

	DETACHED ROLE	PASSIVE ROLE	ACTIVE ROLE	DIRECTIVE ROLE
	Lack of interest No defined policy	No position Allows operation of small programs Maintains distance	Interested Defines its role as coordinator Defines national-level policy	Interested Defines policy Defines role as implementor of programs
Level of Response:				
Early Stage		Honduras Bolivia Brazil	Paraguay Dominican Republic	Nicaragua
Advanced Stage			Mexico	Ecuador Costa Rica Peru Guatemala
Very Advanced Stage				Colombia

Note: This table shows only selected countries, most of which participated in the Inter-American Conference on the Role of Governments and Private Institutions, held in Quito, Ecuador, November 1989.

Stages of Government Response

Most Latin American governments have moved in the direction of becoming active or directive collaborators in informal sector activities. These include policy formulation and program design and implementation; this chapter focuses on the latter two. National or regional policy formulation and regulatory considerations are discussed in other chapters and are discussed here only as they relate to program design and implementation (Liedholm, Franks, Bromley, Márquez, this volume).

Because active and directive collaboration describe a growing number of governments, it is useful to discuss these in greater detail. Within these categories, governments vary considerably in their level of experience and expertise in enacting policy and designing programs, and can be grouped into those that are at early stages of responding to the informal sector and those that have advanced further in developing their approaches. All classifications come from studies discussed at the international conference in Ecuador in 1989.

Early Stages of Government Response.   Governments in this stage are often newly established and are in the process of designing a response. They do not have a clear national strategy nor have they allocated resources to reach the informal sector (Bolivia and Paraguay in 1990). These governments share certain characteristics. First, in comparison with more advanced countries, they have generated less empirical information on the informal sector. Country-level baseline data, national or regional research, and conceptual frameworks exist through private initiatives (research institutions or universities), have received less attention, and are less comprehensive. Fewer people appear involved in analyzing the sector and in promoting approaches to address it.

Second, previous governments in these countries also had no strategy to address the informal sector, leaving new administrations to create new programs rather than dismantle or revise existing ones. In contrast, the Serrano and Fujimori governments in Guatemala and Peru were left to design their responses to the informal sector on the basis of previous governments' approaches.

A third characteristic of this category is that most efforts to extend services reside in the hands of small, relatively autonomous NGOs. Their success raises the government's interest. The Foundation for the Promotion and Development of the Microenterprise (PRODEM) in Bolivia presents an interesting example of the success of a private initiative in this regard. In its first four and half years of operation (1986–1990), this program reached nearly 16,000 microentrepreneurs with over $12 million in loans averaging about $225 each, and maintained a repayment rate of over 99.5 percent (PRODEM 1990). PRODEM's methodology and approach have been studied closely by the government for its own strategy. The Fundación Paraguaya (Paraguay), which developed a successful public education campaign on the informal sector, was asked by the Rodríguez government to assist in the formulation of the country's microenterprise legislation.[11]

Finally, government coordination of efforts to serve the informal sector is missing or incipient in countries at this stage; most private organizations operate on their own. An important exception is ADEMI in the Dominican Republic, which has provided more than 20,000 loans to microentrepreneurs since 1984, operates at a national level, and assumed the role of disseminating information on the sector and coordinating efforts with research and other institutions. This process may later be assumed by the government.[12]

Most governments included in this early stage of response have advanced from a detached role to either a passive collaborator approach or to one that straddles a line between two approaches. Table 10.1 shows the current status of seven countries that fit in this rubric.

More Advanced Government Responses   Governments that exhibit a more advanced understanding of the informal sector and the need to develop a policy and programmatic response to it constitute a second rubric of governments represented at the conference. Colombia and Mexico have pioneered governmental responses that are the most advanced because they have established national-level strategies. Peru and Guatemala initiated a direct service program. In 1990, Ecuador was establishing the structure for a similar program, and Costa Rica had just launched its own program.

By and large, governments in the categories delineated as advanced—or in the case of Colombia very advanced—show a positive assessment of the contribution of informal sector sector production to households and communities and have progressed in formulating their response. Their overall approach represents an official attitude of active support of microentrepreneurial ventures (Portes 1989b). Programs and policies vary according to the specificities of the informal sector in each country and the degree of public attention that the issue has received. The more successful respond to needs, make use of existing expertise, create a favorable environment, and do not implement programs directly. Three types of responses are identified: integration, coordination, delegation of implementation to others.

Countries that display great coherence in approaching the informal sector take a macro level approach and consider its role in the economy, its job creation potential, and its relationship to larger productive units. Incorporation of informal sector strategy into the national development plan is a key characteristic of an advanced response. Colombia presents the most advanced example.

Colombia's National Plan of Microenterprise Development started in 1982 at the request of local private foundations active in microenterprise development, who wanted the government to centralize resources and coordinate activities. The Colombian National Plan channels resources and guarantees lines of credit directed to the informal sector through private foundations (including $8 million from the Inter-American Bank) while the government also contributes (in this case $2 million). The government incorporated intermediary institutions into financial services for informal sector producers and vendors, and the Central Bank lent funds to these institutions that, in turn, lent them to foundations and other NGOs serving microentrepreneurs. The National Plan acknowledged the experience of private organizations, supported their role as primary lenders to the informal sector, and refrained from implementing its own credit program. The plan coordinated lending with the largest and best known government training center in the country, SENA, which trains microentrepreneurs and conducts research on the informal sector.

Governments that make the best use of available resources and organizations coordinate—create space for increased response from diverse sources. They recognize the various players in microenterprise development, and the roles each of them plays. Government seeks to facilitate their interaction and individual work. Ecuador recently initiated its microenterprise program under CONAUPE (Corporación Nacional de Ayuda a las Unidades Pequeñas Económicas) and, like Colombia, coordinates and centralizes activities for the informal sector.

From the perspective of NGOs with experience in reaching the informal sector, their incorporation as recognized program implementors is an essential component for successful government strategies. A different tendency apparent in some countries features the government as the direct implementor of services to the informal sector. Guatemala's SIMME program is a good example.

The implementation of this microenterprise development program, extending credit and technical assistance, became the kingpin of the government's response to the sector. Conducted from the office of the vice president, SIMME selected various NGOs to implement, but management, methodology, and identification of the program remained government based. At a national level, SIMME became identified as the government's centerpiece vis-à-vis the informal sector, and hence the success of this strategy was measured more in terms of clients reached or credit disbursed than in terms of research conducted or policy or legal reform enacted.

Strengths and Weaknesses of Government and NGO Microenterprise Development Programs

Table 10.2 summarizes the general advantages and disadvantages that governments and private institutions bring to the implementation of microenterprise programs. It identifies the areas in which the public and private sectors can contribute in a significant way to forge an effective national plan to address microenterprise development. It also compares the factors that limit the outreach of both entities and become problems when program implementation begins. Observations do not apply to all governments or private sector entities, but provide a basis for comparing the relative merits and shortcomings of each.

Governments' strengths lie in their capacity to mandate the environment necessary for reaching the informal sector. This mandate consists of a variety of factors: widespread dissemination of information; calls for political support at national and regional levels, identification of financial resources and their allocation, and revision of policy and regulatory concerns that affect microenterprise activity. Governments also can call upon both their own entities and private institutions to garner the technical and human resources necessary for national programs.

NGOs have their own strengths, some discussed previously. Their strong methods are based on two decades of experience. Programs they implement exhibit important characteristics of successful efforts: they are agile in their operations, feature a committed staff, seldom suffer from corruption, often are structured to scale up, and consider self-sufficiency the key to long-term sustainability. NGOs reach grassroots communities and organizations in an effective, generally unpoliticized manner, and facilitate their inclusion in designing and planning programs.

The limitations of both governments and NGOs need to be addressed, some of which are inherent to the nature of these institutions. Governments can suffer from corruption and excessive bureaucratization, factors that can quickly decimate a microenterprise program. NGOs, on the other hand, tend to be small and limited in scope. Additional limitations include government lack of experience (potential for serious design and methodological flaws), rapid program growth in the absence of necessary institutional bases, inattention to crucial issues like interest rates and mechanisms for long-term sustainability, exclusion of experienced NGOs and grassroots associa-

Table 10.2 Advantages and Disadvantages of Government and NGOs in Microenterprise Development

ADVANTAGES	DISADVANTAGES
Government:	
Widespread dissemination and political support	Excessive bureaucracy, corruption, politicization of programs
Capacity to obtain significant level of funds	Little or no experience to implement microenterprise programs
Places microenterprise development in context of broader macroeconomic considerations	Can allow programs to grow too large without necessary institutional base
Can address broader policy and regulatory concerns	No incentives to make programs work
Can mobilize institutional and human resources in public and private sectors	Possible lack of consultation with NGOs, grassroots
	No mechanism for long-term sustainability
	Perceived as social welfare and not economic development
NGOs–Private Institutions:	
Strong methodology based on experience	Limited institutional capacity for scaling up
Committed, trained staff	Low level of technical expertise, especially in financial and information systems
Capacity to reach grassroots associations	
Little or no corruption	Often lack sufficient resources to expand programs
Responsive and nonbureaucratic	Operate in isolated manner
Motivated to scale up programs	Little interaction or knowledge about government activity in informal sector
Striving for self-sufficiency	
Capacity to associate among selves to promote a coordinated effort	Limited vision that keeps programs small

tions in the planning stages, and the risk of developing government social welfare programs that are not perceived as an economic development response to assist a productive sector of the economy (Franks, Cartaya, Márquez, this volume).

Government leadership in credit and training programs for microentrepreneurs is problematic because such programs are easily politicized. For instance, if loans become mechanisms for political dividends (votes), borrowers then consider loans "handouts" (which leads to poor repayment and rapid decapitalization of funds). Other political issues are pressure to favor borrowers with a certain political affiliation, allegations of misuse to discredit a political party, bureaucratic procedures, and so forth. The dangers of compromising the integrity of a microenterprise development program can be enormous.

Private development institutions also face important disadvantages. In many cases, NGOs have limited structural and technical capacity and cannot expand their activities in a significant manner. They also have limited resources, which affect the pace of growth of their programs. Deficiencies in technical expertise like financial management and information systems handicap their programs. NGOs lack the vision to organize themselves into larger, coordinated efforts, They tend to operate in an isolated manner and maintain little interaction with the government, leading to fragmented and less effective programs that cannot reach large numbers of borrowers.

Clearly, the nature and scope of governments and NGOs enables them to bring different strengths to the process of planning and implementing programs for the informal sector. Programs should build on the strengths of each.

Conclusions and Recommendations

The following conclusions and recommendations highlight issues governments must address as they seek to respond to (reach and integrate) the informal sector.

1. Effective government response requires that the growth and development of productive activities in the informal sector be an indispensable component of a country's national economic plan and macroeconomic objectives. Successful microenterprise programs conducted by NGOs should be incorporated into the national plan.

2. For government and private programs to reach the informal sector effectively requires a favorable environment in which to operate. Expansion and merging of programs will be determined partly by each country's legal and policy framework. This will provide positive support for the extension of financial services to the informal sector through private and public financial institutions and NGOs.

3. Experience demonstrates that a government's approach to the informal sector should be comprehensive, integrating policy formulation, legal, and regulatory modifications and service extension in credit, training, and other needs.

4. The government is not the most appropriate entity to implement microenterprise programs. Its most useful role is as an active collaborator that integrates other institutions into a national strategy. This builds on the government's mandate to formulate policy and affect the regulatory environment, and it allows the government to provide both moral and financial support to experienced NGOs.

   Because many "players" are involved in microenterprise development and the informal sector in general, the role that the government can play as a coordinating body is crucial. The interaction among policy makers, researchers, financial institutions, program implementing organizations, donors, and other entities is essential for the creation of a coherent, multidimensional strategy. If governments assume a direct role in implementation, they sacrifice the leverage and access necessary to the broader coordinating role.

   Governments must consider broader issues that influence microenterprise development, particularly those related to legal and regulatory concerns. These factors influence every aspect of microenterprise production and marketing and include price controls, trade regulations, allocation of finance capital, and others. The complexity of this issue has been a deterrent to coherence (Liedholm, this volume).

5. NGOs with expertise should continue to operate as financial mediators for microenterprise programs. "Second-tier umbrella" organizations or associations can bring together NGOs to coordinate their strategies and programs as financial intermediaries that on-lend funds to local NGOs and provide technical assistance and training. Such associations foment consensus on proper use of program methodology and maintain quality control among members. Financial intermediary associations are an effective means to identify and allocate resources to programs, monitor performance, and help programs "graduate" to credit from commercial sources.

6. Successful NGOs should be a component of government response because they have proven methodologies, they show high levels of institutional integrity that prevent politicization

and corruption, their staff is motivated to work with the poor, and they have developed a trust relationship with beneficiaries.

7. The financial and managerial capacity of NGOS should be strengthened to assist in scaling up programs to reach more microentrepreneurs. This implies technical cooperation for human resource development, management information systems, experimentation with improved methodologies, and access to increased resources.

8. Donor organizations must assume the responsibility of assisting governments to chart their programs and policies. Therefore, donor agencies must perceive their role not only as resource providers but, more important, as innovators and planners. Bilateral and multilateral organizations can assist in this process by (a) encouraging governments to facilitate direct funding mechanisms to finance microproject activities identified and supervised by specific beneficiary groups; (b) encouraging governments to play a major role in disseminating information to the media on microenterprise development and making a public agenda to assist the productive activities of the poor; (c) bringing international, national, and local private organizations together to create a healthy environment among institutions based on dialogue among planners, researchers, and practitioners; on sharing and standardizing program information; and on linkages among institutions in rural and urban areas.

These conclusions and recommendations represent an initial step toward the development of effective, well-coordinated, sustainable microenterprise programs in Latin America. Governments face many challenges as they venture into this—for them—relatively new area of activity. Similarly, nongovernmental organizations must build on their experience and overcome the constraints that have prevented many of them from becoming even more effective and far reaching.

The approach recommended here combines the expertise of implementing organizations with the resources and collaboration of governments. Effective responses to the informal sector require a model based on cooperation between government and nongovernment institutions. Finally, this approach constitutes an important manifestation of how institutions within a democratic structure can reach the poorer sectors of the society, work with representative associations among the poor, and accomplish more equitable development in each country.

NOTES

1. This chapter focuses on self-employment and other unregulated, unlicensed activities not considered part of the formal economy but that provide opportunities for the poor to generate income (Hart 1973; Sethuraman 1976b; ILO 1972).

2. Throughout this chapter, all organizations not affiliated with government initiatives will be referred to as *NGOs*. In every country, NGOs focus on reaching some segment of the informal sector, especially through credit. Most NGOs consider the terms *informal sector* and *microentrepreneurs* interchangeable.

3. ACCION/AITEC is a United States based, private development organization that provides technical assistance in microenterprise development.

4. INSOTEC (Instituto de Investigaciones Socio-económicas y Tecnológicas) is a private research institution in Ecuador.

5. One measure of the size of the informal sector is to estimate the number of microenterprises or very small productive units operating in each country. Some studies include very small scale agricultural production, whereas others assess only urban units. Official figures are not available in most countries.

6. This approach is less well known in Latin America because most empirical studies have taken place in Africa, but it draws important conclusions about informal production and its contribution to the economy (Liedholm and Mead 1987).

7. Cited in a speech by Enrique Iglesias, president of the Inter-American Development Bank, at the "Microenterprise Development Conference" held at the bank in February 1989.

8. Solidarity groups are formed by individuals who need loans. Each individual receives a loan that is guaranteed by the members of the group, who "cover" for members unable to meet a payment on time (Otero 1986). Subsequent individual loans are tied to the group's repayment history.

9. Some of the best examples are ADEMI in Dominican Republic; FUNTEC and FUNDAP in Guatemala; PRODEM in Bolivia; and the Association of Solidarity Groups (AGS) composed of fourteen NGOs in Colombia (ACCION 1989; Gómez and Saladín 1987; Castello and Guzmán 1988; PRODEM 1990).

10. I was country director for ACCION International in Honduras from 1986 to 1988.

11. Martin Burt, executive director, Fundación Paraguaya, 1990.

12. Pedro Jimenez, executive director, and Camilo Luberes, board member, ADEMI, 1989.

❏ Chapter 11

Training and Technical Assistance for Small and Microenterprise: A Discussion of Their Effectiveness

Cressida S. McKean

Introduction

As indicated by Otero in the preceding chapter, concern with unemployment and underemployment in the developing countries in the 1970s and 1980s prompted both development agencies and private donor agencies (NGOs) to focus on small and microenterprises in the informal sector as a relatively inexpensive source of job creation and to promote the development of assistance programs targeting these enterprises.[1] Small business credit programs are viewed as innovative success stories in terms of their ability to increase income and employment for low-income people, while sustaining high rates of repayment and covering operating expenses out of interest revenues (Tendler 1982, p. 114; Kilby and D'Zmura 1985; Ashe 1985a; Goldmark and Rosengard 1985; Boomgard 1989; Otero, this volume).

This chapter is a revised version of "Training and Technical Assistance for Small and Microbusiness: A Review of Their Effectiveness and Implications for Women," in *Women's Ventures: Assistance to the Informal Sector in Latin America*, ed. Marguerite Berger and Mayra Buvinič (West Hartford, Conn.: Kumarian Press, 1989) pp. 102–120. We wish to thank Kumarian Press for permission to revise and use the paper in this volume.

However, there is considerable controversy over the extent to which the technical assistance and training that some programs provide contributes to the development of the firms that receive it and to the income and welfare of their owners. In fact, several studies are pessimistic about the results of technical assistance programs for very small firms, the programs' limited track record in developing viable enterprises, and the potential improvement in the incomes of poor people (Kilby 1979, p. 319; Kilby and D'Zmura 1985; Tendler 1982, 1983, pp. 101–102; Schmitz 1982a; Boomgard 1989).

Because of two specific trends, the debate over the relative value of technical assistance and training for small business initiatives in Latin America is of particular importance to projects that aim to reach the poor. First, "successful" small enterprise credit programs, managed largely by private voluntary organizations (PVOs, a form of NGO), reach a significant number of poor people, especially when they encourage participation of very small (micro) businesses and commerce.[2] The credit programs that tend to have the highest proportion of poor beneficiaries are those based on solidarity group lending, in which training and technical assistance are considered integral parts of the methodology (Otero 1989).

Second, institutions whose primary function is to provide training and technical assistance are also beginning to develop alternative methodologies for promoting employment through project support for self-employment, home-based firms, associative enterprises, and microenterprises (Corvalán Vásquez 1985; González Chiari 1984; Crandon 1984; Pinilla 1985; Placencia 1985). Because the poor in the informal sector would constitute a primary beneficiary group of such project activities, if properly designed, these initiatives merit examination. The discussion that follows will show that the record of these initiatives has not been promising, especially as regards attempts to start up new enterprises. As we examine recent trends and the programs associated with them, the questions that emerge are these: Under what circumstances do training and technical assistance inputs have an impact on the economic performance of the enterprise, particularly on the beneficiaries' income? And, how can the poor who manage small firms best benefit?

Also at issue is a tendency cited by Buviniè (1986) for women's projects to "misbehave," yielding unexpected and unwanted outcomes and failing to achieve economic goals.[3] But is it only women's projects that misbehave, in the sense that the productive objectives of the undertaking evolve into welfare actions during implementation? Could projects that try to take on too much technical assistance or that seek to develop new enterprises from scratch have similar problems?

This chapter contrasts three approaches to training and technical assistance for microenterprises and assesses the effectiveness of each approach and the degree to which the poor benefit. The first section analyzes the training and technical assistance offered to entrepreneurs who borrow from microenterprise loan programs either as individuals or as members of solidarity groups. The second section looks at the experience of projects that use training and technical assistance to stimulate the creation of new, informal sector enterprises. The third section focuses on the industry sector and trade-based initiatives that provide alternatives to individual, enterprise-specific training and technical assistance programs.

Scope of Analysis

Although varied educational and assistance activities indirectly affect informal businesses and operators, this chapter focuses only on those with the explicit objective of supplementing small business credit programs or promoting self-employment and new enterprise development. The phrase *training and technical assistance* is used to refer to "a flow of services aimed at transferring knowledge and skills which enable the recipients to increase their usable productive capacity" (Kilby 1979). Even this definition encompasses a variety of services, including training in bookkeeping, cost accounting, management, and marketing, as well as leadership and cooperation; business extension and production-specific assistance; and longer term expert technical assistance for other enterprise support services.

In practice, the objectives of small enterprise development programs often go beyond expanding the productive capacity of businesses or increasing income and employment levels. Common complementary goals are (1) to aid beneficiaries in improving self-esteem and changing attitudes on leadership, cooperation, health, nutrition, and child care; (2) to help beneficiaries organize so they can more effectively pressure for improved access to community services, such as child care, water, electricity, and education; and (3) to promote new enterprises by assisting "pre-entrepreneurs."[4] Evaluations and studies of programs have cited important contributions made by this type of training and technical assistance in areas such as participation, solidarity, and access to social services (Reichmann 1984a, 1984b; Ashe 1985b; Placencia 1989; Otero 1986; Rahman 1986). This chapter peripherally considers the effects of small enterprise training and assistance when assessing the role of technical assistance and training in affecting the economic performance of enterprises (principally measured by changes in income). This focus is important, as the 1990s climate of limited development resources makes economic impact and project self-sufficiency fundamental criteria by which programs are judged.

Can Microenterprise Credit Programs Raise Incomes Through Training and Technical Assistance?

Technical assistance and training are common components of microenterprise credit programs in Latin America. An influential program that stresses these elements is the Carvajal Foundation's Program for the Development of Small Enterprises (DESAP) of Cali, Colombia. It has influenced the design of many other credit programs for microenterprises, both in Colombia and elsewhere.[5] Developed in the 1970s, the Carvajal program views comprehensive training and technical assistance, consisting largely of accounting courses and management advice, as integral prerequisites and complements to credit. The Carvajal approach builds on the practical experience of established microentrepreneurs and uses training to change attitudes toward business management and follows this with credit and business extension services (Carvajal 1985; Inter-American Development Bank 1984). By September 1983, thirteen different types of training courses were taught to microentrepreneurs, of which four were mandatory to receive credit. Required courses focused on accounting, costs, investment projects, and personnel management (DESAP records). Individualized managerial assistance to microentrepreneurs is also required before loan authorization; participants receive at least four visits by a DESAP staff member (one visit after each required course) to assure that administrative techniques are put into practice.

Although a number of the firms initially identified drop out before receiving their loans (76.6 percent of microentrepreneurs drop out between the time they are surveyed and the time they receive credit), program results have been very positive for those who remain.[6] The arrears rate was down to 5.7 percent by June 1983. Borrowers also experienced an impressive increase in income and employment. The average real monthly family income of the borrowers increased 13 percent over a period of three years and the average number of jobs per microenterprise increased from 3.8 to 5.1 between September 1982 and September 1983.

The Northeast Union of Assistance to Small Business (UNO), another informal sector credit program, has had less positive experience with training. UNO focused assistance primarily on business extension courses rather than technical assistance, which UNO differentiates as "extension involving the production process." Tendler (1983) reported UNO's extension services to be limited because of cost-minimizing considerations. Even so, UNO spent a considerable portion (30 percent) of its operating budget on a training course that is not mandatory, lasts two weeks, and consists of four "modules": basic management, transactions with banks, basic bookkeeping, and sales promotion. UNO's extension efforts consist of visits by student staff members to clients during the period of loan application and monitoring.

Tendler's evaluation of UNO found that the courses and advice provided to clients had little impact on their businesses. Because course attendance was optional, client participation proved to be low (for example, a 1980–1981 internal evaluation found that out of thirty-five clients interviewed for the study, only thirteen, or 38 percent, had attended the courses). Even worse, interviews of those who attended found most participants unable to put to use anything they learned. The impact of recommendations to clients during visits by student staff members was found to be similarly disappointing. It is not known if clients did not implement recommendations due to lack of time, because they considered the advice inappropriate, or for other reasons; but they put up with monitoring visits to receive their loans. Tendler concluded that, although firms with no prior experience with institutional credit gained access to loans, the unit costs of lending were high, the training courses were of questionable value, and managerial extension had little impact. Moreover, the institution was unable to generate income from the credit operation, and the small firms that benefited were not increasing output or employment (Tendler 1983, pp. 5–8).

Over time, evaluations of microenterprise credit programs and concern about cost recovery have raised questions about the impact of training and technical assistance on enterprise performance. Problems with training and extension commonly cited by beneficiaries are content is excessively general; providers are inexperienced and lack specialized knowledge; and technical assistance has minimal relevance to the practical requirements of the business (Kilby and D'Zmura 1985, pp. 118–119; Tendler 1983, p. 96; Farbman 1981, p. 185; Ashe 1985b). Kilby, in a review of a series of evaluations of small enterprise credit projects, came to a conclusion similar to Tendler's: most forms of technical assistance tried so far are not "appropriate inputs," in that they lack the potential to reduce costs. "In all but a few situations, the recipients and the implementers reported that the results (of technical assistance) were negligible" (Kilby 1982b, p. 119).

Training in Minimalist Credit Programs

In response to these concerns, several microenterprise credit programs adopted what has come to be known as a *minimalist* approach, reducing training and enterprise-specific technical support to a bare minimum. The ADEMI program in the Dominican Republic and the ACCION Comunitaria–Progreso program in Peru started out with the premise that training and business extension should be extremely simple, mostly informal advice to clients imparted in a group setting or during a routine site visit (Reichmann 1984a, 1984b). This approach was one of several measures taken to streamline the credit delivery system, making it more responsive to the cash flow requirements of the beneficiary population. It was also designed to lower costs and thereby expand significantly the number of small firms that could receive credit. Although the training and technical assistance-intensive Carvajal program reaches several hundred firms annually, some of the "minimalist" credit programs, such as those in Peru and the Dominican Republic, reach over 1,000 firms yearly (ACCION 1986; Inter-American Development Bank 1986).

Over time, some formal training and technical assistance have been reincorporated into these minimalist microenterprise credit programs, in some instances on a fee-for-service basis independent of the lending program. In the Progreso program in Peru, the demand for management advice among microenterprise borrowers, including semi-literate women, resulted in a policy decision to provide increased business extension services. Clients in this program are required to pay for monthly technical assistance visits (Reichmann 1984b, p. 30). In the Dominican Republic, ADEMI also retains a minimalist credit delivery system, but it has relied on Peace Corps volunteers and local training institutions to provide one-on-one management extension to larger businesses on a fee-for-service basis (Tippett and McKean 1987; Otero and Blayney 1984, p. 36). A fee-for-service basis does not undermine the streamlining of the credit delivery process.

Training Through Solidarity Groups

Another change in the approach of many microenterprise credit programs has been the adoption of a "solidarity group mechanism" as a guarantee scheme to overcome the institutional constraints and high transaction costs of lending to very tiny businesses. Members of a self-selected group guarantee each other's loans, while the program delivers credit through a financial institution in small amounts with a minimum of paperwork and technical assistance. Commerce, services, and cottage industries—eligible beneficiary sectors for these programs—are often excluded from other microenterprise credit projects that lend to individuals. Therefore, owners of the smallest businesses, predominately women, who were previously denied access to institutional credit, can receive loans (Ashe 1985b; Otero 1986).

Managers of solidarity group credit programs in Latin America consider training to be an essential component of their strategy. Training was mandatory in eight of the ten solidarity group programs underway in 1986 in Latin America (Otero 1986, p. 11). In most solidarity group programs, participants receive an average of three hours of group training monthly in addition to promotional and follow-up firm visits. The training concentrates on entrepreneurial skills, credit management, costs and marketing, and record keeping, as well as on cooperation, leadership, needs assessment, human relations, and self-worth. The solidarity group programs see training as contributing to changing attitudes, solving problems, overcoming existing limitations, and breaking down barriers. Still, the training is not an end in itself, but a means to achieve overall program objectives[8] (Lynton and Pareek 1978; Honadel and Hannah 1982; Kindervatter 1983).

Minimalist versus Standard Training and Technical Assistance

As mentioned earlier, an approach to microenterprise assistance emerged in the 1980s that seeks to reach smaller businesses in larger numbers than previously possible, by reducing the training and technical assistance components, speeding up the loan review process, and granting very small loans (often US$20 or less for the first loan). One organization that has pioneered this "minimalist" approach is ACCION International/AITEC. ACCION contrasts its methodology with that of the "standard," or traditional programs, as shown in Table 11.1.

The "minimalist" approach to training and technical assistance is characterized by a small amount of training aimed at making clients viable borrowers. Usually training, when available, is offered on an informal basis and focuses on administrative or technical problems clients have encountered in their normal business practices. Minimalist technical assistance is often found in microenterprise programs whose beneficiaries have comparatively high levels of education and thus are already more knowledgeable and have less need for technical assistance. It is also used in some solidarity group programs in which most clients have relatively few years of schooling. More important, with this approach, training and technical assistance are not required

Table 11.1 Characteristics of Microenterprise Assistance Programs: Standard (Traditional) and Minimalist (Nontraditional)

	STANDARD	MINIMALIST
Size of beneficiary firms	Large	Small
Main emphasis	Training	Credit
Average loan size	US $800–3,000	Under US $100 initially; can reach US $1,000
Type of loans	Fixed investment and working capital	Working capital
Loan period	6–12 months	2 weeks to 4 months
Time between initial application and loan disbursement	1–2 months	4–7 days
Average number of credit experiences per beneficiary per year	1	4–6

Source: Stephen Gross, ACCION International/AITEC.

prior to borrowing, and the borrowing experience itself is set up to "train" the beneficiary in the effective use of credit; credit itself is the primary training tool (see the ADEMI, ACCION/Progreso experience cited earlier).

On the other hand, the "standard" or "traditional" approach to technical assistance, as discussed previously, was characterized as a wider variety of training courses and programs and technical assistance usually aimed at increasing firm productivity, the number of employees, the level of production, and the borrower's income. Training is offered through group classes, seminars, or prearranged, on-site (field) visits. Standard technical assistance may focus on anything from bookkeeping to investment strategies, and some programs have considered training in such areas as nutrition and child care. Solidarity groups often request a more intense type of assistance because they lack access to outside training and have already established groups that facilitate organized collective assistance.

When microenterprise credit programs retaining significant training and extension services are compared with those retaining minimal technical assistance, available data do not suggest that the standard technical assistance content necessarily results in better economic performance or loan repayment (see Table 11.2 p. 208). Of course, evaluation methodologies differ in many cases, but the results of this rough comparison do not indicate that credit programs with extensive training and technical assistance perform better than those with minimal technical assistance.

It is interesting to note the greater representation of women in the solidarity group programs that lend to smaller borrowers (see Table 11.2). In fact, the size of loans granted and types of activities supported, rather than the amount of training or technical assistance a program offers, seem to be the primary determinants of women's participation in small and microenterprise assistance programs. Women are most active in smaller businesses and in certain industry sectors, particularly commerce and services (Lycette and White 1989; Arias 1989; Reichmann 1989; Otero 1989). In part, this concentration may reflect the relatively low educational levels of women in the informal sector. Therefore, women may need supplementary training of the type used by some solidarity programs to make them viable borrowers. The rise in income and employment of beneficiaries in the solidarity group programs compares favorably with the other minimalist credit programs.[9]

A Reconsideration of Solidarity Group Programs

The solidarity group provides a ready vehicle for training and technical assistance, as well as lending. Although lack of working capital is a primary constraint for the small firm—particularly for the market vendors who predominate in solidarity group programs—lack of business skills needed for expansion may also be a problem (Liedholm and Mead 1987; EPOC 1985; Cohen 1984; Otero 1986). Group based training can help to change attitudes, solve problems and overcome obstacles, and foster the cohesion necessary to sustain group borrowing and repayment.

In minimalist credit programs, one of the primary functions of technical support—firm visits, training, and ad hoc business extension—is to enable credit delivery mechanisms to work efficiently. The minimalist credit model in general and, especially, the solidarity group mechanism have helped the very low-income vendor gain access to credit that is responsive to the rapid turnover characteristic of commerce, with very little use of technical assistance. Making use of working capital and developing skills in credit management have increased

Table 11.2 Comparison of Indicators, Microenterprise Credit Programs, Standard or Minimal Technical Assistance (TA), Women's Participation

	% INCREASE IN INCOME*	% INCREASE IN EMPLOYMENT*	ARREARS RATE (%)	WOMEN'S PARTICIPATION RATE (%)
Credit with High TA Content:				
Carvajal (individual)	19	33	6	23
Corfabricato (individual)	8	36	7	35
BMM/Cali (solidarity group)	38	71	20	65
Minimalist Credit with Low TA Content:				
Progreso (solidarity group)	43	n.a.	4	55
ADEMI (individual)	52	50	21	19
ADOPEM (individual)	36	30	18	100
FED/PRODEM (individual)	39	15	23	33
FED/PRODEM (solidarity group)	24	0	22	66

*Changes in income and employment were measured over a one-year period (1982–1983) for Carvajal and Corfabricato; (1984–1985) for FED/PRODEM; (1982–1983) for Progreso.

Source: Inter-American Development Bank 1984; Trade and Development International 1985; Reichmann 1984a and 1984b; Tippett and McKean 1987; Otero 1986; ACCION International/AITEC 1986; Berger and Buviniĕ 1989.

beneficiaries' productive capacities and incomes, which have remained extremely modest in absolute terms (Otero 1986; Trade and Development International 1985).

In this context, the use of the solidarity group mechanism as a training tool for organizing and developing other activities supplementary to credit runs the risk of complicating (overloading) a relatively efficient method for providing group guarantees. This is evidenced by the fact that demand for supplementary training in literacy and basic bookkeeping, as well as in nutrition and child care, from participants in several solidarity group programs is on the rise. Also, managers of some solidarity group programs in Latin America are considering expanding into complementary training services and group based organizing (Reichmann 1984a, 1984b; Otero 1986; Guzmán and Castro 1989).

The more training seeks to accomplish, the more costly it becomes. At present, the training costs for most solidarity group programs are covered principally by grants from international funding agencies and marginally by service fees (Otero 1986, p. 21). In the case of ADEMI, the costs of training and extension implicit in their solidarity group program were factors in the curtailment of this component (Tippett and McKean 1987). The success of similar credit programs was found to be related to the narrow focus on "minimalist" credit not over-encumbered by large amounts of training and technical assistance (Tendler 1987, p. iv; Boomgard 1989).

Beneficiary Response to Technical Assistance: A Question of Literacy, Scale, and Time

An analysis of the effect of technical assistance must take into account the responsiveness of the beneficiary, which is influenced primarily by level of education, enterprise size, and time availability, as well as by the benefits expected from training. The low educational level of solidarity group beneficiaries, in particular, often makes literacy and basic math training a prerequisite to courses in record keeping (Trade and Development International 1985; Reichmann 1984a). Most microenterprises, especially very small producers and market vendors, do not have an adequate background to absorb accounting courses aimed at calculating a break-even analysis, to act on managerial extension training aimed at reducing costs through improved labor productivity, or to use technical knowledge to increase sales through product diversification. Even the Carvajal program, which reaches primarily better educated operators of larger microenterprises, found it had to simplify its training and business extension services (Inter-American Development Bank 1984).

Responsiveness of firm operators is important to assessing the value of extension services aimed at separating household and enterprise accounts. In microenterprises, particularly home-based activities such as preparing foods or garment production, the economy of the household is often inseparable from the economy of the enterprise. Combining accounts gives small producers a margin of flexibility to respond to the seasonal fluctuations of the business, as well as to medical and educational demands of family members (Lipton 1980). This practice is often a factor limiting expansion of the enterprise; investment decisions are difficult to make without knowledge of existing production costs.

Proposing a separation of accounts again raises a question of the firm owner's capacity to use the technical information provided, given the scale of the enterprise. In the case of market vendors and microproducers, math and literacy skills are rudimentary; capital accumulation is very restricted; and the primary objective is survival of the business, not mobility or expansion. The increased income of participants in solidarity programs is miniscule in absolute terms and it fluctuates daily; a family emergency can wipe out this income overnight (Trade and Development International 1985). Therefore, the risk-averse nature of such microenterprises makes it unlikely that they would make the long-term investment of both time and money that technical assistance implies.

In such a setting, revised record keeping may be of limited value. The time spent in keeping records is a factor restricting, not increasing, flexible market responses—a competitive advantage characteristic of small firms (Lipton 1980; Schmitz 1982). Very small producers have limited interest in expanding their enterprise beyond its current size (Tendler 1982; Schmitz 1982a). Finally, a review of solidarity group programs concluded that service fees and other payments by participants cannot cover the total operating costs of such technical assistance and training (Otero 1986).

The more appropriate beneficiaries of technical assistance to reduce costs and increase productivity and sales are the larger microenterprises. For example, the Fundación Carvajal technical assistance program enabled 53 percent of its beneficiary firms to organize an accounting system and 28 percent to reduce their costs (Universidad de San Buenaventura n.d.); 70 percent of the trainees applied their accounting training to their own firm (Inter-American Development Bank 1984, p. 33). Several factors influenced these outcomes. First, the lengthy nature of the Carvajal program, which requires successful completion of three one-week courses prior to loan approval, probably "weeds out" some of those less likely to succeed. Second, because the Carvajal program reaches predominantly the upper levels of the microenterprise sector, it is selective for entrepreneurs with a greater capacity to absorb such technical training and extension, often due to their higher education levels and greater disposable income (Inter-American Development Bank 1984). Still, the data available on the Carvajal program do not demonstrate that technical training and extension—*in and of themselves*—are the critical factor in reducing costs and improving the economic performance of the beneficiary enterprises (Inter-American Development Bank 1984, 1986; Carvajal 1985; Universidad de San Buenaventura n.d.)

Finally, time is a constraint to the firm owner's ability to benefit from training and technical assistance services (Tendler 1982; Universidad de San Buenaventura n.d.; Arias 1985). In the Carvajal program, 30 percent of the entrepreneurs surveyed identified lack of time—theirs or the advisors—as a major problem (Universidad de San Buenaventura n.d.). In particular, it would be difficult for women who manage both a business and a household to find the time to attend three weeks of required coursework, a fact verified by an evaluation of the small business credit program of the Industrial Bank of Peru (BIP) (Arias 1985). The more important issue in the medium term is the time needed before the enterprise can carry a reliable stream of revenue sufficient to provide income for the beneficiary and his or her family.

Training and Technical Assistance to Develop New Informal Enterprises

The experience of both governmental and nongovernmental institutions in developing training programs for the urban informal sector, at the margin of traditional vocational training programs, dates from the 1970s in Latin America. In some cases, institutions have shifted from purely formal sector training to assistance in the preparation for self-employment and associative enterprise development for the informal sector (Corvalán Vásquez 1985, p. 174; González Chiari 1984). Such programs suffer from the diversity in approaches and the small scale of operation.

Training for informal sector enterprise promotion can be divided into two main categories: training and technical assistance for the formation of new businesses, often in the form of cooperatives or other associative enterprises, and training for existing individual microentrepreneurs. This section focuses mainly on the first type, as the second is less well documented.

In either of its two forms, the addition of training to existing programs may represent an opportunity for poorer individuals, such as women, to gain greater access to technical training. For example, a review of women's participation in technical training institutions in Latin America found that men predominated in the formal training system offering preparation for the modern sector, whereas women predominated in short-term technical courses with a concentration in the service sector (Lembert and Nieves 1986). Thus, established formal training institutions effectively discriminate against women by limiting their access to long-term training for employment in the modern sector (with the exception of service-sector employment such as secretarial positions). An important finding is that low-income women are excluded even from the short-term technical courses and have few, if any, technical training alternatives (Lembert and Nieves 1986, p. 27; Gómez 1984, p. 107).

A number of institutions with enterprise promotion projects have recognized that the inputs required to establish new, viable enterprises commonly go well beyond training of participants. Skills appropriate to the trade, capital (both for initial investment and for operations) needs, technology, and markets are all prerequisites for enterprise development. In a training project for the informal sector in Guayaquil, Ecuador, the technical advisors found that creating new jobs by establishing associative enterprises from scratch was not a large-scale methodology for generating employment, as had been anticipated. In this case, the technical requirements of setting up a bakery and restaurant were excessively complex and costly. The time commitment was too great relative to the number of beneficiaries. In a later phase, the project redirected its attention to providing services to established microenterprises (Placencia 1985; Carbonetto 1985, p. 360).

The experience of several enterprise development projects again illustrates the long time frame, the high costs, and the difficulties of creating economically viable group enterprises. In a project to create enterprises for women in Peru, organized by UNICEF and the Peruvian Ministry of Labor, project managers came to the conclusion that group enterprise creation in the informal sector was inappropriate and unworkable and decided to concentrate on programs for the development of existing enterprises. Plans to establish a group enterprise with a US$150,000 investment were abandoned because of difficulties in execution and irrelevance to the experience of those individuals already working in the informal sector (Pinilla 1985, p. 310).

Another enterprise development project, the Women, Enterprise and Development program executed by the Pathfinder Fund, had similar problems. Over a three-year period, Pathfinder funded projects supporting the development of group-owned productive enterprises in five Latin American countries. An evaluation concluded that the semi-literate women participants benefited most from the training, particularly in production and management skills. They gained skills improving their employability, increased their demand for education, changed their fertility patterns, and became involved in community development activities. But after three years, only three of the five group enterprises were generating sufficient income to meet current expenses; one of these firms has since gone bankrupt (Crandon 1984, p. vii; Yudelman 1987). More important, because the firms were operating at less than full capacity, almost all of the 100 women involved in these group enterprises were working only on a part-time basis. The income stream implicit in wages of one to two weeks per month was insufficient to cover their family expenses (Crandon 1984).

Even though bankruptcy is a common fate for many small businesses, the question that arises in this case is, When are the objectives of creating an enterprise beyond the realistic capacity of project implementers and beneficiaries? In several cases in the Pathfinder program, basic feasibility and marketing studies were not carried out before production was set up in the group enterprise, and supplementary literacy and math training were considered essential for participants to benefit from skills training. Participants undoubtedly benefited as individuals and as members of a community, but did not benefit much from income generated by new enterprises.

The enterprise development methodology designed by the Overseas Education Fund (OEF) for work with the semi-literate in rural areas is the model for a number of projects targeting pre-entrepreneurs as well as established small producers. The priority in the four phases of the OEF approach—organizing, training, credit, and technical assistance—is to encourage the involvement of the women beneficiaries in the organization and management of the enterprise to a maximum extent.[10] Nonformal education methods, a strength of OEF work with illiterate women, have been used increasingly in training programs developed for the urban informal sector as well as in solidarity group programs (Corvalán Vásquez 1985; Otero 1986).

The OEF Women in Business project in Central America has focused on providing services to small established home-based firms, instead of creating larger group enterprises. The high cost per beneficiary and the longer time horizon of group enterprise creation have encouraged the project manager to limit support for group enterprises to less than 10 percent of the portfolio. This microenterprise credit program targets established enterprises as clients, because this group has already been prescreened for motivation and basic skills. Though low-income individuals not engaged in economic activity will be excluded, this criterion increases the potential for improved income for a larger number of individuals in a modest timeframe.[11]

New courses for existing small-scale and microenterprises have been designed by training institutions (for example, the National Training Service in Colombia, SENA) to upgrade or improve the skills of owners, particularly in accounting, marketing, management, and even community development and leadership training. Working alone or in coordination with microenterprise programs, these institutions hope to be able to provide short, part-time courses that will be more useful to owners of informal sector businesses than the typical offerings of training centers, which are oriented toward providing technical production skills to formal sector workers.

The cost effectiveness of recent training programs for the informal sector is still undetermined. A study of SENA programs in Colombia found that the economic benefits of courses for informal sector workers were considerably less than those for the modern sector. Still, the per unit cost of formal sector training is much higher than training for the informal sector.[12] The project's experience indicates that the risks of enterprise creation may outweigh the potential benefits. In general, training programs to develop new businesses tend to have a negative impact on cost effectiveness (Corvalán Vásquez 1985, p. 161).

Efforts of mainstream training institutions like SENA, which capitalize on the more successful training initiatives of small and microenterprise credit programs, seem to hold greater promise than enterprise creation activities and may be carried out at lower cost. Even so, they have limited track records, making evaluation difficult.

Programs to provide training and business extension to lower income beneficiaries assume they suffer from a lack of skills and managerial ability. However, several studies have demonstrated that the skill level of small producers is often not a primary constraint; in some cases, it may even be a source of strength (Schmitz 1982b, p. 179; King 1975). More important are factors beyond the control of individuals, factors that determine their ability to stabilize or increase their incomes and expand production and employment. For example, Schmitz's study of the small-scale weaving and hammock industry in Brazil found that many small producers were skilled workers and that access to raw materials was a more important constraint for them than additional training. The significant increase in beneficiaries' income in "minimalist" microenterprise credit programs also suggests that training and technical assistance inputs may not be essential. Organizational and management assistance to individual firms is most useful when a firm is expanding.

A Note on Training as a Problem

In a number of small business programs, the promotion of training as a solution to problems of program access may be a problem in itself. Several of these programs, such as MUDE in the Dominican Republic, Women's World Banking in Cali, Colombia, and PAME in Ecuador, consider social and women's consciousness raising as an important tool for managerial reorientation (Berger and Buvinič 1989). Although the training itself may be valuable in changing attitudes and increasing self-confidence and participation, the final effect may be the diversion of attention from some of the fundamental external constraints of these small producers.

Industry and Trade-Based Initiatives

Emphasis on a lack of individual entrepreneurial or management skills places the blame for the failure of small enterprises on the people who run them, rather than on the environment in which they operate (Schmitz 1982b, pp. 179–180). Studies of small and microenterprises demonstrate the value of analyzing external constraints on firm development. Analysis of external factors, such as raw material supply and access to technology or product markets, is best approached through a focus on the industry subsector or trade in which the small firms operate. Trade or industry subsector-specific studies are used as a means of identifying points of intervention. The objective is to analyze the forces in the industry that determine the position of small enterprises, such as the pressures of competition, access to raw materials, and subcontracting relations, and then to develop interventions to alleviate the most serious constraints (Schmitz 1982; Boomgard, Davies, Haggblade, and Mead 1986; Cohen 1984; Tendler 1987; McKean 1987).

One type of project activity based on this "subsector" approach is of direct relevance to low-income individuals. Most often, subsector based interventions involve studies of economic activities in which particular groups of individuals predominate, such as the garment and weaving industry or the street food and prepared food trade (Schmitz 1982a; EPOC 1985; Cohen 1984). Trade based organizing and targeting specific obstacles are responsive to these individuals' needs. As mentioned previously, Schmitz's study of the hammock industry found that the lack of access to raw material was the principal constraint. Setting up a raw material deposit was the most viable solution. However, those who finish the hammocks in their homes would still be likely to be excluded from benefits. Given the large number of workers and the lack of work alternatives, trade based organizing, although a difficult objective, was found to be the most advantageous solution for these home-based workers (Schmitz 1982b). EPOC's 1985 review of the street food trade found that police harassment and the lack of legal recognition were major problems, concluding that "perhaps the most important assistance that can be given to vendors is help in organizing" (Cohen 1984).

A review of similar Ford Foundation projects found that the better performing organizations "concentrated on a . . . particular trade, sector or income-earning activity (for example, garbage collectors, food preparers, dairy producers, vegetable vendors, landless groups owning tubwells). The narrow sectoral focus of these organizations forced them to tailor interventions to the needs of that particular sector of trade" (Tendler 1987, p. 9).

In Latin America, vendor and trade based associations of microenterprises slowly grow and expand the provision of services. In Cartagena, Colombia, stall vendors formed an association to limit police harassment (Otero 1986). In the Dominican Republic, the Asociación de Tricicleros (the tricycle association) has an insurance scheme and represents members in negotiations with the municipal government (Reichmann 1984a).

The stimulation of brokering between buyers and producers is another type of sector-specific assistance to small enterprises, but the results of project experience in this area have been limited. In one case, an attempt to link up groups of small handicraft producers directly with buyers allowed buyers to conduct on-site training in product design and quality control, which led to contracts for several groups of small producers. Women, in this case, were the primary beneficiaries (McKean 1985). Technical assistance has been targeted to small furniture enterprises to strengthen their access to buyers and to shrimp farmers to improve the quality of their production in Indonesia. However, it is unlikely that these types of interventions will have a direct effect on income of the beneficiaries in the short term. Again, as in complex enterprise development projects, the risk of failure is inherent in efforts requiring the provision of multiple inputs over a long period of time.

Conclusion: How Can Low-Income Individuals Best Benefit from Training and Technical Assistance?

Several factors influence the capacity of low-income individuals to benefit from training and technical assistance inputs. Illiteracy and lack of education are fundamental constraints, particularly for low-income women. Second, the tiny size and commerce base of the enterprises typically managed by low-income individuals limit their motivation and capacity to absorb complex technical training or business extension. Third, time is a scarce resource particularly for Latin American women responsible both for providing for their families and managing a household.

Solidarity group lending has given the economically active in the informal sector access to credit for working capital. Minimal training and technical assistance inputs have permitted the loan guarantee mechanism to work and have provided some skill upgrading to improve the businesses and solve other problems. Microproducers and vendors may want training in record management, nutrition, or business strategies; and managers also consider training an integral component of the solidarity group strategy. Yet the danger of responding excessively to these demands within the context of the solidarity group credit program is that expectations grow, objectives multiply, and capacity diminishes. The costs of providing these services can overwhelm self-sustaining credit capacity and reduce the ability to lend, interfering with the primary focus of the program. Using the solidarity group mechanism for providing supplementary training in organization, or even nutrition, may unintentionally add unsustainable costs to the credit program.

Market vendors and home-based producers may have little capacity to absorb training and technical assistance aimed at separating household and business accounts. Illiteracy, minute scale, and lack of time can make such efforts a waste of resources. Credit or trade based organizing for established producers or traders may be more immediately relevant to their experience. Training in accounting, business extension, and production-specific assistance have the greatest impact on microentrepreneurs with the capacity and desire for expanding. Still, for those managing these larger microenterprises, time is a constraint to the benefits of valuable accounting assistance.

The opportunity cost of participation is even higher in the case of projects that seek to develop new enterprises. The priority here is to concentrate on economically active individuals, for whom a limited number of inputs are required. Targeting illiterate individuals who are not economically active to create new group enterprises may result in more failures than successes. As Kilby (1979) has argued, supplying the "missing ingredient" is the project activity with the greatest potential for generating income for beneficiaries in a relatively modest time frame.

Finally, it is important to transcend the mind-set that sees factors internal to the firm, such as lack of skills, management capacity, or social consciousness, as the primary constraints. Subsector studies can lead to effective interventions in the informal sector by identifying critical external obstacles to industries and trading activities in which low income groups predominate.

NOTES

1. . The term *informal sector* is used here to refer to economic activity characterized by "ease of entry, reliance on indigenous resources, family ownership of enterprises, small scale of operation, labor intensive and adapted technology, skills acquired outside the formal school system and unregulated and competitive markets" (ILO 1972; see Hart 1971 for original definition).

2. Mazumdar (1976) documents the preponderance of women in the informal sector in his "The Urban Informal Sector," *World Development*. See also Berger (1988) and Lycette and White (1989).

3. Projects "misbehave" when implementation does not conform to objectives. This has been the case of many income-generating projects for women, which are transformed into social welfare projects by (usually male) practitioners so the project shows a better fit with women's role of wife-mother.

4. The term *preentrepreneurs* refers here to individuals not currently economically active, but identified as interested and capable of undertaking activity to generate income. Some projects of the Overseas Education Fund, the Pathfinder Fund, the ILO, and other institutions have targeted preentrepreneurs as beneficiaries.

5. The Carvajal experience inspired the Colombian government to integrate informal sector planning into the National Plan of Development (Otero, this volume).

6. Applicants drop out for a variety of reasons—they obtain funds through other means, abandon the investment idea, find a wage job, become discouraged, and so on.

7. The term *minimalist credit* is used by Judith Tendler (1987) in her recent review of Ford Foundation programs for poverty alleviation.

8. This issue was in the final report of a 1985 solidarity group conference.

9. It should be noted that in the solidarity group programs analyzed, the base figures for income and employment indicators were very low. Starting from such a low base figure results in higher relative increases for the solidarity group beneficiaries compared with those in individual microenterprise credit programs, who have much higher base figures for both income and employment.

10. Personal interview with Suzanne Kindervatter, 1987.

11. Phone interview with Marcy Kelly concerning OEF's Women in Business Project in Central America, September 1987.

12. Information from a study by SENA–Sistema de Planificación de Recursos Humanos, Bogotá, 1982, cited by Corvalán Vásquez 1985, pp. 159–177.

Part IV

A Closer Look at Poverty, Planning, and Power

❑ Chapter 12

Informality and Poverty: Causal Relationship or Coincidence?

Vanessa Cartaya

Introduction

One of the most persistent assumptions made about the informal economy by the general public, academics, and policy makers is that informality is synonymous with poverty. Supporting evidence appears to
abound; the street vendor is the classic example. But not all informals
are poor, nor do all the poor work in the informal sector. A significant
proportion of industrial workers—assumed to be in the "stable, well-
paid modern" sector—receive incomes at or below the poverty level.
Equally important are the significant numbers of successful informal
entrepreneurs whose high incomes were attained without the incentives available to large scale firms. Thus, the informality-poverty relation is complex—a fact that must be understood to achieve efficient
and effective economic restructuring and social policy reform.

Several factors contributed to the oversimplification of the infor-

This chapter is a substantially revised version of "Pobreza y economìa informal: Casualidad or causalidad?" which appeared in *La Economía Informal*, ed.
Gustavo Márquez and Carmen Portela (Caracas: Ediciones IESA, 1991). My
gratitude to Orangel Rivas for his valuable assistance in the preparation of this
chapter and to Jaime Mezzera, Gustavo Márquez, Marisela Montoliú, and
Cathy A. Rakowski for their valuable comments. Cathy Rakowski translated
to English and revised the text.

mality-poverty relation. First, policy makers have not paid enough attention to the existing empirical evidence, despite widespread availability of a proliferation of studies on both informality and poverty in recent years (e.g., studies of crisis and the implementation of structural adjustment policies).[1] Second, analysis of the links between poverty and informality is complicated by the fact that poverty as a policy concept refers to households or families, whereas data on informality or employment refer to the status of individual workers. Confusion is exacerbated by the lack of a clear and fully operationalizable definitions of *informality, informal sector, informal economy*. Proponents of different theoretical or ideological positions all claim these terms for activities and workers who do not conform to the accepted market model of "employment" in some way, but use diverse measures and definitions. This weakens the explanatory power of the terms, and produces conflicting evidence of the informality-poverty relation.

As cited in preceding chapters, the definition most commonly accepted in Latin America is that developed by the United Nations' ILO-PREALC office (Programa de Empleo para América Latina y el Caribe), which posits a strong relationship among size (scale of operations), level of technical sophistication, productivity, and income levels: small scale activities are associated with unsophisticated techniques, low levels of productivity, and incomes below those of "modern" jobs (PREALC 1978). From this assumption, PREALC developed the only widely accepted operationalized concept of informality adapted to available census and survey data[2]—with informality as a form of insertion in the labor market.

An alternative notion also well-known among policy advisors and researchers in Latin America is that offered by Portes and Sassen-Koob (1988), who focus on large, "formal" firms that evade costs of minimum wage and labor benefits by hiring workers on a temporary basis or by subcontracting to unprotected labor. Lack of protection determines "informality" and poverty among workers (see Portes, this volume). But this alternative cannot be verified because censuses and surveys do not include information on social security coverage and other protective measures. The third position influential in Latin America—that of Hernando de Soto (1986) and the Instituto Libertad y Democracia—has limited policy influence (see Bromley, this volume). This approach argues a strong link between informality and poverty, because poverty is believed synonymous with entrepreneurial survival strategies and informality refers to a survival strategy in a context of excessive state intervention. Again, this type of informality is difficult to operationalize because standard surveys do not include information on regulatory controls or registration.

Other conceptual problems that plague the study of poverty include the tendency to ignore the historical and social origins of poverty in Latin America. The recession and debt crisis of the 1980s and 1990s exacerbated poverty and increased its heterogeneity. Poverty was widespread in earlier periods—a fact often ignored by recent labor market studies.[3]

Study Objective and Methods

This chapter presents an overview of a study whose objective is to identify—illustrated by the situation of urban households and their workers—the conditions under which the informal or formal status of workers (hereafter used to refer to PREALC's form of operationalization) is related to poverty across households. To do so optimally requires a consideration of the problems of labor supply (how different types of households allocate labor) and demand for labor (labor market segmentation). The study represents a preliminary analysis of these factors in urban Venezuela.

The study universe included three categories of urban household units with at least one income earner in 1987.[4] "Extremely poor households" show a total income below the level necessary for food subsistence and are at critical risk nutritionally. "Poor households" show total income levels equal to food subsistence requirements, but no possibility of satisfying other needs. "Nonpoor households" show total incomes adequate for satisfaction of food and other needs beyond subsistence. Two types of workers were included—"formal-modern" sector workers and "informals."[5] An underlying assumption of the study is that labor market structure is one of several important variables associated with the expansion of poverty (Rodgers 1987).

Methods and available data imposed limitations. For one, the theories that we postulate as no longer satisfactory to explain poverty are, in fact, supported by the data because data production methods were developed for those theories and implicitly reflect their assumptions. Data production methods do not lend themselves to the use of new approaches. For example, in the 1970s the relationship between firm size and productivity appeared obvious; not so today when new production techniques facilitate capital-intensive, small batch production. But existing methods produce information on firms at and above or below the magical number of five workers. Another critical problem is the implicit assumption that salaried workers have stable, "protected" employment. Existing census and survey techniques do not produce information on benefits or legal protection. Yet, in Venezuela at least, Social Security enrollment (the indicator par excellence of protection) is available only to urban workers and only in certain states, regardless of firm size. Finally, surveys provide information only on the activity that respondents identify as their principle activity (although part-time employment takes precedence over unpaid activities). Thus, we do not have information on second or third jobs of workers with multiple employment—a very common practice, especially during periods of economic crisis. And, although data facilitate analysis of the incidence of informality across different income strata, they do not permit adequate study of the role of labor market structure in poverty.

Hence, a decision was made to stratify households by per capita income and the modest goal was set of calling attention to empirical evidence of the links between poverty and informality, leaving for future study a more exhaustive and sophisticated analysis of these links. Finally, it must be noted that empirical data for one point in time—1987—must be evaluated within the context of a decade-long reality, and conclusions, therefore, suggest the direction for subsequent, time-series analyses.[6]

Background

Diverse theoretical approaches have applied the logic of "exclusion" to explain the evolution of Latin American economies since the Second World War and the persistence of poverty among households excluded from access to the benefits of development and workers excluded from stable and high paid jobs. The most important approaches have been "marginality" and "labor market segmentation" (informal–modern–formal) theories because they shifted the focus of studies from how characteristics of the supply of labor lead to unemployment to how the characteristics of demand perpetuate and expand poverty (Cartaya 1988). The concept of "household survival strategies" (Cornia 1984) added another dimension, a focus on the link between the variety of "arrangements" by households at different stages of a family life cycle[7] and under different economic conditions. The "income generation" approach used for this chapter is a micro level approach that sets aside, at least temporarily, consideration of the macro level conditions that determine income distribution.[8]

None of these popular approaches adequately addresses the links between micro level and macro level processes. Rodgers (1987) argues that to address this issue, four questions must be answered: (1) How is productivity related to wages? (2) What mechanisms determine how workers are allocated to different jobs, and what wages accrue to those jobs? (3) What factors create barriers of access to specific jobs? (4) What factors determine the characteristics of the supply of labor?

In Venezuela, two types of research contribute to the informality-poverty discussion. Labor market segmentation studies by economists provide evidence of a relationship between the form of labor market insertion, productivity differentials, and level of income.[9] Their short-coming is that they identify low income workers as "poor." Survival strategy studies by anthropologists and sociologists provide evidence of the importance of household context to labor market insertion (CENDES 1989). These typically are case studies or limited surveys, however, and their generalizability is questionable. The study discussed in this chapter builds on that research and incorporates lessons learned from other settings.[10] It focuses on labor supply to evaluate the impact of poverty on labor market insertion and asks who and how many generate income and among how many must it be divided? The chapter also analyzes the demand for labor to determine what income alternatives exist, who is employed in what type of enterprise and industry sectors, and how much they are paid.

The Setting

In Venezuela, poverty persisted despite rapid economic growth throughout the 1970s, and worsened during the 1980s. Throughout Latin America, including Venezuela since 1982, increases in poverty resulted from the combined effects of (a) the contraction of production and employment, (b) structural adjustment policies which increased the cost of basic goods and services and depressed wages, and (c) budget reductions that led to a decline in quality and quantity of social services (PNUD 1988). In 1987, year of the study, the Venezuelan economy experienced a period of renewed growth and a decline in open unemployment. Nonetheless, inflation was over 30 percent per year and real wages declined for the ninth consecutive year despite a 75 percent increase in the minimum wage (see Table 12.1).

Economic indicators suggest the relationship between informality and poverty from 1979 to 1987 is not simple or straightforward (see Table 12.1). Even during the growth years of 1985–1987, both the informal sector and poverty continued to expand. Between 1981 and 1987, the proportion of families in poverty had doubled.

Comparisons of price increases and changes in real income are eloquent: between 1978 and 1985 the cost of the basic food basket tripled while household incomes did not even double (Cartaya and

Table 12.1   Evolution of the Economy, Labor Force (LF), and Poverty

YEAR	% RISE IN GNP	INFLA- TION RATE (%)	UNEM- PLOY- MENT RATE	% REAL CHANGE IN WAGE	URBAN INFORMAL SECTOR AS % OF LF	% EXTREMELY POOR HOUSEHOLDS	% POOR HOUSE- HOLDS
1979	0.1	12.2	5.6	-1.4	22.8	**nd	nd
1980	-3.8	18.7	5.7	-1.1	27.1	nd	nd
1981	-0.5	15.3	6.1	-5.6	28.7	4.3	17.0
1982	0.2	11.1	7.1	-7.2	32.1	10.3	22.3
1983	-6.1	5.1	10.3	-1.9	31.9	nd	nd
1984	-2.8	21.2	13.4	-14.2	31.2	10.9	25.1
1985	3.2	11.4	12.1	-4.7	31.4	16.4	29.9
1986	7.0	11.6	10.3	-3.6	33.0	20.5	30.7
1987	4.2	28.1	8.5	-3.1	31.7	*20.5	*32.6

*Figures vary from those of this study due to methodological differences.
** No data available
Source: Banco Central de Venezuela, OCEI (census bureau), CORDIPLAN.

García 1988; Cartaya and Márquez 1990). Between 1985 and 1988, household incomes increased by 50 percent while food prices increased by 379 percent. Consumption patterns changed drastically. In the 1980s, food became the major expenditure for households and the capacity to satisfy other needs declined dramatically (Valecillos 1986). Nutritional levels declined, especially among the poor: between 1985 and 1987 the average annual consumption of calories per person per day declined dramatically (González, Hernández, and Merz 1988).

The incidence of informality increased rapidly at the start of the recession, and the informals have represented over a third of all workers since 1982, despite the fluctuations in economic factors. It would appear that informality will not decline in the short run. However, is this a function of supply side choices or demand for labor?

Labor Supply Among Poor Households

A labor supply approach treats the worker as a social agent and member of a specific social group (Pérez Sáinz 1989) whose job decisions are influenced by cultural and demographic factors. Neo-classical theorists assume that each household or family unit seeks to maximize its satisfaction as a group. Satisfaction results from a combination of domestic production and reproduction and the purchase of marketed goods and services with income earned in the labor market (Blau and Ferber 1986). Fertility rates, age at birth of first child, marital history, gender of household head, and stage of the family life cycle all determine the availability of potential workers.

Models developed to explain labor allocation identify intervening factors: (a) budget constraints, the level of household income at the moment a member decides to enter the labor market (including income of other workers and nonwage income) relative to the cost of goods and services needed to maintain what the household determines as an acceptable life style; and (b) opportunity costs, the income earning potential of a worker compared to the cost of remaining outside the labor market. These widely accepted models explain only part of the variation in labor allocation across households stratified by income levels, because they tend to ignore the relative value of the reproductive activities in which inactive ("unemployed") members engage and the cultural norms that define appropriate social roles for men and women of different income strata. An improvement is introduced with the conceptualization of domestic tasks as a type of job, albeit unpaid (Ward 1990; Collins and Giménez 1990). Thus, different factors contribute to labor allocation decisions for men and women and are related to the relative value of domestic tasks to household welfare (Hossfeld 1990). Women's efforts to balance the demands of household survival with cultural and religious norms varies across income groups and economic conditions. Household income and social class influence how much and what kind of work women carry out at home, a critical factor in variations in household labor supply.

Differences between paid and unpaid domestic tasks are subtle and variable. The same work can be, simultaneously, unpaid, remunerated as informal self-employment, or wage work. Households use a combination of strategies to meet reproduction—including labor intensive strategies, labor saving technology, or contracting tasks to nonhousehold members—and these vary by class. This leads, in general, to a greater availability of female labor for employment in households with higher income levels where the demands on women's reproductive labor are lowered through alternative strategies. Conversely, in the poorest families and despite the need for additional income, the supply of female labor for wage work is restricted.

Characteristics of Poor Households

Approximately half the urban households studied were poor or extremely poor (see Table 12.2): one in six households could not meet minimum food expenses and one third could not meet other basic necessities. Distributional inequities were reflected in the fact that the 15 percent of the households in extreme poverty controlled 5 percent of all earned income whereas 30 percent of the nonpoor households controlled 76 percent.

Household composition appears to be both a contributing factor and a consequence of income level. First, poor households have more members among whom to distribute limited resources and a greater proportion of their members are children.[11] In 1987, half—3.6 of 7—the members per extremely poor household were children under 14 years of age whereas only 1.3 of the average 4.4 members per nonpoor household were children. About one-third of the extremely poor households was headed by a woman, compared with about one-fifth of the poor households and only one-sixth (16.4 percent) of the nonpoor households (see Table 12.2).[12]

Labor Allocation (Supply) and Income

The size and composition of labor supply in the households vary considerably across income strata. Extremely poor households are characterized by *a more limited supply of labor*. They average 1.5 active members, whereas nonpoor households average 2. And, although the gross urban activity rate for 1987 was 41 percent, that of extremely poor households was only 24 percent, a function of the large proportion of children and households headed by women. There are two types of female headed households—those made up of "young" families (with very young children) and those with children old enough to work.

Extremely poor households also show *lower female labor force participation rates* than do nonpoor households. The tension between demands on women's labor for reproductive tasks and demands for income generation are reflected in differential labor force participation rates of men and women, between female heads and nonheads, and across income strata. Female heads show the highest participation rates, but their average rates are lowest in the poorest households (see Table 12.2). However, when only heads aged 25–44 are included, participation rates for both male and female heads in the poorest households increases to about 90 percent.

Although female nonheads are the least likely group to be employed, their participation rates are directly related to household income levels. Numerous studies (Rakowski 1991 and Bethencourt 1988 for Venezuela; Benería and Roldán 1987 for Mexico, among others) have found consistently that, among lower income households headed by

Table 12.2 Characteristics of Household by Income Strata, Labor Force Participation, and Sector

	EXTREMELY POOR	POOR	NONPOOR	ALL
Number of Urban Households:*	379,872	756,243	1,378,558	2,514,643
Households	15.1%	30.1%	54.8%	100%
Population	19.8%	34.0%	46.1%	100%
Average Number of Members	6.9	6.0	4.4	5.3
Female Headed	27.3%	19.0%	16.4%	18.8%
Educational Level (in years)				
All heads of household	5.1	6.4	9.1	7.8
Male heads only	5.2	6.3	9.1	—
Female heads only	4.8	6.5	9.4	—
Labor Force Participation:				
Active members**	1.54	1.80	2.06	1.90
Employed members	1.34	1.67	2.01	1.80
Dependents per worker	5.15	3.57	2.20	2.93
Activity rate for all members**	24.1%	31.2%	51.1%	41.1%
Activity rate heads**	78.0%	84.5%	90.0%	86.5%
Male heads	88.2%	92.0%	96.1%	93.8%
Female heads	50.9%	52.4%	58.8%	55.1%
Unemployement rate	6.8%	2.8%	2.3%	2.3%
Male heads	7.7%	2.9%	2.4%	2.4%
Female heads	2.3%	1.6%	1.3%	1.3%

Proportion of Workers in Modern and Informal Sectors by Household Strata:

Informal	46.7%	37%	28.9%	
Modern	53.3%	63%	71.1%	

*Excludes households without earned income.
**Number or proportion of adults in the labor force or seeking work.
Source: OCEI, Household Survey, II Semester 1987, processed by IESA.

men, women are employed primarily when household survival is threatened or the male head is unemployed. Employment of female nonheads is more common in middle and upper income strata.[13]

Poor households show *lower educational levels among adults*. The average educational level of heads of household—the primary income earner in most households—is significantly lower (less than sixth grade) among the poorest households than among the nonpoor (ninth grade). Conventional social policy wisdom supports universal primary education (to sixth grade) as the most important instrument for overcoming poverty, but this study found secondary education appears to make the difference between being poor or nonpoor.

Extremely poor households show *higher levels of open unemployment* (see Table 12.2). This finding contradicts the commonly accepted notion (PREALC 1978) that unemployment is a luxury the poor cannot afford. In Venezuela, previous studies of change in unemployment rates across income strata showed that the "luxury assertion" held true before 1982. The deepening of the crisis and contraction in employment and expansion of poverty in the 1980s changed this situation and is one feature of the increasing heterogeneity of poverty. An additional factor in unemployment among the poor since 1985 is the increase in previously inactive members entering the labor market as a household survival strategy (Cartaya 1990b). Survival strategies are conditioned by the number of potential workers and the availability of their labor for wage work; 18 percent of the extremely poor households have only one income earner and 40 percent depend on income exclusively from one sector (informal or modern). Lack of diversification may be a factor in extreme poverty.

The study reveals that the income of the head is the most important factor in determining household income and *this is particularly true among the extremely poor*. In these households, the head contributes 90 percent of the income; among the nonpoor, the head's contribution is about two-thirds of total income.[14] This exerts tremendous pressure on income earners in poor households. Workers in extremely poor households support over 5 dependents, whereas those in nonpoor household support only 2.2. In the case of female heads, poverty is exacerbated by a combination of low educational levels and demands of reproductive tasks that interfere with women's possibilities to accept paid employment outside the home. Female-headed households show average per capita incomes 23 percent below those of male-headed households, but households headed by nonemployed women show incomes 16 percent higher than those headed by employed women (nonemployed women are likely to be older with children of working age who support the household).

Poverty is not merely a function of labor allocation strategies. The success of these strategies depends on the demand for labor and job opportunities for workers with specific characteristics. Employed members of extremely poor households concentrate in the lowest paying jobs; having two employed members or fewer dependents cannot be counted on to raise these households above the poverty level.

Demand for Labor: Jobs and Income

Labor market studies in Latin America have explained income differentials among workers as a function of segmentation, discrimination, human capital differences, and institutional factors such as unionization and labor legislation. Segmentation studies focus on the structure and function of distinct labor markets whose jobs are distinguished by marked differences in requirements for human capital, stability, conditions of work, and monetary and nonmonetary rewards for workers (Portes and Sassen-Koob 1988; Lacabana 1990). Through segmentation of the labor market different kinds of people are tracked into different kinds of jobs or are excluded from employment. A major focus of segmentation studies in Latin America has been the formal-informal or modern-informal breakdown. Some studies treat these "sectors" as dichotomies, others as intersecting or overlapping pieces of a whole (see Moser, this volume). Additionally, some research has approached segmentation as it affects industry sectors or occupations, stressing differences in productivity, forms of organization, technologies, and class factors (López Castaño 1984).[15] Finally, discrimination based on personal characteristics of workers (gender, age) also explains some wage differentials. The following sections evaluate these factors among urban Venezuelan workers.

Labor Market Segmentation and Household Income

The notions of segmentation and structural heterogeneity in production entered the poverty debate in Venezuela in the 1970s (Souza and Tokman 1976). They emerged as tools to explain why, following decades of sustained economic growth, relative levels of poverty had not declined substantially and large numbers of workers were found in conditions that were unstable and low paid (contradicting "trickle down" theories of development). The explanation given was that rapid population growth in urban areas and indiscriminate adoption of capital intensive technologies made it difficult for increases in demand for labor to match rapid growth in the supply of labor. This created a "structurally based excess supply of labor" (Mezzera 1987).

Under these conditions, workers were obliged to generate their own incomes through activities with low requirements for capital or training. Resulting enterprises showed low capital-to-labor ratios, relatively simple technologies, low levels of productivity, and low profits. Because of small size and scale of operations and the markets they targeted (poor and working class neighborhoods), these enterprises paid high prices for inputs and sold at relatively low prices. Efforts to control costs of production focused on labor inputs, depressing wages. Because they employed few workers (frequently family members), depressed wages were facilitated by the fact that minimum wage and other legislation did not apply to small firms (PREALC 1978). These studies confirmed the belief in an informality-poverty link.

Cartaya and Márquez (1991) found that the modern-informal breakdown alone does not explain poverty very well.[16] A great proportion of the poorest households' income in 1987 was earned in informal activities, with a linear relationship between proportion of income from informal jobs and level of household income. However, more than half the workers in these households had jobs in the "modern" sector, and a third of the workers in nonpoor households held informal jobs (see Table 12.2).

In general, the relationship between household income and individual income is as follows. Informal employment does imply a cost; the average informal wage is lower than the average modern wage. But wage gaps are more marked for those workers who reside in extremely poor households, suggesting that informality alone does not explain the difference. For instance, among poor households, informal-modern wage differentials are greatest among workers who are not heads of households and virtually nonexistent among heads. Among all workers in nonpoor households, only moderate wage differentials are found between modern and informal sector workers and the largest gaps are found among female heads of household.

Because of discrimination, gender has costs. Informal sector female heads' incomes are about half those of modern sector female heads. In comparison, informal sector male heads' incomes are only 12 percent lower than those of modern sector male heads (see Table 12.3).

Economists argue that human capital, especially education, is a critical factor to explain income differentials.[17] Table 12.4 reveals significant differences in educational levels between men and women, between informal and modern sector workers, and between household income strata. But, the problem is not solely one of differences in educational levels; it is a problem of education having a different income

Table 12.3   Income Levels by Household Income Strata

	EXTREMELY POOR	POOR	NON POOR	ALL
Average household income (Bs.)*	2,184	4,026	8,972	—
Male headed	2,267	4,068	9,300	—
Female headed	1,964	3,872	7,296	—
Per capita income	316	675	2,025	—
Income per employed member	1,630	2,411	4,463	—
% income from head—all	64.4	64.9	63.1	63.8
Employed male head	89.0	80.0	70.9	
Employed female head	86.4	71.6	69.2	
% income from informal activities	46.7	35.4	30.5	34.4
% households with income from				
Informal sector only	39.8	22.2	14.4	19.3
Modern sector only	42.7	44.6	47.6	46.2
Both sectors	17.5	33.4	38.2	34.5
Index of monthly average income**				
Data on all workers:				
Informal Sector	70.9	89.0	86.2	
Men	83.5	100.0	98.9	
Women	50.2	58.6	56.8	
Modern Sector				
Men	101.0	104.1	111.7	
Women	93.7	89.3	78.8	
Data on household heads:				
Informal sector	84.8	109.6	115.0	
Men	96.1	115.6	119.6	
Women	52.8	68.8	73.2	
Modern Sector	108.0	115.2	122.8	
Men	110.4	118.7	124.8	
Women	95.6	91.1	105.2	

*All income in 1987 bolívares. US$1 = Bs. 16–22.

**Index of modern sector average = 100. Real averages are
Bs.2,018 = extremely poor households, Bs.2,568 = poor households,
Bs.4,702 = nonpoor households.

Source: OCEI, II Semester 1987, processed by IESA

payoff for different groups of workers. Educational differences alone explain only a small proportion of income differences. For instance, among female heads of extremely poor households, two years' difference in educational attainment between modern and informal sector workers translates into a 50 percent difference in income. For men, however, especially male heads, differences in educational attainment between modern and informal sector workers does not translate into significant differences in income levels between those sectors, even though differences in educational attainment among modern sector workers are associated with income differences within that sector. On the other hand, higher educational attainment of women in the modern sector does not give them an edge over less educated males. Women's incomes in the modern sector are consistently lower than those of men, and increases in education are not strongly associated with increases in income for women (as they are for men).

As mentioned previously, the notion of "survival strategies" implies that when faced with changes in the economic context and over the life cycle of the family, the incorporation of men, women, and the very young varies according to household needs for domestic labor and for wage income. Recently, Pérez Sáinz (1989) and Giménez (1990) have documented the existence of diverse combinations of wage and non-wage strategies among the urban poor. Within the context of macroeconomic policies that emphasize wage and cost controls, stable wage work has declined in importance as an option to maximize survival.

There is a growing body of evidence suggesting households must maintain a delicate balance to overcome vulnerability and achieve optimal allocation of labor resources. Their major dificulties lie in con-

Table 12.4   Educational Attainment by Household Income Strata

| | AVERAGE YEARS EDUCATION FOR HEADS OF HOUSEHOLD | | | |
	EXTREMELY POOR	POOR	NONPOOR	ALL
Informal sector	4.4	5.5	7.2	6.2
Men	4.6	5.5	7.3	6.3
Women	4.0	5.0	6.6	5.3
Modern sector	5.7	6.3	10.1	8.7
Men	5.7	6.8	10.0	8.6
Women	5.9	7.3	10.4	8.9

Source: OCEI, II Semester 1987, processed by IESA.

fronting educational barriers and demands for women's labor at critical points in the family life cycle. The characteristics of labor allocation
(supply) in 1987 suggest a sophisticated household decision making
process, which considers demand factors, including differential pay-
offs to education, relative demands on labor time of men and women,
and the need for diversifying resources in an uncertain economy. Furthermore, where more than one worker is available, there is a relationship between the household's income level and mixed strategies for
allocation of labor. One-third of the poor households and 18 percent of
the extremely poor households show mixed strategies in which members with the lowest educational levels are allocated to activities in the
informal sector where their income levels are higher than would be
possible if they were hired into the modern sector.

Heterogeneity in Informal Sector Employment and Production

The informal sector is extraordinarily heterogeneous and large
(between 20 percent and 50 percent of the urban labor force throughout most of Latin America). In fact, as pointed out by Márquez (this
volume) at least two kinds of informal activities have been identified
by analysts (López Castaño 1984), and this breakdown is supported by
my analysis of 1987 data. One set of informal activities are unstable,
easy to enter, and show low productivity and low incomes. Women,
the very young, the very old, the less educated, minorities, and the
handicapped tend to be overrepresented among its workers. This set
of workers fit the definition of a surplus supply of labor and the self-
employed. The second set of informal activities are dynamic and
somewhat more difficult to enter. Its workers are skilled or semi-
skilled entrepreneurs, primarily men, who earn high average incomes
and their workers who tend to earn very low wages. These activities
are associated with subcontracting and production for a particular
market that demands goods and services produced most cheaply
through simple technologies and small-scale units (López Castaño
1984; Rakowski 1984, 1987). This latter informal sector generates average incomes similar or above (in the case of entrepreneurs-owners)
those in the modern sector.

The Role of Industry Sector in Poverty

In general, the industry sectors with the lowest levels of productivity
and incomes are in commerce and personal services. The industry sec-

tors that are the most dynamic and show the highest productivity and incomes are manufacturing, transportation, construction, and nonpersonal services.[18] In 1987, 90 percent of all workers concentrated in five industries: manufacturing, services, commerce, construction and transportation (see Table 12.5). A simple comparison of employment in these industries for workers from poor and extremely poor households reveals a complex relationship between industry sector and poverty. As indicated already, the proportion of workers from poor and extremely poor households who work in the modern sector is larger than that in the informal sector and this holds true for most industries. The only exceptions are construction (in a recession in 1987), where the poorest households have more workers in informal construction, and transportation, where more households with higher income levels have workers in informal transportation.[19] A closer look at the distribution of employment and incomes by industries and segments is warranted (see Table 12.5).

In commerce, the overwhelming majority of poorly paid workers in both the informal and modern sectors—and the lack of income differentials across sectors—suggest that a limit of five workers to define informality in this industry is inappropriate. Informal activities in commerce tend to concentrate among the self-employed. There is a strong association between income levels and type of worker. The self-employed (all in the informal sector) show much lower income levels than owners and employees in both the modern and informal sectors. However, the average modern sector income is significantly lower than in other industries. Lower skill requirements and low levels of unionization contribute to this pattern.

In the manufacturing industry (for which a lower limit of from ten to fifty workers might be a better indicator of informality than the five used in this study), higher capital inputs required per worker are reflected in the low proportion of informal workers in this industry sector and in significant wage differentials between the modern and informal sectors. Manufacturing shows the clearest delineation between large-scale, modern production with well-paid workers and smaller-scale and informal production with low-paid workers.[20]

Services present a different picture. The modern sector includes a high proportion of workers because it includes public sector services and a wide variety of communal and personal services. The proportion of poorly paid workers in both sectors is high, but the heterogeneity of this industry sector is associated with significant income differentials between the sectors. Income differentials are owed to the diverse nature and characteristics of two types of activities—domestic and other personal services (including repair), on the one hand (with low productiv-

Table 12.5 Labor Force Participation and Income by Sectors and Household Income Strata

	EXTREMELY POOR	POOR HOUSEHOLDS
All workers, total N	515,833	1,287,191
% modern segment	53.3%	63.0%
Manufacturing	11.4%	16.7%
Commerce	7.8%	8.9%
Services	15.6%	18.8%
% informal segment	46.7%	37.0%
Manufacturing	5.5%	4.2%
Commerce	14.1%	11.8%
Services	11.8%	7.7%
Heads of household		
% modern segment	52.6	61.7
Manufacturing	10.5	15.8
Commerce	6.5	7.4
Services	17.4	18.1
% informal segment	47.3	38.3
Manufacturing	4.9	5.4
Commerce	14.8	12.6
Services	8.5	5.5
Average income, all workers*		
Modern segment average	100.0	100.0
Manufacturing	104.8	91.2
Commerce	95.2	95.7
Services	100.2	99.9
Informal segment average	71.0	88.0
Manufacturing	52.2	84.7
Commerce	74.9	89.0
Services	56.1	71.9
Average income, heads		
Modern segment average	100.0	100.0
Manufacturing	102.2	102.2
Commerce	94.7	96.5
Services	96.1	93.2
Informal segment average	78.2	92.5
Manufacturing	70.1	96.7
Commerce	77.6	93.3
Services	71.3	94.1

Income Index based on Modern sector average = 100 within each household strata.

Source: OCEI, II Semester 1987 processed by IESA.

ity levels), and social and communal services that employ a significant proportion of professionals. This industry sector is highly segmented.

Finally, transportation is an industry sector in which informal workers are well paid, more so than the majority of their counterparts in the modern sector. This can be attributed to the selective nature of informal employment, which favors those able to invest the necessary capital to purchase a vehicle (taxi, van, bus, truck). This investment, in turn, is protected by the high level of organization of driver-owners and the high user fares mandated by municipal councils (Rakowski 1983). There has been much debate over including it as "informal."

Class Differentiation

Workers change jobs frequently and this includes moving from the modern to the informal sector or vice versa. This and the fact that wage levels also fluctuate widely within sectors and across sectors are evidence that informal workers cannot be identified as members of a particular or static class (Portes and Sassen-Koob 1988; Benería and Roldán 1987; Pérez Sáinz 1989).

This study found that the majority of workers who live in extremely poor households tend to be private modern sector wage workers or self-employed and informal wage workers, whereas half the workers in poor households are private wage workers in the modern sector. Among informal sector workers, almost equal proportions are self-employed or wage workers (in small firms) who reside in poor and extremely poor households. But the self-employed earn much higher wages than wage workers. Many of the self-employed are older heads of household with longer work experience than the nonhead wage workers, factors that give them advantages as self-employed entrepreneurs, whether or not they employ others. This same general pattern is repeated among those in petty commerce, those in services, and those in construction. But the inverse is true for manufacturing. The self-employed earn significantly less in manufacturing than in other industry sectors, probably because of technological constaints.[21]

Other Mechanisms that Depress Wages

Legal and institutional factors contribute to income differentials within and across modern and informal activities. The absence of regulation and labor protection in the informal sector, including for workers subcontracted by modern firms contributes to poverty, even as its presence in the modern sector cannot guarantee better than poverty level incomes. But, in periods of high inflation and recessionary conditions, the decline in real income of all workers, including "protected" modern sector workers, also contributes to poverty. Structural adjustment policies usually entail a decline in real wages.

A decline in wages is not uniform—different sectors respond in different ways and show greater or lesser sensitivity to market pressures. For instance, during recessions, the volume of informal workers increases absolutely and relative to the modern sector, and this is accompanied by a rapid decline in wages in both sectors. At the same time, modern sector wages do not decline as quickly as does the level of employment. This can be explained not only by protective legislation but also by the strategies of modern sector employers, who maintain a stable, skilled labor force through salary incentives (Márquez 1990). But, as the findings of this study show, this holds true for skilled workers. Less skilled workers—easily substitutible—would be subject to conditions of competition and wage decline similar to those in the informal sector and, hence, subject to increasing poverty among households that rely on the income of these modern workers.

A complementary explanation is provided by Portes (this volume): in Latin American economies characterized by a structurally induced labor surplus, the costs implied by protective labor legislation encourages modern firms to decentralize production and distribution processes to avoid such costs. This factor, facilitated by technological innovation, contributes to the proliferation of subcontracting that— given the form of operationalization of modern-informal sectors— leads to expansion of the informal sector (as detected through statistical analyses of survey data) and of precarious employment in modern firms. This process—supported by studies by Portes and Sassen-Koob (1988), Pérez Sáinz (1989), and Rakowski (1984)—means that the links (as hypothesized by economists) between income differentials and productivity differentials throughout the urban economy are weakened. These studies question the notion that formal sector work is stable and well paid.

Although a time series analysis and information on labor protection would be necessary to detect this process in the Venezuelan case, the 1987 study suggests, given the numerical importance of both informal and modern sector workers among extremely poor and poor households, that such a process characterized the decline in incomes since 1982. Other studies in Venezuela (Lacabana 1990) find that the assumption of legal protection for modern sector workers is unrealistic—almost half those workers defined as modern and 73 percent of those in informal firms (determined by firm size) show work histories characterized by instability and absence of minimum guarantees established in labor law.

Occupational Segregation and Sex Discrimination

We return to a consideration of occupational segregation and sex discrimination, which operate on both the supply and demand sides. Across all households, within the modern and informal sectors, across industry sectors and occupational categories, and within educational levels, women workers earn less than do men in the same or similar jobs, a result that has been obtained also in other studies of Venezuela (Márquez 1990; Winters 1991). Men employed in the modern sector show higher incomes than men in the informal sector and men in non-poor households show higher incomes than those in poor and extremely poor households. Women's incomes do not follow a similar pattern; they are irregular and not clearly related to differences in skill and education. Women's income levels are associated with demands of their reproductive role that, in turn, are associated with occupational segregation.

For women, the link between informality and poverty probably originates in the need to engage in informal work that can be carried out in the home, providing a means to combine demands for income generation and domestic responsibilities. In fact, women's domestic skills tend to be "capitalized" and put to use for income generation. The price of this choice is a lower income potential (Fernández-Kelly and García 1988; Rakowski 1987). When women's informal employment is linked to subcontracting for modern firms (the case of seamstresses) they lose control over the rates at which their labor will be remunerated (Benería and Roldán 1987). Other options are domestic service and preparation and sale of food stuffs.

Women's income disadvantage is associated also with their lower tendency to be self-employed or owners of small firms. Women in the informal sector tend to be wage workers in small firms not covered by labor legislation. Other studies suggest more women enter the informal sector as a survival strategy whereas more men enter as a means of social mobility through entrepreneurship (see Ward 1990).

But supply-side factors are not the only explanation for women's segregation in the lowest paying jobs. The demand for female labor is highest for the production of goods and services that can be produced at home and that are extensions of those activities they perform as wives and mothers. These domestic tasks—unpaid—are devalued; their remunerated counterparts also are devalued and characterized by low wages or income. Employers' assumptions that women are secondary workers, even when they are heads of household, also depresses their wages (Hossfeld 1990).

This study found that female employment varies little in characteristics across household income strata. Regardless of whether a woman is a member of an extremely poor or a poor household, she is likely to work in personal services, petty commerce, or subcontracted manufacturing (foodstuffs and textiles). Women of nonpoor households also concentrate in community services like health care and education—but still in activities that pay lower average wages. Male employment is more diversified across household income strata.

Conclusion and Policy Implications

Is there a causal or coincidental relationship between informality and poverty? Although public policies and NGO efforts aimed at poverty alleviation target the informal sector, especially entrepreneurs-microenterprises, the preliminary analysis presented here suggests the causes of poverty are diverse, complex, and conditional. Whereas informality is associated with poverty, not all informals live in poor households and not all poor households include informal sector workers.

I have presented evidence that poverty in urban Venezuela in 1987 was heterogeneous, as was informality. The expansion of some informal activities is associated with the expansion of poverty, but the expansion of others is not. Furthermore, if a causal relationship exists, it is equally likely to be one where poverty contributes to the expansion of informality as one where informality produces low-income workers and the impoverishment of their households.

In general, this study suggests that informality is strongly associated with the *intensity* of poverty. But this relationship appears only when informal workers are analyzed by industry sectors and type of employment (employer, worker, self-employed). Within the poorest households are concentrated the lowest paid informal and modern sector workers. The poorest households also are those whose characteristics increase their vulnerability to poverty, including characteristics of labor supply that, when matched to the demand for labor (segmentation of the labor market), leave them open to discrimination. Thus, the poorest households frequently are those with elderly workers, those headed by young women, those whose workers have low educational levels, and those where children constitute an important proportion of all household members. Although the "feminization" of poverty that characterizes households is linked to gender differences in education and social roles, it also must be understood within the context of structural barriers, including policies that determine access to credit programs, training to improve human capital, and access to child care services.

The study also reveals that the *expansion* or *widespread incidence* of poverty in urban areas cannot be explained solely by the relative importance of informality in urban employment. Within the poorest households are found those workers who receive the lowest incomes, especially within the informal sector. However, an important proportion of the households whose source of income is "modern" activities are poor also, and they concentrate in those same industry sectors and occupations where the poorest informals concentrate. This suggests that a standardization of work conditions and demand for labor has taken place within particular industry sectors, and this exacerbated poverty since 1982. Even so, the poorest of the poor are those workers employed by the same informal employers-entrepreneurs targeted by poverty alleviation policies and microenterprise promotion programs.

Poverty in 1987 appears as a pyramid. At the base are both modern and, especially, informal workers who concentrate in the same industry sectors, possibly linked through "production chains" and subcontracting. Future research on production chains, among others, could identify links between informal and formal workers within a same industry sector (e.g., textiles). Such links would demand a shift of attention from policies that address an assumed relation between poverty and informality to very different kinds of policies needed to address links between poverty and certain industry sectors.

Gender and age differences in poverty go beyond the supply and demand problems indicated by the study. Policy analyses identify gender barriers in access to credit programs directed at the informal sector and discrimination implicit in widely accepted policies designed to improve "human capital" (Berger and Buvinič 1989).

Additionally, economic experts assume that the expansion of the market combined with short-term economic and social programs will alleviate the intensity of poverty. This ignores the reality of discrimination and the impact of conflicting demands on the labor time of vulnerable groups of workers. This is the case of women. Credit programs and subsidies may alleviate their situation temporarily, but are unlikely to have a sustained impact once they are withdrawn. Of great concern is the reality that even when women improve their "human capital," they do not command the same pay nor do they have access to the same jobs as men. Women need not only credit or training for nontraditional jobs, they need support systems to alleviate other demands on their time, and they need the erradication of discrimination.

Some links between some poverty and certain activities, both modern and informal, are at least partly conjunctural. Policies that depress salaries and maximize flexibility in production (which predominated throughout the 1980s) created pressures for informalization of production and, undoubtedly, contributed to impoverishment. Within the framework of structural adjustment programs "new policies" are proposed to alleviate poverty. Yet these depend on liberalization of the markets for goods and money, and the "opening up" of the Venezuelan economy to increased international trade (expected to generate new employment opportunities for the poor). International experts propose that in the short run this process could exacerbate poverty, and human capital interventions may be needed (World Bank 1990a). Therefore, emergency programs to alleviate poverty have been created that include direct subsidies and focus attention on social services such as health, nutrition, primary education (see Cartaya and Márquez 1990). In theory, these will not "interfere" with the operation of the market but will contribute to a "virtuous cycle" of improved human capital and more equitable and efficient growth. Implicit in these programs is a shift from attention on workers to attention on families, although programs still include credit to informal firms. Given these assumptions, studies of the consequences of structural adjustment policies, and the findings from this study of poverty and informality, this shift is unlikely to achieve its objective of alleviating poverty.

More important, these programs cannot deter the expansion of poverty because by 1987 many workers in poor families already were wage workers in the modern sector, and their wages were depressed by regulatory and market mechanisms as well as by discrimination. Furthermore, the assumption long held by economists that modern workers' wages are subject to less decline than informal workers' wages simply has not held up in Venezuela, as evidenced by longitudinal data from the Central Bank and the census bureau. Low-skilled "modern" workers in ample supply, subject to high rates of turnover or layoffs, and whose wages are close to the legal minimum are subject to the same forces of supply and demand as informal workers. It is unlikely that "social" programs intended to compensate the devastating effects of poverty can make up for depressed wages and likely that opening the market to foreign competition will contribute to more flexibilization in production, more informalization, and more depressed wages (Bourgignon 1991).

These programs also cannot alleviate poverty because they do not consider the heterogeneity of informality. This can be illustrated through consideration of specific cases of informal workers. For instance, the study found informals, especially self-employed and owners, whose incomes approach those of modern sector counterparts despite lower educational levels. This group provides the rationale for credit, management training, and other programs to support microenterprise development. In the absence of sectoral policies based on knowledge of different markets for goods and services, promoting these firms can increase competition in already crowded markets and depress incomes. In addition, no evidence shows the benefits that accrue to entrepreneurs are passed on down to their workers. Microentrepreneurs are no more altruistic than their "modern" counterparts.

Finally, the emphasis on expanding primary education as a mechanism for improving human capital ignores the reality of the interaction between education and poverty. There are nonpoor workers who have less than a primary (sixth grade) education, and for women primary level or higher has little impact in the face of other factors described earlier. On the other hand, secondary education can have an impact on income levels in an economy where employment opportunities expand to meet the supply of well-educated workers. If not, employers may simply feel free to demand higher levels of education for jobs that now require less than a secondary education.

This study reveals the critical need for further research, including time series analyses of highly stratified groups of households and of workers within households. Although standard household surveys permit preliminary analyses like that discussed previously, the complexity of the linkages and the heterogeneity of the phenomena demand better survey instruments, more adequate indicators and concepts, and more sophisticated statistical techniques. Survey data alone, however, are insufficient because poverty cannot be explained through an exclusive focus on the characteristics and allocation of labor within households. What goes on inside households must be evaluated within the context of what goes on outside of households. In the case of Venezuela, an understanding of poverty and informality requires the study of economic and social indicators that can document how the crisis, adjustment policies, and restructuring affect the demand for labor. Better studies are needed to distinguish between genuinely conjunctural factors and those that are or can become long-term factors affecting the demand for labor. Case studies of production chains and firms also will be critical to understanding firm dynamics and response to internal and external factors.

NOTES

1. Many structural adjustment policies directly affect informality and poverty, including cutbacks in public sector employment and budget allocations for public services, removal of subsidies for foodstuffs, income tax reform, currency devaluation, privatization of state industries, and so forth.

2. Informal workers are those who are self-employed in non-professional or technical occupations, unpaid family workers, domestic servants, and owners and workers in firms that employ fewer than five persons. Modern sector workers include self-employed professionals and technicians, public sector workers, and owners and workers in firms that employ five or more persons.

3. The contraction of real income among formal sector workers, linked to the implementation of cumulative adjustment programs, provides clear evidence of the role played by factors other than sector of employment in poverty generation.

4. Data are from the second semester Household Survey (Encuesta de Hogares por Muestreo) produced twice yearly by the Venezuelan census bureau (OCEI, Oficina Central de Estadísticas e Informática). This is the only data source that permits integrating a household level analysis with a labor market analysis. To determine income strata, the *per capita income* of each household unit was compared with the per capita cost of the basic food basket (*canasta alimentaria*) established by CORDIPLAN, the national planning agency, for 1987. "Extremely poor households" are those whose income is below the cost of the basic food basket. "Poor households" are those whose per capita income is above but less than double the cost of the basic food basket. "Nonpoor households" are those whose per capita income is more than twice the per capita cost of the basic food basket.

5. The study uses the PREALC form of operationalization as adopted by the OCEI (Venezuelan Census Bureau) for its labor market analyses. See note 2.

6. An analysis for a particular economic conjuncture like that in 1987 implies contrasting two realities that became increasingly heterogeneous in the preceding decade. Therefore, the outcome of the analysis might vary in greater or lesser respects when applied to other points in time and other economic conjunctures.

7. Life cycle approaches consider the division of labor and competing time demands of productive and reproductive tasks within households, usually with reference to the ages and numbers of children.

8. This approach ignores other ways to satisfy basic needs, including nonwage income or goods and services obtained through networks of family and friends or from private and public agencies.

9. Many studies were carried out between 1982 and 1984 at CORDI-PLAN, the national planning agency, with the technical assistance of PREALC

advisors. The author was, for several years in the early 1980s, the director of employment and in charge of employment research and policy recommendations.

10. Jatobá (1988) provides a comprehensive review of the Latin American literature regarding the relationship between poverty and labor markets. Rodgers (1987) provides empirical evidence from a variety of regional contexts.

11. Income differences may be distorted slightly by the failure to adjust per capita consumption by age and weight of members. However, most studies that have made such adjustments find only a small and often statistically insignificant decline in the proportion of poor households (Pollack 1986).

12. These figures probably should be higher. Cultural factors (which affect both respondents and interviewers) contribute to underreporting of female heads even when they support the household (Rakowski 1991).

13. Methodological issues must be kept in mind when assessing female participation rates. For many women, the similarity and overlap between their domestic tasks and their income-generating tasks lead to underreporting of employment. The magnitude of underreporting was illustrated in a study of low-income neighborhoods in Venezuela (FUDECO 1986). Of those who identified themselves as housewives or unemployed (almost all women), 21 percent were found to carry out activities in the home for which they received payment.

14. This study used the standard form of calculating household income: the sum of all individual incomes reported for household members. This underestimates household income by not including transfers from other households and overestimates income by failing to account for transfers to other households or discretionary income not contributed to the household income "pool."

15. Different types of informal workers (employers, employees and laborers, self-employed) do not have equal access to productive resources; therefore, class position helps explain wage differentials (Pérez Sáinz 1989; Benería and Roldán 1987).

16. This study was supported by subsequent analyses (Cartaya, unpublished data analyses; Márquez 1991).

17. Human capital is a supply-side variable that is transformed into a demand-side variable through job descriptions and requirements.

18. To test this hypothesis fully, data would need to be disaggregated to two or three digits. This was not possible due to sample size.

19. Informal construction is the final level in the subcontracting chain that characterizes the construction industry in Latin America; many informal construction workers are highly skilled artisans or machinists whereas others

are menial laborers. Transportation is an anomaly because drivers tend to be owners (mandated by law) and members of cooperatives whose vehicles represent significant outlays of capital (Rakowski 1983).

20. Many informal workers in manufacturing report themselves as self-employed when, in reality, they are subcontracted by modern sector firms and are impossible to detect with data from household surveys.

21. Although data do not permit such an analysis, studies by Llona (1983) for Venezuela, Pérez Sáinz (1989) for Ecuador, and López Castaño (1979) for Colombia suggest that modern sector unskilled wage workers concentrate at the base of the income pyramid and reside in the poorest households. The legal minimum wage in 1987 would not allow a worker to meet the basic needs of the average household (five members).

Chapter 13

Transaction Costs, Formal Plans, and Formal Informality: Alternatives to the Informal "Sector"

J. Douglas Uzzell

Introduction

Focusing attention on an informal "sector" has led to studies primarily of poor entrepeneurs and employees working outside the prescriptions of formal institutions—but *not* to inquiries into the kinds of institutional processes that generate a preponderance of informal solutions to economic problems. Programs designed to help informal entrepreneurs, although enjoying some localized success, appear to have had little effect on the systems that produce patterns of production and exchange. Some writers point out that employment without official government protection—and much work contracted for legally constituted companies—is exploitative, but no means have been found to

Research in Peru was supported by a Fulbright–Hays Graduate Fellowship (1969–70), a brief contract with USAID (1983), and contracts with the Instituto Libertad y Democracia (1983, 1984). Research in Mexico and Texas was supported by the National Science Foundation (1968), Rice University (1975, 1977), and the Wenner–Gren Foundation (1981). My gratitude to those organizations. Data on urban, human services, and corporate planning was gathered while a research and management consultant (Texas and Florida) and a human services administrator.

encourage or enable governments to correct this situation. This chapter suggests an alternative that may prove productive for future studies. The discussion is organized around the following four questions.

1. What are the uses and implications of the major definitions of the *informal sector* and should the concept be retained?

2. What are the real effects of attempts by Third World formal institutions to regulate economic activities (including sale of labor) and might a Coasian analysis of transaction costs illuminate issues obscured by the formal-informal sector dichotomy?

3. Where and how should power be factored into deliberations about economic relations and in assessments of various actors who try to promote change?

4. What is the role of formal planning in the whole process of investigation, discussion, and intervention?

A Note about Planning

Three aspects of planning are included in the discussion:

1. the role of social science in development planning,

2. the lack of fit between formal planning as it is usually carried out and the planning styles of those who are the subjects of programs, and

3. the likelihood that formal planning acts largely as a mechanism for maintaining the systemic status quo (Uzzell 1990).

Though not usually framed as such, most social science discussion about development has implications for planning and, indeed, most chapters of this book contain explicit or implied policy recommendations. When Otero (this volume) complains that so far debate about the correctness or utility of particular analytical models has not led to action plans, the implication is that they are expected to do so. More directly, descriptions and evaluations of programs are, or should be, an integral part of the planning process. That being the case, it is appropriate in this book to take a look at the possible effect of formal planning on generating or sustaining the conditions we are studying (Rees and Murphy 1990).

Questions

Definitions of the Concept (Question 1)

What are the uses and implications of the major definitions of the *informal sector*, and should the concept be retained? Although I do not wish to replow ground already cultivated by others in this volume and most tellingly by Peattie (1987), the manner in which the central concept is formulated is crucial to the outcome of studies. Currently there are two major ways of defining the *informal sector*, loosely termed the *Portes-ILD model* (a focus on regulation) and the *ILO-PREALC model* (a focus on firm or worker characteristics). Each model has its uses. The ILO-PREALC model is simple and relatively easy to use for identifying samples for study. The Portes-ILD model, though less handy operationally, lends itself to analysis of relations between the defined informal sector and the formal sector. However, proponents of both models appear to be chafing against paradigmatic restrictions.

Working with the ILO-PREALC model, Márquez and Cartaya (this volume) and Tokman (1989) express concern with the problem of heterogeneity of the enterprises in the "sector" as they define it; Márquez and Cartaya both suggest additionally breaking down the economy into functional industry subsectors, which presumably would cut across the formal-informal partition.

Portes, Castells, and Benton (1989) conclude that their analysis of actual situations where informal enterprises (defined according to the Portes-ILD model) have successfully expanded calls into question a fundamental tenet of theories of modern industrial development:

> This is the belief that economic development leads inexorably to the incorporation of the working-age population into regular labor relations dominated by the wage bond . . . the assumption of progressive incorporation of the labor force into modern wage and salary relations is enshrined in both orthodox liberal and neo-Marxist theories of development. Depending on the school, the belief is labeled "full" labor utilization or "proletarianization." (1989, p. 307)

At the same time de Oliveira and Roberts and Cartaya (this volume) express concern that proliferation of informal economic activities blurs class boundaries.

As far as these concerns go, conservative solutions may be feasible. The PREALC studies could expand, as Tokman and Márquez suggest, by adding functional factors, although it would be simpler just to set out a list of characteristics considered important, such as size, income, wages, kind of activity, and legal status, and treat them as factors without recourse to an informal sector at all. On the other hand, some Marxist theorists are already incorporating radical institutional economics (Grunchy 1987; Stanfield 1989), and in general it may be wise to take Peattie's advice (1987) and focus upon analysis of institutions (as anthropologists have for some time). Presumably, econometric models could be upgraded in the direction of systems models that sacrifice the elegance of linear equations for more complex, context-sensitive algorithms that permit bifurcation in Prigogine and Stenger's (1984) sense or allow for transformations among capital, power, and information.

I find it useful, however, to go further: to think of informal activities and the strategies that lie behind them not necessarily as located in a particular class or set of categories of entrepreneurs or workers, but as being the characteristic mode of operation of most people most of the time. This formulation breaks with the major models in two ways. First, it does not create sectors of actors with other social and economic characteristics (e.g., class, ethnicity, or income) that have to be mapped over the formal-informal dichotomy. This clears the way to studying the informal activities of nonpoor, non-working class players as well as the partial strategies of all players. The implications of this are important to consider and will be discussed in the following.

Second, my formulation treats informal activities as normative rather than deviant[1]. Defining *informal activities* as normative leads in several directions. For one thing, it serves as a partial corrective to the ethnocentric tendency to approach the informal activities of the poor (but not those of the nonpoor) as a problem to be solved. More important, it now becomes possible to ask what special conditions lead to people following the formal rules in the first place. An institutional economist might ask a similar question: "Under what conditions is it the optimal strategy to cooperate?"—in this case, with the government.

Given the customary focus on people who act informally—particularly in light of the received development wisdom that it is always in their best interests (or the inexorable path of development) to follow formal rules—it usually follows that the subjects of our inquiries must, through ignorance or some other disability, be unable to meet their needs by following codified behavioral prescriptions.

A year's resident fieldwork in *pueblos jóvenes* in Lima during 1969–1970 (Uzzell 1972, 1974a, 1974b, 1976) suggested to me that, although this was often true, the reality perceived by the players involved was much more complex than the literature would lead one to believe. Participant observation and, more formally, analysis of the life histories of a sample of approximately 400 heads of households revealed family economic strategies to be mixed and constantly changing in response to feedback actively sought from external and internal developments.

Selling one's labor to a single, formally constituted firm over a long period of time was not necessarily viewed as an optimal strategy in itself. Indeed, the least successful group in the sample (lowest income, least desirable housing, least productive personal networks) were those most likely to choose that pure strategy. Shorter periods of fieldwork in the United States and in southern Mexico have tended to confirm the notion that mixed strategies are common and that following formal rules is no more than one option among others, with situationally constituted utilities like the rest (Uzzell 1980a).

When Portes and the ILD define as informal any activities that do not follow formally codified prescriptions, *informal* encompasses both idiosyncratic actions and those that follow prescriptions of informal institutions: cultural norms, voluntary associations, kinship groups, and so forth. To go farther and look at primarily economic informal activities distributed throughout the socioeconomic system (to understand why and how, under some circumstances, people develop formal rules for some kinds of economic transactions) leads to a consideration of the costs of transactions and the ways in which formal rules can affect those costs. This puts the discussion squarely in the domain of institutional economics and its treatment of transaction costs (costs of quality control, guarantee of usufruct, standardization of weights and measures, and enforcement of contracts).

Transaction Costs (Question 2)

What are the real effects of attempts by Third World formal institutions to regulate economic activities (including sale of labor) and might a Coasian analysis of transaction costs illuminate issues obscured by the formal-informal sector dichotomy? Coase has been convinced for sixty years that the cost of doing business must be considered in any complete economic model. In his Nobel Prize acceptance speech, he said,

> Not to include transaction costs in the theory leaves many aspects of the working of the economic system unexplained, including the emergence of the firm, but much else besides. In fact, a large part of what we think of as economic activity is designed to accomplish what high transaction costs would otherwise prevent or to reduce transaction costs so that individuals

can freely negotiate and we can take advantage of that diffused knowledge of which Hayek has told us. (1992, p. 716)

Microeconomic models assume zero transaction costs (Coase 1960). Yet avoiding the high costs of doing business may be the central motive for informal economic activities. This view is especially persuasive if one considers transaction costs to be fundamentally the cost of information (Dahlman 1979, cited in Coase 1988, p. 6; North 1990). Much of the literature that treats the "informal sector" as a development problem to be solved would lead one to believe either that transaction costs are irrelevant or that, where formal regulatory institutions exist, they always reduce transaction costs. However, as North points out, "Institutions are not necessarily or even usually created to be socially efficient; rather they, or at least formal rules, are created to serve the interests of those with the bargaining power to devise new rules" (1990, p. 16). North goes on to say that transaction costs tend to be much higher in Third World countries than in more affluent countries because "The institutional structure in the Third World lacks the formal structure (and enforcement) that underpins efficient markets," and underground economies under such conditions "attempt to provide a structure for exchange" and, in so doing, may actually reduce transaction costs (1990, p. 67). It is probably fair to suggest that reduction of transaction costs is de Soto's main goal, although his notion that the goal can be reached through radical deregulation is probably naive.

When we speak of transaction costs, we are speaking of the cost of information. On this point North says: "The costliness of information is the key to the costs of transacting, which consist of the costs of measuring the valuable attributes of what is being exchanged and the costs of protecting rights and policing and enforcing agreements" (1990, p. 27).

Elsewhere (Uzzell 1980b) I have suggested approaching an understanding of regional socioeconomic systems by tracing the flows of capital, power, and information through the systems and noting the points of transformation of each aspect into the others. Such analysis quickly reveals that all three tend to pool in certain subsystems of socioeconomic systems, and that the movement of either tends to predict system changes affecting the quantity and distribution of the others. The original formulation had in mind all kinds of information, including technology, prognostication, and the generation of values through control of the media, but the concept appears to serve as well in the special case of transaction costs.

Any thorough treatment of the problem of transaction costs must include the costs connected with selling one's labor. This implies a very complex and fluid array of kinds of information in addition to the education or technical knowledge required actually to perform the work. Some examples include

1. learning of the availability of jobs, how to apply, behavioral requirements (demeanor, dress, deference to superiors, accent, other speaking patterns, eye contact, etc.), and other requirements, such as bribery or the use of personal influence;

2. knowing the appropriate wage and benefits to request or contract for;

3. predicting the stability of the firm and the likelihood of firm actions to deprive one of formal guarantees, such as keeping working hours below a level that qualifies a worker for union membership, routinely firing employees before they complete probationary periods or firing employees before they reach retirement age.

All these and many more kinds of information required for selling one's labor are likely to be unevenly distributed in any given population. From this point of view, choosing to allocate one's labor informally may be as much an attempt at reducing transaction costs (avoiding the cost of acquiring new information) as is the decision not to declare one's furniture factory to the government.

This is not to say that no transaction costs are associated with informal economic activities (see Table 13.1). On the contrary, some costs are probably higher than in formally regulated transactions. A difference is that the player has more freedom to choose the information actually needed to get a job, buy and sell, or manufacture. It is instructive to look at what passes for technical support of entrepreneurs in the NGO credit programs that include training (Ashe 1985a; Bromley 1985; McKean, this volume). Following standard accounting procedures is an activity in which business people engage (and bear the expense of) that reduces regulative organizations' costs of monitoring and enforcing formal rules. This becomes an appropriate expenditure for an entrepreneur only if one is working under the aegis of a formal organization, in this case an NGO credit program that requires accounting. In other words, the NGO is adding a transaction cost as the price of getting loans and calling the process technical support. From the point of view of the recipient, it is one more cost of doing business, to be weighed against the cost and feasibility of borrowing the capital from various alternative lenders.

More is involved in the general situation than failure of govern-

Table 13.1   Comparison of Transaction Costs

	"INFORMAL"	"FORMAL"
Credit	X	
Police protection (including avoidance of harassment)	X	
Guarantee of usufruct	X	
Quality control	X	
Organizational costs (including communication)	X	
Any kind of long-distance activity	X	
Marginal labor costs		X
Accounting		X
Taxes and legal registration		X

Note: X indicates that the cost tends to be high on this item relative to the cost for the other "sector."

ments and other formal organizations to lower or equalize transaction costs. Frequently the informal activities of formal institutions raise transaction costs. One danger of providing the state with coercive force is that "those who run the state will use that force in their own interest" (North 1990, p. 59). The other danger is that lacking adequate coercive force and means of monitoring, the state may be forced to act informally in ways that increase transaction costs.

An example of the latter is the Peruvian government's manner of awarding microbus routes in Lima (Uzzell 1987). Although formal procedures for obtaining permission to drive a particular route are clearly set out by the Ministry of Transportation, these procedures are honored more in the breach than in the observance. The normative (informal) procedure is for a group of microbus owners to invade a route already assigned to another group, then through a combination of bribery, public relations, legal actions, and allegiance pledges to some political faction or party, to gain from the Ministry retroactive sanction for the invasion. Meanwhile, those whose route was invaded take similar action to ward off the invaders.

The positive side of this kind of competition is that bus lines are constantly being remapped over the riding public in something approaching a continuously optimizing redistribution of an inadequate fleet. In other words, lacking the power or other resources to regulate services efficiently, the government gives informal sanction to a process that will accomplish at least one aspect of the regulation at no cost to the government. The negative side is that the cost to the microbus owners is high and contributes substantially to the continued inadequacy of the fleet.

Both official informality, such as that carried out by Peru's Ministry of Transportation, and the informal activities of officials raise transaction costs, while sustaining the operational status quo. In the sample of *pueblo jóven* householders in Lima mentioned previously, one of the most common successful employment strategies was to take a job in government or in a formally constituted firm (e.g., as a teacher, police officer, government clerk, dispatcher, bank teller, or as a counterperson at a parts or construction equipment store) that put the employee in the position of keeper of the gate to the formal system so that one could collect bribes. Not only is such bribery a transaction cost, but it also amounts to regressive taxation, because the cost falls disproportionately on the poor.

My intent here is not to extend a list of inequities in the systems, but to suggest that focusing exclusively upon certain categories of people who choose to break the economic game rules some or most of the time does not tell us very much. High and poorly distributed transaction costs have deleterious effects on markets generally, not just among marginal players, and it is not necessarily undesirable to try to reduce costs informally at any point in the system. The informal sector literature has partially addressed the problem of production costs, though usually only in terms of the use of informal labor arrangements by employers seeking to avoid paying minimum wages or legally sanctioned employee benefits. However, transaction costs can become production costs or offset them, and it makes sense (particularly given the dismal record of attempts to enforce wage and hours regulations in many Third World countries), to look at possible reduction of transaction costs as an incentive to employers to tolerate regulation of the cost of labor.

In the aggregate and over time people's decisions make sense. It is more than likely, given this assumption, that large scale informal economic activity represents a viable adaptation to real conditions, an optimal choice where transaction costs are high and information, power, and capital are correspondingly scarce. The traditional approach focuses upon the symptoms and not on the configuration and operation of the systems that generate them. If we were to turn that emphasis upside down many of our favorite topics of debate, such as whether or not the informal sector can become the "engine of development," would lose all meaning. That, in turn, might free us to get on to more productive enquiry.

Power (Question 3)

Where and how should power be factored into deliberations about economic relations and into assessments of various actors who try to promote change? So far the discussion has concentrated on scarcity of operational information and the capital required to obtain that information. It is now time to consider the ways in which operational information is kept scarce and that brings up the issue of power, the third aspect of socioeconomic systems. Like information, power has attracted little attention from traditional development economists, though it has been a central concern of followers of Coase and Williamson. Power is a broad topic; this chapter will focus only on the effects of political power on transaction costs.

Because we are concerned in this book with economic activities that violate or avoid formal prescriptions, it will be well to begin with questions about the coercive power necessary to enforce formal economic regulations. The case of the microbus routes in Lima shows that the government lacks the power to carry out its regulations. That statement should be qualified. It can be assumed that officials in the government wanted to enforce their own regulations but could not; that can be taken as evidence of lack of power. There is, of course, no way to know what they wanted to do or what they could not do, only what they did.

An illustration of this kind of situation comes from another account recorded during research in 1969. A retired Peruvian senator (instrumental in drafting the progressive 1961 legislation that sought to recognize and formalize squatter holdings) told me during an interview that the legislation had been the result of the government's perceived lack of power. According to the senator, he and some of his colleagues had examined census figures showing the dimensions of a massive wave of rural-urban migration to Lima, decided that the government was powerless to stop the migration and lacked capital to provide government-built housing, and so concluded that their best course was to jump in front of the wave and hope to gain some measure of control through cooptation. The following paragraphs assume that government officials and others charged with regulation prefer to regulate directly ceteris paribus and that informal or indirect actions (or inaction) follow from lack of power to do so.

Power, like information, is hard to calibrate, though both can transform into capital. It is probably safe to say that many Third World governments—short on capital, lacking secure domestic political bases, threatened with military takeover, and subjected to coercion from the outside—operate in a chronic power deficit. The government's task in reducing transaction costs is twofold: (1) create rules that will assure property rights and contracts and (2) enforce the rules. Lack of power makes it unrealistic or irrelevant to promulgate new, or to enforce existing, regulations.

Transaction costs can be diminished informally if the parties to exchanges are known to each other and have a history of exchanging with each other in a mutually beneficial way. This is true with or without formal intervention, and it describes the transactions of both the elite and the poor in a country such as Peru. Given the ability of a small elite to reduce their transaction costs informally, it is to their advantage to keep costs high elsewhere to avoid competition. In the Peruvian case, there has historically been a tendency to formalize elite informality, using legislation to create market distortions of which, with privileged access to information and capital, only the elite can take advantage. This practice is not limited to developing countries. However, under import substitution it may have at times attained the status of development policy. Both of these forces work against support by the most powerful players for legislation that would uniformly lower transaction costs.

Legislation is relatively inexpensive, but enforcement is dear, and under conditions of normative informality, enforcement must be backed up with sufficient power to overcome its original disruptive effects. Enforcement is already expensive in Third World countries where accounting systems, communications networks, and data storage and retrieval methods are weakly developed. Also, for enforcement to take place, it must be worth more to the responsible parties to carry out the enforcement than not to, either because the rewards of carrying it out are high or because the punishment for not carrying it out is severe. Up to a certain point, each time an official takes a bribe the cost of transactions goes up because of the uncertainty (the need for information) of outcome that is introduced. However, when this kind of informality becomes normative, the players can calculate their costs because the cost of bribing a judge or police officer becomes more or less standard. In this situation, a government that seeks suddenly to begin enforcing regulations itself introduces uncertainty, thus temporarily raising the costs of transactions. The power required for enforcement in this case is, in the short term, higher than in situations where enforcement is normative, and it is likely to be resisted more generally.

Where lack of enforcement (itself a kind of official informality) is normative, it is easy to pass sham legislation that serves purposes other than those it claims to serve. The widespread existence of progressive labor laws in societies where labor exploitation is extreme is a notorious case in point (see Portes, this volume).

This raises a third point about power in socioeconomic systems: if normative formal regulation and enforcement is not in the interests of primary power holders, it must be supported by significant secondary power holders. The history of worker protection legislation in the United States is illustrative, coming as it did only after vigorous labor activism early in this century, followed by labor scarcity during the First World War, followed by the social upheavals of the Depression and the Second World War. It is also interesting to observe in this case that as the power of labor increased so did the formal recognition of its institutions, a process in which informal activity (casual groupings and unlawful assemblies and strikes) evolved into formal activity (labor organizations, legal strikes, political action).

Tendler's (1987) discussion of six programs in India and Bangladesh that successfully enhanced the previously informal activities of entrepreneurs is instructive on this point. Tendler reports that each program had a narrow focus on a particular trade or sector and had strong connections with powerful institutions: the government (1), trade unions (3), a bank (1), and a private consulting firm (1). On the one hand, it may be assumed that the power of the mentors and their informal activities were available. On the other, it is likely that the narrow focus of the activities involved rendered the players harmless in the eyes of other powerful actors in the system.

North (1990) makes the point very forcefully and at length that lowering of transaction costs takes place in situations where there is a concerted mixture of formal and informal enforcement, the latter implying some sort of consensus that it is optimal to have regulations enforced. The lesson to be learned here is that *lowering of transaction costs may require power from a variety of subsystems and may be beyond the abilities of any government acting only from an official power base.*

Where nonenforcement is common, governments are free to gain temporary popular support by passing laws with only the appearance of effecting changes. However, it appears that when it is not in the interest of powerful elements in society to reduce transaction costs, either there must be counterbalancing power to reduce costs (as in the case of labor unions) or there must be a tacit agreement not to enforce—or the laws, plans, or projects must be made innocuous or invisible to the power holders. I return to the last point in the conclusion, but first it is necessary to address the role of formal planning in regulative power relations and the maintenance of the status quo.

Formal Planning (Question 4)

What is the role of formal planning in the whole process of investigation, discussion, and intervention? Elsewhere (Uzzell 1987, 1990), I have argued that the dominant formal planning style in government, business, and human services (which I call *formal, regulative,* or *coercive planning* interchangeably) has the following characteristics. It relies primarily on power instead of operational information. It seeks to create new systems instead of accommodating to existing systems. It implements plans on a large scale, even where implementation is incremental. It prefers standardization and mass production. And it treats incremental actions as final, rather than experimental.

Probably the most controversial assertion is that formal planning is not based upon operational information, but upon power. The quickest and easiest defense of this position probably would be to refer to the chronic disjunction between the data contained in what are called *needs assessments* in human services programs and the design and implementation of programs or to the manner in which productivity goals are set in most U.S. firms. It may be more useful logically, though, to develop the concept of "information deficits," and to use this concept to explain what is meant.

The prototype of power-based planning is the large-scale planned intervention in an ecological system. In natural ecological systems, self-regulation (upon which the continuing organization of the system depends) implies massive transmissions of information (by analogy, transaction costs) following each minute transfer of matter and energy—more information than humans and computers can process. Forceful introduction of an irrigation system, for example, sets off chains of events at least some of which are always surprising to human planners, precisely because the effects exceed predictions and information. What may be called the *planning information deficit* is the difference between the planner's information and the information necessary to maintain the natural system.

Sociocultural systems are a special case of natural systems, where operational information plays the same role (Prigogine and Stengers 1984; Campbell 1982). The predominant pattern of human interventions, at least since the agricultural revolution, is that when undesirable side effects arise from an intervention, we then intervene to eliminate the side effects. At that point, though we may have reduced the original information deficit, we add to it the new deficit arising from the subsequent intervention. Thus in power-based planning the deficit in operational information always grows faster than the power to offset it.

In human systems, a planner's ability to understand the context in which a plan is implemented is undermined by the secondary learning that occurs when an organism learns a task and secondarily learns about learning tasks (Bateson 1972). Not only will the environment respond to interventions in ways the planner cannot anticipate, but also secondary learning about the intervention and its environmental effects will enable people to respond in ways not envisioned. Secondary learning is a major source of information used in informal responses to coercive plans.

In contrast with formal planners, people with relatively little power to intervene in ecological systems, such as hunter-gatherers or wet rice farmers, operate with less of an information deficit. This is partly due to the scale of their interventions: the smaller the intervention, the smaller the deficit. But more important, it is the result of a process of intervention, followed by observation of the systemic response, followed by corrections in the plan—in other words a feedback process between one intervention and the next. This, in effect, turns every intervention into an experiment, and that process— arguably the central mechanism of secondary learning—is a sine qua non of successful informal activities. (This is also echoed in the maxim that transaction costs are ceteris paribus reduced by repetition.)

The main business of formal planning, as enshrined by positivism, is assumed to be collecting, packaging, and delivering information. However, the information purveyed by formal planners tends to be "manufactured" for purposes other than operational decision making and, in terms of information theory, is not information at all; for example, when human services needs assessments list irrelevant census data or a business manager lists last year's productivity figures and increases them by a magical percent useful only for terrorizing middle managers. This kind of information does not reduce uncertainty about operational questions. Operational information is needed to answer questions such as can we do X? how? how much can we do? does it work?

In coercive planning, the preferred mode of operation is to create a new system, a new program, a new organizational form and to force those affected to conform to it. But where power is scarce, these plans do not work. The purpose of information used in such planning appears not to be to gain understanding or answer operational questions about the appropriateness and feasibility of the plan, but to produce explanation and with that—particularly in the absence of power to impose official reality—mystification and an illusion of control. Thus, what passes for information in coercive planning is largely a covert instrument of elite domination through manipulation of reality.

Following this line of thinking, it is predictable that the NGO projects that are least intrusive and make greatest use of existing informal institutions have tended to be the most successful. They are the ones that rely the least upon power and the most upon operational information. It is also predictable that most governmental actions that work to the benefit of the elite are the result of elite informal activity, not formal "planning," which in this case supplies formal sanction to faits accomplis.

In Latin American countries such as Peru, one direction that formal planning has taken in relation to the poor in the last forty years is the creation of new official organizational forms that either increase transaction costs or handicap participants. Examples of such organizational forms are government prescribed residents' associations for irregular settlements, social interest companies, and cooperatives.

Cooperatives are a mechanism that allows the poor to reduce some transaction costs, but not those that would put them in competition with the elite. Governments of various political persuasions have promoted cooperatives, and they are a common organizational device. Participants form cooperatives to conduct their business because of government incentives such as tax breaks intended to encourage use of the form. For some purposes they work well, but decision making in cooperatives is so cumbersome and slow that they function in a limited venue. The structure also lends itself to ruinous divisions among members. In 1983 a group of ambulatory vendors in Lima formed a cooperative to build a shopping mall. Although they had resources to complete the project and a general agreement on what they wanted to do, two factions developed within the organization and not only was the project blocked, the factions embroiled each other in lawsuits that exhausted the resources of both sides.

In 1970, the government decreed that all irregular settlements would thenceforth have to organize according to a particular government plan to gain government assistance. In many cases, this form of organization proved less effective and efficient than settlement organizations that had evolved locally. In Villa El Salvador, a large informally developed settlement that the Velasco government attempted to turn into a showcase of socialist planning (Bejar 1976), despite hugely disproportionate infusions of public aid and formally planned "assistance," it was not until after a decade (during which the planned organizations atrophied and locally generated organizations developed) that the locality began to realize its potential as a center of entrepreneurial development.

Another unsuccessful organizational form of the period was the "social interest company." This scheme appears to have gone straight from the drafting table to operation without testing. The resulting disasters were legion. For example, one such company was formed to absorb a number of failed bus cooperatives. This was a perfect example of formal planners mounting an additional intervention to correct the undesirable effects of an earlier intervention and thus increasing the deficit of planning information. Members of the new company were thrown into a situation for which they had no training and their operations were capitalized through government loans, at the government's direction, without any investigation of the ability of the company to generate sufficient capital to maintain the fleet, let alone repay the loans. The result was a money sump for the government and an inefficiently operated fleet of rapidly deteriorating buses for the public and the "owners."

With some notable exceptions, the role of formal planning in Third World development has been to maintain the status quo. This is done by implementing plans that require power for their realization where power is lacking or by implementing shams (not always cynically, I assume) whose main purpose is to diffuse and disorganize the power of the poor, while failing to reduce transaction costs at critical points.

Successful informal planning, particularly that engaged in by those with little power, is based on operational information. This style of planning, which I have referred to elsewhere as *generative planning* (Uzzell 1987; 1990), is possible for formal planners, although an array of political and cultural factors reduce the likelihood that it will be carried out. Absent development of distributed centers of power, it is unlikely that such planning will be applied to equalizing transaction costs, although it may be the only approach with a chance of succeeding.

Conclusion

Shifting focus from an imagined informal "sector," however defined, to the systemic processes that may be generating the phenomena we propose to understand raises many new possibilities. For one, transaction costs seem to be an appropriate point of entry because they occur throughout the system, because they are affected (albeit perhaps differently) by formal and informal actions, and because they appear to be central to the decisions of players about whether to act formally or informally (see Table 13.1). Not to be neglected is the fact that a large literature on transaction costs and their institutional correlates is already available.

My purpose has been briefly to sketch in some of the effects of high transaction costs, to suggest ways in which the scarcity and distribution of power prevents formal steps from reducing or equalizing transaction costs, and to point out the perhaps unwitting collusion of formal planners (including those of us who only plan from the sidelines) in maintaining the status quo. My hope is that these may point the way for further work.

The valued good in transaction costs is information. This information can be purchased (or created) if one has the capital. Its cost can be formally lowered or redistributed if the formal institution has the power and informal support to do so. Or to some extent it can be lowered or redistributed informally for relatively small groups of cooperating players without coercive power. In most Third World countries capital, power, and information reside together in a few subsystems, and probably the best bet for change is to change the distribution of power.

It is not surprising that, in the mean time, some groups maintain other subsystems in which cooperation substitutes for power and some transaction costs are kept low. However, when transactions reach across boundaries of such subsystems to other subsystems, system wide information costs are in effect. Meanwhile even within subsystems, adaptations that make bad situations tolerable discourage change.

In Latin America, sheer growth in the numbers of the relatively powerless population has been the main force behind a multidimensional process that has been responsible for such empowerment as has taken place in the past seventy years. In Peru, politicians from Sánchez Cerro in the early 1930s, and the Odría government of the late 1940s and 1950s, through conservative and relatively liberal governments of the 1960s (Collier 1976), Velasco's progressive experiment of the late 1960s and early 1970s, the García and Fujimori governments, and a wide array of declared and undeclared parties and factions (Rodríguez, Riofrio, and Walsh 1980) have wooed this large potential constituency assiduously. In the dialectical development of informal institutions, which have been well developed in Peru for some time (Uzzell 1976), formal action has always followed informal initiative and has always been followed in turn by further informal responses. Nevertheless, elite informality and other characteristics of the system have so far operated to keep transaction costs high and unequally distributed.

In part, the formal plans and programs that partially and locally reduce transaction costs and make capital and information available to a few of the poor are allowed to succeed precisely because they do not openly involve use of power or threaten a general reduction of transaction costs. This is why micro level interventions have been able to proliferate, while changing little in the basic structures where they occur.

In another context Serrano-García lists the reasons for the limited success of an empowerment project in a village in Puerto Rico: "I am convinced that our project achieved the goals it did because its goals and strategies were and are unknown to the people in power, because we are working with low-status people who are not recognized as a threat, and because we did not choose to deal with problems which directly confront governmental institutions" (1984, p. 198). When the poor openly use power they either succeed in lowering costs of formally sanctioned transactions to the point that it is optimal for them to follow formal prescriptions (i.e., they cease to be "informals") or they become guerrillas or outlaws.

Most formal plans are far from irrelevant to all this; they are just not what they seem. As I have suggested elsewhere,

> The implementation of a coercive plan, whatever other goals are stated, [is] a ritual playing out of power, wherein the reality of the powerless is symbolically subordinated to the reality of the powerful. This may be one reason that information deficits are tolerable in coercive planning. In this regard it is also appropriate to observe that formalization itself is only a manifestation of power and that all power transactions are carried out informally and grow out of generative plans. Thus coercive plans may be nothing more than the way in which informal power relations are ritually reinforced. (1990, p. 127)

My personal conviction is that in our attempts to understand and assist those of the poor who labor, manufacture, truck, and barter without official sanction, we have been looking in the wrong places and proposing interventions that too often have been either unworkable, irrelevant, or trivial, or at worst help sustain the status quo. This may be unavoidable, but I believe that we have an obligation to try out new paradigms and formulations. At the very least let us look closely at our own work to make sure that we are not unwittingly the agents of homeostasis, rather than change.

NOTES

1. In normalizing informality, I come closer than Portes to the formulation of Hernando de Soto (1986) and the Instituto Libertad y Democracia (ILD). The resemblance is more than coincidence, because I was employed by the ILD in 1983 and 1984 to help develop its research design and participate in research. I undoubtedly had some influence on the ILD's formulations, and though my

own views were already well developed by the time I joined them, I was certainly influenced by de Soto and the excellent research team he assembled. However, as pointed out by Bromley (this volume), the ILD research focused primarily upon entrepreneurs and was interested in locating, measuring, and describing a sector. In contrast, I wish to include workers and do not want to be bound by a sector. Any disagreement I may have with aspects of de Soto's formulations are beyond the scope of this chapter.

Part V

Conclusion

❏   Chapter 14

Contrapunto: Policy, Research, and the Role of the State

Cathy A. Rakowski

Introduction

The authors of the preceding chapters reveal a multidimensional and complex informal sector debate. This debate addresses (a) definitional and conceptual issues, (b) methodological issues, (c) questions regarding the nature of linkages between informal and so-called modern activities and the informal sector and the state, and (d) the role of informal activities in development and democratization.

This chapter summarizes points of agreement and disagreement and organizes the research and policy recommendations discussed. The emphasis is on highlighting the degree of convergence among diverse positions and the fact that there are few insurmountable differences among authors. In fact, common themes thread through the chapters, only some of which are explained by our prior agreement to address certain issues in all chapters. Other common themes emerged spontaneously, including attention to the role of the state and a preoccupation with issues of power, gender, markets, and social-political-economic context.

The task of this chapter is to integrate the perspectives and alternatives of the authors. The following sections outline points of agreement and differences and summarize recommendations for research and policy and program design.

General Points of Agreement

The following are points on which most, if not all, authors can agree:

1. The activities that have been classified as informal share at least two characteristics.[1] They tend to be *small scale* and their workers usually are *not protected* by labor law. Transactions seldom are included in national accounts or taxed.

2. Beyond these shared characteristics, the informal sector is *heterogeneous*. Although *some activities* (e.g., petty commerce, personal and repair services) and *worker types* (e.g., self-employed) *may predominate*, overall the activities classified as informal span industry sectors, geographic space (rural, urban), occupational groups, demographic characteristics (age, gender), and other variables. This indicates the need for heterogeneous policies.

3. The set of activities known as the informal sector are *dynamic*; they contribute to employment, production, personal incomes, and the generation of wealth. As such, they cannot be considered traditional forms of production or indicators of development gone wrong. Rather, study of informal activities, their links to so-called modern activities, and their roles in socioeconomic systems can be a "window" to the changing nature of capitalism and the functioning of socioeconomic systems. Research in diverse settings can contribute to understanding the range of alternative forms of development or change that can achieve economic growth and human well-being or, alternately, suppress change and maintain the status quo at the expense of large segments of the population.

4. Because informal activities are not independent of the context in which they arise and operate, to understand the behavior of those who engage in such activities, it is important to understand their experience with the state, large firms, and social institutions *within specific historical and spatial contexts.*

5. Authors tend to agree that equal attention should be focused on the characteristics of activities, units, and forms of production and on the characteristics of the individuals engaged in those activities. For instance, when research and policy focus on individual characteristics (e.g., human capital variables), they tend to "blame the victim" and attribute informality to

only supply side variables. They miss the rich *interplay of supply and demand* and fail to understand the importance of contextual factors (Cartaya, de Oliveira and Roberts, Liedholm). Individuals respond to opportunities and constraints, vary in their ability to do so, and have different choices open to them because of their characteristics (Cartaya, Uzzell, Portes).

6. Authors *question fundamental tenets of economic development theory and planning,* including the notion that proletarianization is inevitable (Portes, Moser) or that development is about accumulation of wealth through competition (Uzzell, Bromley); that modern technologies, capital-intensive production, and hiring well-paid, skilled workers is rational; that informal sector policies are the exclusive domain of macroeconomics *or* of social welfare agencies (Márquez, Franks, Cartaya); that state policies, plans, and labor standards are rational (information based) or promote well-being (Uzzell, Bromley, Portes); that to be small scale and self-employed is synonymous with poverty (Cartaya) or entrepreneurial spirit (McKean, Márquez); or that informality is undesirable or deviant (Otero, Franks, Uzzell).

7. There is general agreement that the *actions of the state are problematic.* But there is disagreement over whether the state is too intrusive in economic undertakings (Bromley), not involved enough (Otero), or should change the form of its involvement (Portes, de Oliveira and Roberts, Cartaya, Márquez, Liedholm, Franks, Uzzell).

8. Some authors argue the state should recognize the informal sector as both a macroeconomic phenomenon and a social welfare phenomenon.

9. Authors tend to agree that among the factors affecting growth in the informal sector, three stand out: economic conditions, regulation and policy, and people's rational assessment of options and needs. Hence, policies and programs should be *heterogeneous and flexible.*

These common themes lead logically to recommendations for research, policy and action. The following sections summarize and contrast the positions of authors on research issues and policy recommendations.

Recommendations for Research

This volume confirms that, although some disciplinary approaches may provide more information than others, a multidisciplinary approach can spare embarrassment (from narrow research findings) and help prevent potentially harmful policy recommendations (based on incomplete information). No one perspective has the answer to the questions of what is the informal sector, what roles it plays in socioeconomic systems, or how the state and other actors should deal with the informals. Some details may not be knowable and their relative importance may be obscured by the overall picture. But, piecing together descriptions and interpretations from a variety of ideological, conceptual and methodological approaches can weave a richly textured tale of the multidimensional and complex reality of Latin American peoples and the socioeconomic and global systems within which they construct their lives.

Research efforts should include factors appropriately the domain of historical research, political and class analysis, sociological "big picture" work, macroeconomic modeling, micro level analyses of production chains and product markets, ethnographic research, feminist analysis, and so forth. Research must incorporate different levels of analysis for concrete research problems. These include the macroeconomic level, policy-regulatory environment, social institutions, labor markets, subsectors, power relations, communities, and economic units and households (see Table 14.1). Some specific research questions raised by authors follow.

A Focus on the Macroeconomy

Research is needed on the impact of specific policies on the growth and nature of informal sector activities (Liedholm, Uzzell, Bromley, Márquez); links between macroeconomic restructuring and restructuring in the informal sector (de Oliveira and Roberts, Portes, Márquez); the impact of informal sector restructuring on the implementation of macroeconomic policies (Franks); and links between the type or source of data, political process and power, and the nature of macroeconomic plans (Uzzell).

Questions include the following: What are the full range of economic conditions and constraints under which specific informal activities thrive or struggle? What is the division of labor between different forms of production, and what productive or service role is played by specific informal activities? Under what conditions do the social opportunity costs of informal activities prevail over traditional approaches to

Table 14.1   Selected Recommendations for Research and Policy

Future Research Needs

Multidisciplinary

Focus on the macroeconomy
  Impact of restructuring on informal sector
  Impact of informal sector on macroeconomic programs

Focus on the policy-regulatory environment
  Costs and benefits by enterprise size
  Economic versus social welfare approach

Focus on power and democratic principles
  Who benefits, who loses
  Authority of the state

Focus on firms, labor markets, and subsectors
  Internal constraints versus external constraints on firms
  Interplay of labor supply and demand factors
  Subsector characteristics: markets, competition, technology

Biases
  Disciplinary: conceptual, methodological
  Ideological, value-based

Policy Considerations

Flexibility and sensitivity
  Heterogeneous and flexible policies and programs
  Periodic evaluation and revision
  Variations in socioeconomic context and conditions
  Nature of planning

Constraints on small firms
  Competition and access to markets, raw materials, and credit
  Government discrimination

Exploitation and subcontracting
  Impact of legislation and job security, competitive markets
  Protecting minimum labor standards

Direct subsidies for social welfare

Education, training, and technical assistance

Targeting beneficiaries
  Informal elite versus vulnerable groups
  Reaching larger numbers
  Needs assessment

Problems with promoting informal activities
  Efficiency and effectiveness
  Challenge to state authority and status quo

investment and growth? What happens when microenterprise programs selectively benefit subsectors or activities deemed important to
national goals, target only the most viable activities, benefit activities
with low viability that serve as survival strategies, support activities
whose competitive advantage is the exploitation of workers?

A Focus on the Policy-Regulatory Environment

Research should assess which policies or regulations in a particular setting encourage informalization and exploitation or discriminate
against small firms and the self-employed (Liedholm, Bromley, Uzzell,
Franks, Portes). Which factors are most critical given simulations of the
costs and benefits of specific policies or laws and of formal forms of
production versus informal forms of production? Which increase
transaction costs? How do "economic" and "social welfare" policies
interact to promote or disadvantage informal activities and workers?
Furthermore, given the range of work-related welfare policies and
standards, which are deemed critical to national development goals or
to social welfare goals (or both)? For instance, economic policies could
focus on supporting the most viable activities; the least viable would
be targeted by social welfare programs or allowed to die off (Márquez),
reducing competition and maximizing efficiency. Who will benefit the
most from legal and regulatory reform, small firms or large firms?

A Focus on Power and Democratic Principles

Power is one of the most commonly neglected variables in studies of
labor markets and enterprises (Uzzell, Liedholm, Bromley). Who benefits and who loses through specific regulations, policies, and programs; and what are the vested interests that make difficult reform and
change? What economic conditions facilitate incorporating the poor
and powerless into political processes? How do firm behavior and
employment patterns interact with, support, or threaten the authority
of the state? Analyses need to be sensitive to ideological positions and
ethical issues.

A Focus on Firms, Labor Markets, and Subsectors

Research with a triple focus on firms, labor markets, and subsectors can
increase understanding of the heterogeneity in the informal sector and

help overcome the mindset of policy makers and advisors who tend to see factors internal to firms as their primary constraints (Márquez, Portes, Moser, McKean, Cartaya, de Oliveira and Roberts). Such research can lead to an appropriately broad array of policy measures adapted to specific beneficiary needs and specific socioeconomic contexts. Some research questions include these: What balance of large, medium and small firms is most likely to benefit and to survive in the system? What do microenterprises and the self-employed need to make the transition from petty producer to small-scale capitalist firm without being replaced by large firms when an activity becomes profitable? What forces (e.g., productive, market) in a specific subsector determine the position and role of small versus large enterprises? Research also is needed on the impact of state and private sector or NGO initiatives on specific activities. For instance, has microenterprise promotion increased competition beyond the capacity of the market for a particular product or service?

More research is needed on the interplay between the characteristics of the supply and demand of labor to understand reasons for growth and the role played by informal activities in a specific setting (Cartaya, McKean). A critical problem in labor market analysis is the use of surveys that generate selective information on the behavior of individual workers and nonworkers. Household analyses and studies of labor demand in productive units are needed to understand the allocation of labor at the household level and how certain cultural and life-cycle variables determine entry into and exit from wage labor and self-employment.

Biases

At the very least, researchers should acknowledge the assumptions underlying and limitations imposed by their choice of concepts, models, instruments, and methods of analyses. Choices should be made clear in reports and publications so findings can be compared with those of studies using alternative methods, concepts, and so on. A comprehensive, interdisciplinary approach would be ideal. Researchers also need to keep in mind that their findings are likely to be used for policy formulation. This demands a consideration of the ethical problems that may arise from research findings that do or do not point fingers of blame or make value judgments regarding the "worthiness" of particular actors. Issues of exploitation, power and privilege are more complex than most research acknowledges. The notion of "findings scenarios"—alternative explanations for patterns detected through analysis—might be useful.

Policy Recommendations for the Informal Sector

Policy Issue 1: Flexibility and Sensitivity

A blanket policy approach should be avoided (Márquez) and the relative short and long-term benefits of direct and indirect policies should be assessed for each policy problem. As stated earlier, policies and programs need to be *heterogeneous and flexible*, because informal sector activities change in response to economic expansion and recession and may, in turn, influence expansion and recession (Franks, Cartaya, de Oliveira and Roberts). For instance, some activities change in response to shifts from import-substitution industrialization to export-oriented industrialization (de Oliveira and Roberts, Portes), others in response to discriminatory market policies and industrial subsidies (Liedholm, Franks), others as a result of poverty alleviation programs and microenterprise promotion (Cartaya, Otero, McKean, Márquez). Not all changes are anticipated.

Policies and programs need to be *evaluated* and *revised periodically* to take into account the changing socioeconomic context and real-world impact on people and institutions. For instance, the informal sector seems to show the greatest possibilities of increasing income and production during economic expansion, a period in which the sector tends to decline in relative importance as a source of employment. Periods of prosperity lead to demand for specialized products and services that may be best produced by small firms and the self-employed and lead to lower competition levels as some workers leave informal activities for newly created well-paid jobs in protected employment (de Oliveira and Roberts). During economic recession, however, employment in the sector tends to expand rapidly even though productive units may show involutionary tendencies and heightened competition, especially in the absence of state provided welfare (de Oliveira and Roberts). Economic conditions also create pressures for large firms that informalize a portion of production to maintain competitiveness under changing market and trade conditions (Portes). Thus, the number of persons employed in informal activities is likely to be highest during recessions, whereas the average incomes and levels of production of informal activities would be highest during periods of prosperity. Policies need to take this into account.

Policy recommendations should be grounded in knowledge of the nature of planning, the production of information or knowledge, state objectives, needs assessments, and the impact of specific policies on the balance of power and the authority of the state. Policies too often promote the interests and values of some groups at the expense of others and are based on outdated information produced by methods and models that include implicit ideological biases. Therefore, policy makers should solicit input from "target" groups, not merely from "experts," as a means of improving the potential of policies to address real problems and as a mechanism for democratizing the policy process. Policy makers should acknowledge and correct for biases that are unacceptable morally, for example, that reinforce inequality and exacerbate social problems like poverty (Uzzell).

Policy Issue 2: Constraints on Small Firms

Private organizations and some government agencies have targeted the problems of the self-employed and small firms. But they tend to emphasis internal factors that have to do with input and operations, rather than external structural factors. Among the most important constraints reported by informals or researchers are (a) high levels of competition and restricted access to alternative markets, (b) restricted access to and cost of raw materials and credit, (c) technological deficiencies, and (d) government discrimination (Moser, de Oliveira and Roberts, McKean, Otero, Liedholm, Márquez). Each of these needs to be addressed and not all can be addressed through direct intervention with microentrepreneurs.

Credit has been the program of choice *extraordinaire* of microenterprise promotion. The most successful credit programs (in terms of disbursement of funds, rates of repayment and program sustainability) are minimalist programs—those that focus almost exclusively on credit (McKean). Solidarity group approaches are particularly effective in reaching the poor and women and have the additional benefit of contributing to organizational problem solving, networking and cohesion, attitude change, and guaranteeing repayment (Otero, McKean). However, credit can hurt productivity and income if it leads to an increase in competition within restricted markets. Some innovative suggestions follow.

Obvious means of reducing competition or expanding markets include direct promotion of new products for new markets, feasibility and market studies, and state purchases of goods and services (de Oliveira and Roberts, Liedholm). A less direct way to increase markets is through reform of agriculture and trade policies in ways that increase the demand for the goods and services produced by informal activities. Others include provision of infrastructure (e.g., roads) that can open previously inaccessible markets and direct assistance in marketing (Liedholm, Bromley, Uzzell). (These are unlikely if support programs are relegated to the realm of "poverty alleviation" and "social welfare" rather than to the realm of "economic development" or "business development.") Other indirect means include providing social welfare benefits so fewer persons need engage in informal activities as a survival strategy (Márquez, Cartaya) or supporting higher wages so fewer household members need enter the labor force (de Oliveira and Roberts).

Restricted access to and the cost of raw materials is frequently cited by informals as their most important constraint (McKean). Governments can improve access and reduce costs by eliminating monopoly control over raw materials, for example, through trade liberalization and consumer cooperatives, among others. More research is needed on this problem and the feasibility of potential solutions.

Policy Issue 3: Exploitation and Subcontracting

By linking benefits to employment, the state distorts the supply of labor (creating a division between workers) and gives incentives to employers to informalize employment practices (de Oliveira and Roberts). Labor is more expensive to firms that abide by labor standards; this encourages subcontracting and exploitation (Liedholm, Portes, de Oliveira and Roberts).[2] The single most important factor that encourages subcontracting and exploitation is the guarantee of job security. Flexibility in conditions of employment is necessary to reduce the pressures for informalization and exploitation (Portes). This does not mean denying basic rights to workers; it means looking for ways to equitably distribute the costs of those rights and to discourage exploitation and labor market segmentation.

Subcontracting is not always considered problematic. Under some conditions, governments may advocate closer links between some informal and "modern" firms as a means to guarantee markets and revenues to the goods and services produced by informal firms or to maximize "complementarity" (each set of firms concentrates on those activities in which it has comparative advantage) (Moser). Fair marketing and production arrangements in sectors where subcontracting exists could help avoid exploitation (Márquez). Subcontracting should not be encouraged as a policy without thorough evaluation of potential outcomes and the implementation of safeguards. For instance, support should be denied to large *and* small firms whose main competitive advantage is violation of accepted wage and labor standards (Portes, Márquez, Otero). Trade-based organizations could help advise and defend the interests of home-based workers (McKean, Márquez).

Policy Issue 4: Direct Subsidies

Microenterprise support programs do not address the structural origins of poverty and disadvantage, and poverty alleviation policies cannot help workers in formal jobs with depressed wages (Cartaya). Welfare subsidies may be appropriate to alleviate poverty and are known to have at least a short-term positive impact on nutrition, health, and education of children (Cartaya). But, direct subsidies are justified only in periods of recession or structural adjustment and only for the most vulnerable groups (Márquez). Policies should avoid spillover to the nonpoor (Márquez).

Policy Issue 5: Education, Training, and Technical Assistance

Although one of the most common strategies suggested to move workers into formal jobs and improve the productivity of informal workers is human capital development (Márquez), studies of human capital variables suggest that primary education is not strongly associated with employment (Cartaya). Human capital improvement cannot guarantee good jobs because jobs depend on factors such as the level of demand for labor and discrimination against certain workers (Cartaya).

    Extensive training and technical assistance also do not seem to improve the impact of credit programs, and their costs typically are not recovered through affordable service fees. Many entrepreneurs lack the time to take courses, the content of training can discriminate against women by promoting service activities, and technical assistance often turns into social welfare actions with limited impact on profitability (McKean). Larger (elite) microenterprises are the most likely to benefit from technical assistance, if combined with credit and other support (McKean).

Policy Issue 6: Targeting Beneficiaries

Policies and programs must be adapted to the characteristics and needs of intended beneficiaries. Some beneficiaries may need basic literacy and math training which require simplified services, not sophisticated training in accounting and management (McKean). Most programs tend to target or reach the elite of the informal sector because this group shows the greatest potential for growth. Targeting elites can help diversify economies (the missing middle), but will not alleviate poverty (Márquez). "Massification," reaching greater numbers of people, should be a policy goal (Otero).

Policies need to consider the special circumstances and constraints of certain populations, for example, women and the elderly. Social norms regarding gender roles and life-cycle stages of family units place special constraints on women. Furthermore, training programs should try to avoid channeling them into "feminine" occupations (office, sewing, services, food preparation, etc.) that are devalued and low paying. Credit programs have made headway in overcoming laws regarding the management of community property that discriminate against their access to collateral.

Although not directly addressed as a policy issue by the authors, age is a factor that crops up persistently in empirical studies of informal activities. Policies to support informal activities and conceptualizations of informals need to consider age as a variable of importance. Recent research suggests that public and private sector workers are being pressured to retire early or are simply fired from their jobs as they age. Many use severance pay to start businesses in the informal sector. For this group, education and training will not lead to stable, wage work, and health needs may limit their ability to manage and expand their enterprises. They may not want to expand either. Research is needed as an input to understanding their needs and developing innovative policies for this group.

Policy Issue 7: Problems with Promoting Informal Activities

In their fervor to alleviate poverty, both NGOs and governments have jumped on the "microenterprise promotion bandwagon." There are potential benefits to promoting some informal activities: the efficient use of resources (capital, labor, recycled technology), savings on foreign exchange through the use of local materials and financing, poverty alleviation in some cases, and potential income redistribution (Franks, Moser). But there also are potential dangers to promoting informal activities: because they do not comply with all regulations, they challenge the authority of the state and can erode the tax base; informal construction (through invasions) reduces state control over urban planning and zoning, health and safety, environmental quality; informal products can undercut formal production and lead to a flood of low-quality, noncompetitive products; program benefits may not be sustainable in the long run, especially under changing economic conditions (Franks, Márquez, McKean). Feasibility studies are needed to assess costs and benefits (social, political, and financial).

The Role of the State

Various roles have been suggested for the state. Hernando de Soto argues that development requires debureaucratization, privatization, and deregulation—the state should leave the market alone (Bromley). There may be no alternative to state intervention in the market, however (Portes, Bromley). What seems to be needed are new and unorthodox ways for the state to intervene to facilitate more efficient and equitable growth and poverty alleviation (Portes, de Oliveira and Roberts, Márquez, Cartaya, Uzzell, Bromley, Liedholm). State intervention should not consist of enacting unrealistic laws and then erratically enforcing them (Portes, de Oliveira and Roberts) or enforcing them through coercion and cooptation and in ways that defend the status quo (Uzzell).

The state's strength may lie in its capacity to mandate the institutional and policy environment necessary for reaching informal activities, for example, maintain law and order, disseminate information widely, call for political support, allocate financial resources, carry out policy reform, garner needed technical and human resources (Otero, Moser). The state also needs to guarantee the welfare and protection of its citizens from the impact of structural adjustment and from exploitation and discrimination (de Oliveira and Roberts, Liedholm, Portes, Cartaya, Márquez). However, the state has its own vested interests and these are likely to interfere in policy formulation and implementation. It is a paradox that only a strong state can comprehensively plan and reform the policy environment; but no strong state apparatus ever dramatically reduced its own powers and roles (Bromley, Uzzell). A system of checks and balances is needed; for example, citizen evaluations and research at diverse levels capable of capturing diverse ideological positions.

The state needs to be realistic in its assessment of options and needs. Informal activities should not be romanticized in state policy and planning. Many can benefit socioeconomic systems, but they also create problems for economic and social welfare planning, taxation and regulation, the legitimacy of state authority, and implementation of economic policies. They represent potential constituencies in democracies, but as such threaten the status quo. Certainly, the state should not encourage informality by selectively applying labor standards and other regulations, creating a division between protected and unprotected workers (Portes).

Identification of problems and opportunities can lead to a set of appropriate policy recommendations targeting specific problems rather than a group of people lumped into a "sector." States typically construct plans on information that is outdated and, at the very least, based on research that contains its own implicit or explicit biases. This introduces serious bias and endangers the implementation of plans intended to promote economic growth and recovery (Franks). The state should achieve generative planning based on real, changing, and useful information—not based merely on political imperatives or outdated standardized indicators and surveys (Uzzell, Otero, Franks). States can learn from both large firms and informal sector firms and from microenterprise programs which regulations should be removed and which could be enforced (Portes, de Oliveira and Roberts, McKean, Márquez, Bromley). The state also should assess the potential impact of institutional change prior to mandating such change. This makes testing policies, reforms, and programs in diverse settings a critical step prior to widespread implementation (Bromley).

Conclusions

This volume has presented the cogent issues of the as-yet-unresolved debate that began in the early 1970s on the nature and evolution of the informal sector. The volume has attempted to clarify and compare the reasons for and merits of competing empirical findings and conceptual theories, the implications of competing paradigms for policy and intervention, and the issues involved in developing policy and programs to promote economic growth and social welfare, including those meant to reach and support informal activities. In particular, the volume has focused on concrete policy issues identified by competing approaches, research, models, and theories. Key issues identified include the role of the state in promoting, regulating, and organizing informal activities; the way in which the heterogeneity and complexity of those activities complicates the task of the state and private agencies; the ethical issues involved in policy and intervention; and the potential, unintended outcomes of direct and indirect policies and programs.

This is an ongoing debate. No one approach, paradigm, policy, issue, or problem analysis holds the answer to the role of the informal sector in development or the position the state should take in interacting with informals. It is hoped, however, that the discussion of the relevant problems and issues has succeeded in clarifying how the debate has evolved over time and why, has helped to simplify the conceptual confusion, has successfully illustrated points of convergence and divergence across approaches, has helped explain the myriad policy recommendations under debate, and has indicated the conceptual, research, and policy issues that require further research and analysis. The task now is to refine and reform, continue dialogue and research, develop more appropriate instruments and techniques, identify the ideological and ethical considerations behind recommendations, and test recommendations in appropriate settings. Then politicians, policy makers, development economists, intellectuals, social welfare advocates, and citizens will be better able to rank specific policies and actions from the "shopping list" of measures that promise to improve productivity and expand jobs and income, alleviate poverty, level the playing field and redistribute power and privilege, democratize Latin American socioeconomic systems, and contribute to genuine development

NOTES

1. The authors of this volume have, in one form or another, addressed and corrected for the nine deficiencies of the original ILO informal sector concept discussed by Bromley (1978a). These nine deficiencies are: 1) a two category classification is too crude and simple; 2) the informal/formal division is logically inconsistent and not based on variables tested through multivariate analysis; 3) the sectors are too often assumed separate and independent; 4) often a single policy prescription is touted for the whole informal sector; 5) the informal sector is too quickly assumed to be an urban phenomenon; 6) it is not clear how other "sectors" intersect with or are separate from the formal/informal sector division (e.g., State sector, rural sector, etc.); 7) the informal sector has been depicted as having a present but not a future; 8) there is a tendency to confuse neighborhoods, households, people, activities, and enterprises; and 9) the informal sector is considered synonymous with poverty. For a complete discussion of these deficiencies, see Bromley (1978a).

2. In some contexts, the cost of labor and of complying with regulations simply is not identified by employers as a significant problem (de Oliveira and Roberts).

Bibliography

ACCION International/AITEC. 1990a. "Internal Memorandum on Status of Bridge Fund." Cambridge: ACCION International.

———. 1990b. "Informe Anual de Estadísticas 1989." Cambridge: ACCION International.

———. 1989. "Estadísticas del Año 1988: Programas de Microempresas Afiliados." Cambridge: ACCION International.

———. 1986. "Programas de Microempresas Afiliados." Statistical review of microenterprise credit programs prepared for ACCION.

———. c. 1986. "The Informal Economy in Latin America: Problem or Opportunity?" Pamphlet. Cambridge: ACCION.

———, and the Calmeadow Foundation. 1988. *An Operational Guide for Micro-Enterprise Projects*. Toronto: Calmeadow Foundation.

Acharya, Shankar. 1983. "Informal Credit Markets and Black Money: Do They Frustrate Monetary Policy?" *Economic and Political Weekly*.

———, and Srinivasa Madhur. 1984. "Informal Credit Markets and Monetary Policy." *Economic and Political Weekly* 19, no 36: 1593–1596.

Adams, Dale W., Douglas H. Graham, and J. D. von Pischke, eds. 1984. *Undermining Rural Development with Cheap Credit*. Boulder, Colo.: Westview Press.

ADEMI (Asociación Para el Desarrollo de Microempresas). 1990. "Informe Trimestral (Julio–Septiembre 1990)." Santo Domingo: ADEMI.

———. 1989. "Informe Trimestral (Julio–Septiembre 1989)." Santo Domingo: ADEMI.

Alba, Carlos, and Bryan R. Roberts. 1990. "Crisis, Adjustment and Employment in the Manufacturing Industry of Jalisco." Working Paper 24. Washington, D.C.: Commission for the Study of International Migration and Development.

Amaro, Raymundo. 1988. *Desburocratización de la Administración Pública*. Santo Domingo: Editorial Tiempo.

Andreas, Carol. 1985. *When Women Rebel: The Rise of Popular Feminism in Peru*. Westport, Conn.: Lawrence Hill.

Anker, Richard, and Catherine Hein. 1987. "Empleo de la mujer fuera de la agricultura en países del tercer mundo: Panorama general de las estadísticas ocupacionales." In *Desigualdades entre hombres y mujeres en los mercados de trabajo urbano del tercer mundo,* ed. OIT, pp. 11–36. Geneva: International Labour Office.

Annis, Sheldon, and Jeffrey R. Franks. 1989. "The Idea, Ideology and Economics of the Informal Sector: The Case of Peru." *Grassroots Development* 13, no. 1: 9–23.

Arias, María Eugenia. 1989. "The Rural Development Fund: An Integrated Credit Program for Small and Medium Entrepreneurs." In *Women's Ventures: Assistance to the Informal Sector in Latin America,* ed. Marguerite Berger and Mayra Buvinič, pp. 201–213. West Hartford: Kumarian Press.

————.1985. "Peru: Banco Industrial de Peru—Credit for the Development of Rural Enterprise." In *Gender Roles in Development Projects: A Case Book,* ed. Catherine Overholt, Mary B. Anderson, Kathleen Cloud, and James E. Austin, pp. 243-82. West Hartford, Conn.: Kumarian Press.

Arias, Patricia. 1988. "La pequeña empresa en el occidente rural." *Estudios Sociológicos* 6, no. 17: 405–436.

————, and Bryan R. Roberts. 1985. "The City in Permanent Transition: The Consequences of a National System of Industrial Specialization." In *Capital and Labour in the Urbanized World* ed. John Walton, pp. 149–175. London: Sage Publications.

Armstrong, Warwick, and Terence G. McGee. 1985. *Theatres of Accumulation: Studies in Asian and Latin American Urbanization.* London: Methuen.

Arrow, Kenneth. 1963. *Social Choice and Individual Values.* New Haven, Conn.: Yale University Press.

Ashe, Jeffrey. 1985a. "Extending Credit and Technical Assistance to the Smallest Enterprises." In *Planning for Small Enterprises in Third World Cities,* ed. Ray Bromley, pp. 277–291. Oxford: Pergamon Press.

————. 1985b. "The PISCES II Experience: Local Efforts in Micro-Enterprise Development, Vol. I." Washington, D.C.: United States Agency for International Development (USAID).

Axelrod, Robert. 1984. *The Evolution of Cooperation.* New York: Basic Books.

Balassa, Bela, Gerardo M. Bueno, Pedro Pablo Kuczynski, and Mario H. Simonsen. 1986. *Toward Renewed Economic Growth in Latin America.* Washington, D.C.: Institute for International Economics.

Bateson, Gregory. 1972. *Steps to an Ecology of Mind.* New York: Ballantine Books.

Bejar, Hector. 1987. "Reflexiones sobre el sector informal." *Nueva Sociedad* 90 (July–August): 89–92.

————. 1976. *La Revolución en la Trampa.* Lima: Ediciones Socialismo y Participación.

Benería, Lourdes. 1984. "Gender, Skill, and the Dynamics of Women's Employment." Paper presented at the Conference on Gender in the Work Place, The Brookings Institution, Washington, D.C.

————. 1989. "Subcontracting and Employment Dynamics in Mexico City." In *The Informal Economy: Studies in Advanced and Less Developed Countries*, ed. Alejandro Portes, Manuel Castells, and Lauren Benton, pp. 173–188. Baltimore: Johns Hopkins University Press.

————, and Martha Roldán. 1987. *The Crossroads of Class and Gender: Industrial Homework, Subcontracting, and Household Dynamics in Mexico City.* Chicago: University of Chicago Press.

Bental, Benjamin, Uri Ben-Zion, and Alois Wenig. 1985. "Macroeconomic Policy and the Shadow Economy." In *The Economics of the Shadow Economy*, ed. Wulf Gaertner and Alois Wenig, pp. 179–192. Berlin: Springer-Verlag.

Benton, Lauren. 1989. "Industrial Subcontracting and the Informal Sector: The Politics of Restructuring in the Madrid Electronics Industry." In *The Informal Economy: Studies in Advanced and Less Developed Countries*, ed. Alejandro Portes, Manuel Castells, and Lauren Benton, pp. 228–244. Baltimore: Johns Hopkins University Press.

Berger, Marguerite. 1988. "Introducción." In *La Mujer en el Sector Informal: Trabajo femenino y microempresa en América Latina*, ed. Marguerite Berger and Mayra Buvinič, pp. 13–34. Quito: Editorial Nueva Sociedad and ILDIS.

————, and Mayra Buvinič, eds. 1989. *Women's Ventures: Assistance to the Informal Sector in Latin America.* West Hartford, Conn.: Kumarian Press.

Bethencourt, Luisa. 1988. "La Organización Doméstica y la Condición de la Mujer en los Sectores Populares." *Cuadernos del CENDES* (September–December).

Bidegaín, Gabriel, and Hernán Nuñez. 1988. "Transición Demográfica en Venezuela y la Región Centro Occidental (1786–1986)." Mimeo. Barquisimeto: FUDECO–ILDIS.

Bienefeld, Manfred. 1975. "The Informal Sector and Peripheral Capitalism: The Case of Tanzania." *IDS Bulletin* 6, no. 3: 53–73.

Biggs, Tyler, Merilee S. Grindle, and Donald R. Snodgrass. 1988. "The Informal Sector, Policy Reform, and Structural Transformation." In *Beyond the Informal Sector: Including the Excluded in Developing Countries*, ed. Jerry Jenkins, pp. 133–171. San Francisco: ICS Press.

————, and Jeremy Oppenheim. 1986. "What Drives the Size Distribution of Firms in Developing Countries?" EEPA Discussion Paper No. 6, HIID, Harvard University.

Birkbeck, Chris. 1979. "Garbage, Industry, and the 'Vultures' of Cali, Colombia." In *Casual Work and Poverty in Third World Cities*, ed. Ray Bromley and Chris Gerry, pp. 161–183. New York: Wiley.

Blanes Jiménez, José. 1989. "Cocaine, Informality, and the Urban Economy in La Paz, Bolivia." In *The Informal Economy: Studies in Advanced and Less Developed Countries*, ed. Alejandro Portes, Manuel Castells, and Lauren Benton, pp. 135–149. Baltimore: Johns Hopkins University Press.

Blau, Francine, and Marianne Ferber. 1986. *The Economics of Women, Men and Work.* Englewood Cliffs, N.J.: Prentice-Hall.

Blayney, Robert G., and Heather Clark. 1987. *Honduras: A Small and Microenterprise Development Strategy*. Washington, D.C.: United States Agency for International Development (USAID), ARIES.

———, and María Otero. 1985. "Small and Microenterprises: Contributions to Development and Future Directions for A.I.D.'s Support." Washington, D.C.: United States Agency for International Development (USAID).

Boomgard, James. 1989. "A.I.D. Microenterprise Stock-Taking: Synthesis Report." Washington, D.C.: United States Agency for International Development (USAID).

———, Stephen P. Davies, Steve Haggblade, and Donald C. Mead. 1986. "Subsector Analysis: Its Nature, Conduct and Potential Contribution to Small Enterprise Development." International Development Paper, East Lansing, Michigan State University.

Bose, A. N. 1978. *Calcutta and Rural Bengal: Small Sector Symbiosis*. Calcutta: Minerva Associates.

Bourgignon, Francois. 1991. "Optimal Poverty Reduction, Adjustment and Growth." *The World Bank Economic Review* 5, no. 2: 315–339.

Bowles, W. Donald. 1988. *A.I.D.'s Experience with Selected Employment Generation Projects*. A.I.D. Evaluation Special Study No. 53, Washington, D.C.: United States Agency for International Development (USAID).

Breman, Jan. 1976. "A Dualistic Labour System? A Critique of the Informal Sector Concept." *Economic and Political Weekly* 11, 48:1870–1876; 11, 49:1905–1908; 11, 50:1939–1944.

BRI, Planning Research and Development Department. 1990. "Briefing Booklet: KUPEDES Development Impact Survey." Jakarta: Bank Rakyat Indonesia.

Bromley, Ray. 1992. "Small Enterprise Promotion." In *Urbanization, Migration and Development*, ed. John D. Kasarda and Allan M. Parnell. Newbury Park, Calif: Sage Publications.

———. 1990. "A New Path to Development? The Significance and Impact of Hernando de Soto's Ideas on Underdevelopment, Production, and Reproduction." *Economic Geography* 66: 328–348.

———. 1985. "Small May Be Beautiful, But It Takes More than Beauty to Ensure Success." In *Planning for Small Enterprises in Third World Cities*, ed. Ray Bromley, pp. 321–341. Oxford: Pergamon Press.

———, ed. 1979. *The Urban Informal Sector: Critical Perspectives on Employment and Housing Policies*. Oxford: Pergamon Press.

———. 1978a. "Introduction—The Urban Informal Sector: Why Is It Worth Discussing?" *World Development* 6, nos. 9–10: 1033–1039.

———. 1978b. "Organization, Regulation, and Exploitation in the So-called Urban Informal Sector: The Street Traders of Cali, Colombia." *World Development* 6: 1161–1171.

———, and Chris Gerry. 1979. "Who Are the Casual Poor?" In *Casual Work and Poverty in Third World Cities*, ed. Ray Bromley and Chris Gerry, pp. 3–26. New York: Wiley.

Bruno, Michael, Stanley Fischer, Elhanan Helpman, and Nissan Liviatan with Leora (Rubin) Meridor. 1991. *Lessons of Economic Stabilization and Its Aftermath*. Cambridge, Mass.: MIT Press.

Bruschini, C. 1989. "Tendencias da força da Trabalho Feminina Brasileira nos Anos Setenta a Ochenta: Algunas Comparaçoes Regionais." Paper No. 1/89. Sao Paulo, Brazil: Department of Educational Research, Carlos Chagas Foundation.

Brusco, Sebastiano. 1982. "The 'Emilian' Model: Productive Decentralization and Social Integration." *Cambridge Journal of Economics* 6: 167–184.

Bujra, Janet. 1982. "Prostitution, Class and the State." In *Crime, Justice and Underdevelopment*, ed. Colin Sumner, pp. 145–161. Exeter: Heinemann Educational Books.

Buvinič, Mayra. 1986. "Projects for Women in the Third World: Explaining their Misbehavior." *World Development* 14 (May): 653–64.

———, Marguerite Berger, and Cecilia Jaramillo. 1989. "Impact of a Credit Project for Women and Men Microentrepreneurs in Quito, Ecuador." In *Women's Ventures: Assistance to the Informal Sector in Latin America*, ed. Marguerite Berger and Mayra Buvinič, pp. 222–246. West Hartford, Conn.: Kumarian Press.

Cagatay, Nilufer. 1988. "Economic Development Policies and Worker's Rights: The Case of Turkey." Paper presented at the Symposium on Labor Standards and Development organized by the U.S. Department of Labor, Georgetown University.

Cain, Glen G. 1976. "The Challenge of Segmented Labor Market Theories to Orthodox Theory: A Survey." *Journal of Economic Literature* 14, no. 4: 1215–1257.

Cameron, Maxwell. 1989a. "Party Competition for Working Class Votes in Peru: Continuity and Change Since Military Rule." Unpublished paper, Carleton University.

———. 1989b. "The Politics of the Urban Informal Sector in Peru: Populism, Class, and 'Redistributive Combines'." Paper presented at the Latin American Studies Association meetings.

Campbell, Jeremy. 1982. *Grammatical Man: Information, Entropy, Language, and Life*. New York: Simon and Schuster.

Campos, Luís. 1990. "Paraguay: Emerging Cooperation in Support of the Informal Sector." In *The Critical Connection: Governments, Private Institutions, and the Informal Sector in Latin America*, ed. Katherine Stearns and María Otero, pp. 127–137. Cambridge: ACCION International.

Canak, William L. 1989. "Debt, Austerity, and Latin America in the New International Division of Labor." In *Lost Promises, Debt, Austerity and Development in Latin America*, ed. William L. Canak, pp.9–30. Boulder, Colo.: Westview Press.

Capecchi, Vittorio. 1989. "The Informal Economy and the Development of Flexible Specialization in Emilia-Romagna." In *The Informal Economy: Studies in Advanced and Less Developed Countries*, ed. Alejandro

Portes, Manuel Castells, and Lauren Benton, pp. 189–215. Baltimore: Johns Hopkins University Press.

Carbonetto, Daniel. 1984. "Políticas de mejoramiento en el sector informal urbano." *Socialismo y Participación* 25: 109–139.

———. 1985. "Políticas de Mejoramiento del Empleo en el SIU." In *El Sector Informal Urbano el los Países Andinos*, ed. Santiago Escobar, pp. 329–62. Quito: ILDIS/CEPESIU.

———, and María Ines Carazo de Cabellos. 1986. *Heterogeneidad Tecnológica y Desarrollo Económico: El Sector Informal.* Lima: Instituto Nacional de Planificación–Fundación Friedrich Ebert.

Cardoso, Fernando Henrique and José L. Reyna. 1968. "Industrialización, estructura ocupacional y estratificación social en America Latina." In *Cuestiones de Sociología del Desarrollo de América Latina*, ed. Fernando Henrique Cardoso. Santiago: Editorial Universitaria.

Carrasco, Santiago. 1990. "Ecuador: Government and Private Projects for Microenterprise Development." In *The Critical Connection: Governments, Private Institutions, and the Informal Sector in Latin America*, ed. Katherine Stearns and María Otero, pp. 73–87. Cambridge: ACCION International.

Carrillo, Jorge. 1989. "The Restructuring of the Automobile Industry of Mexico: Adjustment Policies and Labor Implications." Texas Papers on Mexico 89–07, Mexican Center, University of Texas at Austin.

———, and Alberto Hernández. 1985. *Mujeres fronterizas en la industria maquiladora.* Mexico City: SEP/CEFNOMEX.

Cartaya, Vanessa. 1990a. "Costos de legalización de empresas informales. El caso de Venezuela." In *Más allá de la Regulación*, ed. Victor Tokman, pp. 247–274. Santiago: PREALC.

———. 1990b. "La desocupación y la teoría económica: Explicaciones alternativas." Paper prepared as part of the requirements for a doctorate in Development, CENDES, Caracas.

———. 1988. "El sector informal urbano: La controversia alrededor de la definición y utilidad del término." Unpublished paper presented at the conference of the Urban Informal Sector in Barquisimeto, Venezuela.

———. 1987. "El Confuso Mundo del Sector Informal." *Nueva Sociedad* 90: 76–88.

———, and Haydee García. 1988. *Infancia y pobreza. Los efectos de la recesión sobre la infancia en Venezuela.* Caracas: UNICEF–Ministerio de la Familia, Editorial Nueva Sociedad.

———, and Gustavo Márquez. 1990. "Social Policy During Adjustment: The Poor and Beyond." Paper presented at the Latin American Senior Policy Seminar sponsored by The World Bank, Caracas.

———, Juan Carlos Rodríguez, and José Luís Bernardo. 1989. "Los Programas de Apoyo al Sector Informal en América Latina: Lecciones de la Experiencia." Report prepared for seminar on Financing Microenterprise in Venezuela and Latin America: The Experience of Credit Programs. Barquisimeto, Venezuela: FUDECO.

Carvajal, Jaime. 1985. "Fundación Carvajal: Un Caso do Apoyo a las Microempresas de Cali, Colombia." Regional Meeting of Latin American Sponsoring Agencies for Microenterprise Development, Quito, Ecuador.

Castello, Carlos, and Diego Guzmán. 1988. "Expansion and Replication of Benefits in Micro-enterprise Programs: The Colombian Model" (draft).

Castells, Manuel. 1986. *The Shei-Kip-Mei Syndrome*. Hong Kong: Center for Urban Studies and Planning, University of Hong Kong.

———. 1975. "Immigrant Workers and Class Struggles in Advanced Capitalism: The Western European Experience." *Politics and Society* 5: 33–66.

———, and Alejandro Portes. 1989. "World Underneath: The Origins, Dynamics, and Effects of the Informal Economy." In *The Informal Economy: Studies in Advanced and Less Developed Countries*, ed. Alejandro Portes, Manuel Castells and Lauren A. Benton, pp. 11–40. Baltimore: Johns Hopkins University Press.

CENDES (Cecilia Cariola, Miguel Lacabana, Luisa Bethencourt, J. Gregorio Darwich, Beatriz Fernández, and Ana Teresa Gutiérrez). 1989. *Crisis, sobrevivencia y sector informal*. Caracas: ILDIS-CENDES, Editorial Nueva Sociedad.

CEPAL. 1989. *Transformación Ocupacional y Crisis Social en América Latina*. Santiago de Chile: United Nations, CEPAL.

———. 1986. "América Latina: Las mujeres y los cambios socio-ocupacionales 1960–1980." Document LC/R.504 prepared by the Division of Social Development, CEPAL.

Chamorro, Amália, Mario Chávez, and Marcos Membreño. 1991. "El sector informal en Nicaragua: Entre la acumulación y la subsistencia." In *Informalidad Urbana en Centroamérica*, ed. Juan Pablo Pérez Sáinz and Rafael Menjívar, pp. 217–258. Caracas: Editorial Nueva Sociedad.

Chávez O'Brian, Eliana. 1990. "Peru: Governmental and Non-Governmental Support Programs: Reflections and Assessment." In *The Critical Connection: Governments, Private Institutions, and the Informal Sector in Latin America*, ed. Katherine Stearns and María Otero, pp. 139–152. Cambridge: ACCION International.

Chenery, Hollis, and coworkers. 1974. *Redistribution with Growth: Policies to Improve Income Distribution in Developing Countries in the Context of Economic Growth*. London: Oxford University Press.

Chuta, Enyinna. 1989. "A Nigerian Study of Firm Dynamics." Draft Paper, Department of Economics, Michigan State University.

———, and Carl Liedholm. 1985. *Employment and Growth in Small-Scale Industry: Empirical Evidence and Policy Assessment from Sierra Leone*. Basingstoke, U.K.: Macmillan.

Coase, Ronald H. 1992. "The Institutional Structure of Production." *The American Economic Review* 82, no. 4: 713–719.

———. 1988. *The Firm, the Market, and the Law*. Chicago: University of Chicago Press.

————. 1960. "The Contractual Nature of the Firm." *Journal of Law and Economics* 17.

Cohen, Monique. 1984. "The Urban Street Food Trade." Report prepared for the U.S. Agency for International Development, Office of Women in Development. Washington, D.C.: Equity Policy Center.

Collier, David. 1976. *Barriadas y Elites de Odría a Velasco.* Lima: Instituto de Estudios Peruanos. Available in English as *Squatters and Oligarchs: Authoritarian Rule and Policy Change in Peru.* Baltimore: Johns Hopkins University Press.

Collins, Jane. 1990. "Unwaged Labor in Comparative Perspective: Recent Theories and Unanswered Questions." In *Work Without Wages: Comparative Studies of Domestic Labor and Self Employment Within Capitalism,* ed. Jane Collins and Martha Giménez, pp. 3–24. Albany: State University of New York Press.

————, and Martha Giménez, eds. 1990. *Work Without Wages: Comparative Studies of Domestic Labor and Self Employment Within Capitalism.* Albany: State University of New York Press.

CORDIPLAN. 1988. "La Cuantificación de la Pobreza en Venezuela." Caracas: Dirección de Planificación del Empleo, Producción y Precios. Mimeo.

Cornia, Giovanni. 1984. "Ajuste a nivel familiar: Potencial y limitaciones de las estrategias de sobrevivencia." In *Ajuste con rostro humano: Protección de los grupos vulnerables y promoción del crecimiento,* ed. Giovanni Cornia, Richard Jolly, and Frances Stewart. Madrid: Siglo XXI.

Corvalán Vásquez, Oscar, in cooperation with Alfonso Lizarzaburu. 1985. "Un programa de capacitación de trabajadoras del Sector Informal en América Latina." Research Report prepared for IIPE 53. Paris: UNESCO.

Crandon, Libbet. 1984. *Women, Enterprise and Development: The Pathfinder Fund's Women in Development—Projects, Evaluation and Documentation (WID/PED Program).* Boston: The Pathfinder Fund.

Cueva, Agustín. 1988. *Las Democracias Restringidas de América Latina.* Barcelona: Planeta.

Culbertson, W. Patton. 1989. "Empirical Regularities in Black Markets for Currency." *World Development* 17, no. 12: 1907–1919.

Davies, Richard, and Peter Elias. 1990. "The Relationship Between a Husband's Unemployment and His Wife's Participation in the Labour Force." Mimeo, Centre for Applied Statistics, University of Lancaster, United Kingdom (draft chapter for Unemployment volume of Economic and Social Research Council of the United Kngdom's research initiative on Social Change and Economic Life).

Davies, Stephen P., Donald C. Mead, and James L. Seale, Jr. 1990. "Small Manufacturing Enterprises in Egypt." *Economic Development and Cultural Change.*

De Barbieri, Teresita. 1984. "Incorporación de la mujer a la economía en América

Latina." In *Memoria del Congreso Latinoamericano de Población y Desarrollo*, ed. PISPAL-COLMEX-UNAM, pp. 355–389. Mexico City: UNAM (Universidad Nacional Autónoma de México).

————, and Orlandina de Oliveira. 1987. *La presencia de las mujeres en América Latina en una década de crisis*. Santo Domingo: Research Center for Feminine Action (CIDAF) and Editora Bho.

de Oliveira, Orlandina, and Brígida García. 1988. "Expansión del trabajo femenino y transformación social en México. 1950–1987." Mimeo, Center for sociological Research, Colegio de Mexico.

————, and Bryan Roberts. 1989. "Los antecedentes de la crisis urbana: urbanización y transformación ocupacional en América: 1940–1980." In *Las Ciudades en Conflicto: Una Perspectiva Latinoamericana*, ed. D. Veiga and M. Lombardi. Montevideo: Ediciones de la Banda Oriental.

de Soto, Hernando. 1992. "Carta Abierta: Encomendándose a San Antonio." *Carétas* (Lima) no. 1199: 16–19 and 82–83.

————. 1989. *The Other Path: The Invisible Revolution in the Third World*. New York: Harper and Row. English translation of *El Otro Sendero*.

————. 1988. "Constraints on People: The Origins of Underground Economies and Limits to Their Growth." In *Beyond the Informal Sector: Including the Excluded in Developing Countries*, ed. J. Jenkins, pp. 15–47. San Francisco: Institute for Contemporary Studies.

————. 1986. *El Otro Sendero: La Revolución Informal*. Lima: Editorial El Barranco.

Devarajan, Shantayanan, Christine Jones and Michael Roemer. 1989. "Markets under Price Controls in Partial and General Equilibrium." *World Development*, 17:1881–1893.

Deyo, Frederic C. 1987. "State and Labor: Modes of Political Exclusion in East Asian Development." In *The Political Economy of the New Asian Industrialism*, ed. Frederic C. Deyo, pp. 182–202. Ithaca, N.Y.: Cornell University Press.

Díaz, Mario Alberto. 1990. "Mexico: Developing the Microenterprise Sector: Public and Private Initiatives." In *The Critical Connection: Governments, Private Institutions, and the Informal Sector in Latin America*, ed. Katherine Stearns and María Otero, pp. 111–125. Cambridge: ACCION International.

Dickens, William, and Kevin Lang. 1985. "A Test of Dual Labor Market Theory." *American Economic Review* 75, no. 4.

Dietz, Henry. 1991. "Electoral Behavior Under Sustained Economic Crisis: The Urban Informal Sector in Lima, Peru." Paper presented at the 1991 World Congress of the International Political Science Association, Buenos Aires.

Doria Medina, Samuel. 1986. *La Economía Informal en Bolivia*. La Paz: EDOBOL.

Drabek, Anne Gordon. 1987. "Development Alternatives: The Challenge for NGOs—An Overview of the Issues." *World Development* 15 (Supplement): ix–xv.

Duarte, Isis. 1978. "Marginalidad Urbana en Santo Domingo." Paper presented at the First Congress of Dominican Sociology, Santo Domingo.

Echeverría, Rafael. 1983. "Empleo Público en América Latina." Employment
    Research Collection No. 26. Santiago: PREALC.
ECLAC (Economic Commission for Latin America and the Caribbean). 1989.
    "The Dynamics of Social Deterioration in Latin America and the
    Caribbean in the 1980s." LC/G 1557. Paper for Regional Prepara-
    tory Meeting, San José, Costa Rica. Santiago: ECLAC.
EPOC (Equity Policy Center). 1985. "Final Report: Utilizing Street Food Trade
    in Development Programming." Prepared for the U.S. Agency for
    International Development and the Equity Policy Center.
Escobar, Agustín. 1988. "The Rise and Fall of an Urban Labour Market: Eco-
    nomic Crisis and the Fate of Small Workshops in Guadalajara,
    Mexico." Bulletin of Latin American Research 7, no. 2: 183–205.
————. 1986. Por el sudor de su frente. Guadalajara: Jalisco College and CIESAS.
————, and Bryan R. Roberts. 1989. "Urban Stratification, the Middle Classes,
    and Economic Change in Mexico." Texas Papers on Mexico, 89–04,
    University of Texas at Austin.
Escobar de Pabón, Silvia. 1990. Crisis, Política Económica y Dinámica de los Sec-
    tores Semiempresarial y Familiar: La Paz, Cochabamba, Santa Cruz,
    1985–1989. La Paz: CEDLA.
Fadul, Miguel. 1990. "Colombia: A Collaborative Effort to Serve the Urban
    Informal Sector." In The Critical Connection: Governments, Private
    Institutions, and the Informal Sector in Latin America, ed. Katherine
    Stearns and María Otero, pp. 45–71. Cambridge: ACCION Inter-
    national.
Fajardo, José Carlos. 1990. "'El Otro Sendero' al Trasluz." Socialismo y Partici-
    pación 49: 47–61.
Farbman, Michael, ed. 1981. The PISCES Studies: Assisting the Smallest Economic
    Activities of the Urban Poor. Washington, D.C.: United States
    Agency for International Development (USAID).
Feldman, Shelley. 1991. "Still Invisible: Women in the Informal Sector." In
    Women and Development Annual, vol. 2, pp. 59–86. Boulder: West-
    view Press.
Felix, David. 1986. "Import Substitution and Late Industrialization: Latin
    America and Asia Compared." Working Paper No. 97, Depart-
    ment of Economics, Washington University, St. Louis.
Ferguson, Adam. 1767. An Essay on the History of Civil Society. Edinburgh: A.
    Kincaid and J. Bell.
Fernández-Kelly, María Patricia. 1983. For We Are Sold I and My People: Women
    and Industry in Mexico's Frontier. Albany: State University of New
    York Press.
————, and Anna M. García. 1988. "Economic Restructuring in the United
    States: Hispanic Women in the Garment and Electronics Indus-
    tries." In Women and Work: An Annual Review, Volume 3, ed. Bar-
    bara Gutek, Ann Stromberg, and Laurie Larwood, pp. 49–65.
    Beverly Hills, Calif.: Sage Publications.
Fields, Gary S., and Henry Wan. 1986. "Wage-Setting Institutions and Eco-

nomic Growth." Paper presented at the Conference on the Role of Institutions in Economic Development, Cornell University.

Fishlow, Albert. 1986. "Latin American Adjustment to the Oil Shocks of 1973 and 1979." In *Latin American Political Economy*, ed. Jonathan Hartlyn and Samuel A. Morley, pp. 54–84. Boulder, Colo.: Westview Press.

Fortuna, Juan Carlos, and Suzana Prates. 1989. "Informal Sector Versus Informalized Labor Relations in Uruguay." In *The Informal Economy: Studies in Advanced and Less Developed Countries*, ed. Alejandro Portes, Manuel Castells, and Lauren Benton, pp. 78–94. Baltimore: Johns Hopkins University Press.

Fowler, D. A. 1978. "The Informal Sector of Freetown (Sierra Leone)." Working Paper No. 26, Urbanisation and Employment Programme, WEP 2–29. Geneva: ILO.

Franks, Jeffrey R. 1991. "Sector Informal y Crecimiento Económico en Bolivia." *Informe Confidencial* 67 (November): 1–97.

———. 1989. "Unravelling the Riddle of the Informal Sector: A Survey." Harvard University–World Institute of Development Economic Research, unpublished.

———. 1987. "Economic Stabilization in Peru: 1985–87." Unpublished M.Sc. paper, Oxford University, June.

Frey, Bruno S. 1984. "Hidden Economy as an 'Unobserved Variable'." *European Economic Review* 26, nos. 1–2: 33–53.

———, and Hannelore Weck. 1983. "Estimating the Shadow Economy: A 'Naive' Approach." *Oxford Economic Papers* 35, no. 1: 23–44.

FUDECO. 1986. *Modalidades de ocupación e ingresos en sectores sociales de bajos ingresos de la ciudad de Barquisimeto*. Barquisimeto, Venezuela: FUDECO.

Fundación Paraguaya de Cooperación y Desarrollo. 1988. "Memoria y Balance: Cuarto Ejercicio, 31 de Diciembre de 1988." Asunción: Fundación Paraguaya.

Gabayet, Luisa. 1989. "Women in Transnational Industry: The Case of the Electronic Industry in Guadalajara, Mexico." Texas Papers on Mexico, Mexican Center, University of Texas at Austin.

García, Brígida. 1988. *Desarrollo económico y absorción de fuerza de trabajo en México: 1950–1980*. Mexico City: El Colegio de Mexico.

———, Humberto Muñoz, and Orlandina de Oliveira. 1981. "Migration, Family Context and Labour-Force Participation in Mexico City." In *Why People Move*, ed. Jorge Balán, pp. 211–229. Paris: UNESCO.

———, and Orlandina de Oliveira. 1990. "Work, Fertility, Women's Status in Mexico." Paper presented at Xll World Congress of Sociology, Madrid.

GEMINI. 1990–. *GEMINI Newsletter*. Washington, D.C.: GEMINI.

Gereffi, Gary. 1989. "Rethinking Development Theory: Insights from East Asia and Latin America." *Sociological Forum* 4, no. 4: 505–533.

———. 1987. "Industrial Restructuring in Latin America and East Asia." Paper presented at the Conference on Taiwan: A Newly-Industrialized Society, National Taiwan University, Taipei.

Gerry, Chris. 1978a. "Petty Production and Capitalist Production in Dakar: The Crisis of the Self-Employed." *World Development* 6, nos. 9–10: 1147–1160.

————. 1978b. "Employment and Income Stability in the Gambling Sector: A Study of Lottery-Ticket Selling and Allied Occupations in Cali, Colombia." Unpublished paper, Swansea Centre for Development Studies, University College of Swansea.

————. 1974. "Petty Producers and the Urban Economy: A Case Study of Dakar." Working Paper No. 8, Urbanization and Employment Programme, WEP 2–19. Geneva: ILO.

————, and Chris Birkbeck. 1979. "The Petty Commodity Producer in Third World Cities: Petit Bourgeois or Disguised Proletarian?" In *The Petite Bourgeoisie: Comparative Studies of the Uneasy Stratum*, ed. Brian Elliott and Frank Bechhofer, pp. 121–154. New York: Macmillan.

Ghersi, Enrique. 1991. "El otro sendero o la revolución de los informales." In *Economía Informal*, ed. Gustavo Márquez and Carmen Portela, pp. 43–64. Caracas: Ediciones IESA.

Giménez, Martha. 1990. "The Dialectics of Waged and Unwaged Work: Waged Work, Domestic Labor and Household Survival in the United States." In *Work Without Wages: Comparative Studies of Domestic Labor and Self Employment Within Capitalism*, ed. Jane Collins and Martha Giménez, pp. 25–45. Albany: State University of New York Press.

Ginsburgh, V., P. Michel, F. Padoa Schioppa, and P. Pestieau. 1985. "Macroeconomic Policy in the Presence of an Irregular Sector." In *The Economics of the Shadow Economy*, ed. Wulf Gaertner and Alois Wenig, pp. 194–216. Berlin: Springer-Verlag.

Goldmark, Susan, and Jay Rosengard. 1985. "A Manual for Evaluation of Small Scale Enterprise Development Projects." AID Program Design and Evaluation Methods Report No. 6. Washington, D.C.: United States Agency for International Development (USAID).

————, et al. 1982. "Aid to Entrepreneurs: An Evaluation of the Partnership for Productivity Project in Upper Volta." Washington, D.C.: Development Alternatives.

Gómez, Martha Isabel de. 1984. "Efectos de la Capacitación Técnica sobre la Mujer en el Mercado de Trabajo en Colombia." Report prepared by the International Center for Research on Women (ICRW) for a study on technical assistance.

Gómez, Arelis, and Vanessa Saladín. 1987. *Programa de Financiamiento a Microempresas y Grupos Solidarios: Informe de Evaluación de Impacto*. Santo Domingo: Asociación Para el Desarrollo de Microempresas (ADEMI).

González, Bernardo, Juan Luís Hernández, and Gabrielle Merz. 1988. "Consumo y alimentación en los estratos pobres. Criterios para instrumentar políticas compensatorias del ingreso." Mimeo. Caracas: ILDIS.

González Chairi, José María. 1984. "Capacitación y Desarrollo de la Población de las Areas Suburbanas de Guayaquil." Report prepared for the International Labour Office. Guayaquil, Ecuador: CADESURB.

González de la Rocha, Mercedes. 1988. "Economic Crisis, Domestic Reorganization and Women's Work in Guadalajara, Mexico." *Bulletin of Latin American Research* 7, no. 2: 207–223.

———. 1987. "Crisis, economía doméstica y trabajo femenino en Guadalajara." Paper presented at the Colloquim on Women's Studies, Mexico City, Colegio de Mexico–PIEM.

———. 1986. "Los recursos de la pobreza: Familias de bajos ingresos en Guadalajara, México." Working Paper, Colegio de Jalisco/CIESAS/SPP.

Gregory, Peter. 1985. *The Myth of Market Failure.* Baltimore: Johns Hopkins University Press.

Grompone, Romeo. 1985. *Talleristas y Vendedores Ambulantes en Lima.* Lima: DESCO.

Grunchy, Allan G. 1987. *The Reconstruction of Economics: An Analysis of the Fundamentals of Institutional Economics.* New York: Greenwood Press.

Guzmán, María Margarita, and María Clemencia Castro. 1989. "From a Women's Guarantee Fund to a Bank for Microenterprise: Process and Results." In *Women's Ventures: Assistance to the Informal Sector in Latin America,* ed. Marguerite Berger and Mayra Buvinič, pp. 185–200. West Hartford, Conn.: Kumarian Press.

Haggblade, Steven. 1989. "Agricultural Technology and Farm-Nonfarm Growth Linkages." *Agricultural Economics* 3, no. 4: 345–364.

———, Stephen P. Davies, James J. Boomgard, and Donald C. Mead. 1990. "A Subsector Approach to Small Enterprise Promotion and Research." Unpublished manuscript.

———, Peter B. Hazell, and James Brown. 1989. "Farm-Nonfarm Linkages in Sub-Saharan Africa." *World Development* 17, no. 8: 1173–1201.

———, Carl Liedholm, and Donald Mead. 1986. "The Effect of Policy and Policy Reforms on Non-Agricultural Enterprises and Employment in Developing Countries: A Review of Past Experiences." EEPA Discussion Paper No. 1. Cambridge, Mass.: Harvard Institute for International Development and Discussion Paper No. 1. Washington, D.C.: United States Agency for International Development (USAID).

Harrison, Lawrence. 1985. *Underdevelopment Is a State of Mind: The Latin American Case.* Lanham, Md.: University Press of America.

Hart, Keith. 1973. "Informal Income Opportunities and Urban Employment in Ghana." *Journal of Modern African Studies* 11, no. 1: 61–89.

———. 1971. "Small Scale Entrepreneurs in Ghana and Development Planning." *Journal of Development Planning* (July).

Hartlyn, Jonathan, and Samuel A. Morley. 1986. "Bureaucratic-Authoritarian Regimes in Comparative Perspective." In *Latin American Political*

Economy, ed. Jonathan Hartlyn and Samuel A. Morley, pp. 38–53. Boulder, Colo.: Westview Press.

Hatch, John, and Arelis Gómez. 1989. *An Evaluation of the Microbusiness Promotion Project in Guatemala*. Bethesda, Md.: Development Alternatives.

Havel, Vaclav. 1992. "A Dream for Czechoslovakia." *New York Review of Books* 39, no. 12: 8–13.

Helzner, Judith, and the Overseas Education Fund. 1982. "Improvement of the Socio-Economic Conditions of Low-Income Women Age 25–50 through Strengthening of the Union of Moroccan Women." Prepared for the Union of Moroccan Women (des Femmes Morocaines) and OEF.

Honadel, George, and John P. Hannah. 1982. "Management Performance for Rural Development: Packaged Training or Capacity Building." *Public Administration and Development* 2: 295–307.

Hopenhayn, Martín. 1987. "Nuevos enfoques sobre el sector informal." *Pensamiento Iberoaméricano* 12 (July–December): 423–428.

Hossfeld, Karen J. 1990. "Their Logic Against Them: Contradictions in Sex, Race, and Class in Silicon Valley." In *Women Workers and Global Restructuring* ed. Kathryn Ward, pp. 149–178. Ithaca, N.Y.: ILR Press, School of Labor Relations, Cornell University.

Hurtado, María Elena, and Anita Coulson. 1988. "The Smuggling Boom." *South* (June): 15–17.

ILD (Instituto Libertad y Democracia). 1990a. "Anteproyecto de la Ley de Democratización de las Decisiones de Gobierno, y Resúmen Explicativo." Lima: ILD.

———. 1990b. "A Reply." *World Development* 18, no. 1: 137–145.

———. 1989a. "Estimación de la Magnitud de la Actividad Económica Informal en el Perú." Lima: ILD.

———. 1989b. "La Simplificación Administrativa: Primer Paso hacia la Desburocratización." ILD Working Paper 4. Lima: ILD.

———. 1987. "Las Leyes de Estabilidad Laboral y sus Efectos Económicos." Working Paper No. 2. Lima: ILD.

ILO (International Labour Office). 1989. *World Labour Report, 1989*. Geneva: International Labour Office.

———. 1972. *Employment, Incomes and Equality: A Strategy for Increasing Productive Employment in Kenya*. Geneva: ILO.

———. 1970. *Towards Full Employment: A Programme for Colombia*. Geneva: ILO.

IMF (International Monetary Fund). 1987. Theoretical Aspects of the Design of Fund-Supported Adjustment Programs, Occasional Paper No. 55. Washington, D.C.: IMF.

INEGI. 1989a. *Información Oportuna*. Aguascalientes, Mexico: INEGI.

———. 1989b. "Encuesta Piloto sobre el Sector Informal: Documento Metodológico, Presentación de Tabulados y Breve Análisis." Mimeo, Inegi/Orstom, Mexico.

———. 1988. *Indicadores Trimestrales de Empleo—Guadalajara, México y Monterrey, Enero-Marzo de 1987*. Aguascalientes, Mexico: INEGI.

Inter-American Development Bank. 1986. "Internal Document on the Financial Status of the Small and Microenterprise program." Cali, Colombia: IDB.

———. 1984. *Ex-Post Evaluation of Two Microenterprise Projects: Small Projects Program. Colombia.* Washington, D.C.: IDB Operations Evaluation Office.

Jatobá, Jorge. 1988. "Latin America Labour Market Research: A State of the Art." Geneva: Discussion Papers, International Institute for Labour Studies.

Jelin, Elizabeth. 1978. "La mujer y el mercado de trabajo urbano." *Estudios CEDES* 1, no. 6.

Jenkins, Jerry. 1988. "Informal Economies: Emerging from Underground" and "Transforming the Formal Sector and Transcending Informality." In *Beyond the Informal Sector: Including the Excluded in Developing Countries*, ed. Jerry Jenkins, pp. 1–14 and 221–233. San Francisco: ICS Press.

Jolly, Richard, and Rolph ver der Hoeven, eds. 1991. "Adjustment with a Human Face—Record and Relevance." *World Development* 19, no. 12: 1801–1864.

Jones, Christine, and Michael Roemer, eds. 1989. "Parallel Markets in Developing Countries." *World Development* 17, no. 12.

Junguito, Roberto, and Carlos Caballero. 1982. "Illegal Trade Transactions and the Underground Economy in Colombia." In *The Underground Economy in the United States and Abroad*, ed. Vito Tanzi, pp. 285–313. Lexington, Mass.: Lexington Books.

Kennedy, P. 1979. "Workers and Employers in the Sphere of Petty Commodity Production in Accra: Towards Proletarianization," BSA Development Studies Working Paper. London: British Sociological Association.

Khundker, Nasreen. 1988. "The Fuzziness of the Informal Sector: Can We Afford to Throw out the Baby with the Bath Water? (A Comment)." *World Development* 16, no. 10: 1263–1265.

Kilby, Peter. 1985. "Breaking the Entrepreneurial Bottleneck in the Late-Developing Countries: Is There a Useful Role for Government?" Paper presented at the World Conference on Microenterprises, Washington, D.C., Committee of Donor Agencies for Small Enterprise Development.

———. 1979. "Evaluating Technical Assistance." *World Development* 7, no. 3: 309–329.

———, and David D'Zmura. 1985. *Searching for Benefits.* AID Evaluation Special Study No. 28. Washington, D.C.: United States Agency for International Development (USAID).

Killick, Tony. 1989. "Economic Development and the Adaptive Economy." ODI Working Paper No. 31.

Kindervatter, Suzanne. 1983. "Women Working Together." Washington, D.C.: Overseas Education Fund.

King, Kenneth J. 1979. "Petty Production in Nairobi: The Social Context of Skill Acquisition and Occupational Differentiation." In *Casual Work and Poverty in Third World Cities*, ed. Ray Bromley and Chris Gerry, pp. 217–228. New York: Wiley.

———. 1975. "Skill Acquisition in the Informal Sector of an African Economy: The Kenya Case." *Journal of Development Studies* 11, no. 2: 108–122.

———. 1974. "Kenya's Informal Machine-Makers: A Study of Small-Scale Industry in Kenya's Emergent Society." *World Development* 2, no. 4–5: 108–122.

Klein, Joyce, Kathryn Keeley, and Rick Carlisle. 1991. "Treading Through the Micromaze." *Entrepreneurial Economy Review:* 3–10, 26.

Kochan, Thomas A., and Willis Nordlund. 1988. "Labor Standards and Competitiveness: An Historical Evolution." Paper presented at the Symposium on Labor Standards and Development organized by the U.S. Department of Labor, Georgetown University.

Korten, David C. 1987. "Third Generation NGO Strategies: A Key to People-Centered Development." *World Development* 15 (Supplement): 145–159.

Lacabana, Miguel. 1990. "La precariedad laboral en el mercado de trabajo urbano: Las inserciones laborales de los habitantes de los barrios segregados de Venezuela." Paper presented in the seminar on Flexibilization of the Labor Force. Caracas: ILDIS.

Langdon, Steven. 1975. "Multinational Corporations, Taste Transfer and Underdevelopment: A Case Study from Kenya." *Review of African Political Economy* 2 :12–34.

Lanzetta de Pardo, Mónica, Gabriel Murillo Castaño, and Alvaro Triana Soto. 1989. "The Articulation of Formal and Informal Sectors in the Economy of Bogota, Colombia." In *The Informal Economy: Studies in Advanced and Less Developed Countries*, ed. Alejandro Portes, Manuel Castells, and Lauren Benton, pp. 95–110. Baltimore: Johns Hopkins University Press.

Lebergott, Stanley. 1964. *Manpower in Economic Growth: The American Record Since 1800*. New York: McGraw-Hill.

LeBrun, Olivier, and Chris Gerry. 1975. "Petty Producers and Capitalism." *Review of African Political Economy* 3: 20–32.

Lembert, Marcella, and Isabel Nieves. 1986. "Technical Assistance and Labor Force Participation of Women in Latin America: A Comparative Review." Report prepared for the Ford Foundation and the International Development Research Center.

Levitsky, Jacob, ed. 1989. *Microenterprises in Developing Countries: Papers and Proceeding of an International Conference*. London: Intermediate Technology Publications.

———. 1988. "Summary Report of the World Conference on Microenterprises." Washington, D.C: Committee of Donor Agencies for Small Enterprise Development.

Lewis, W. Arthur. 1954. "Economic Development With Unlimited Supplies of

Labour." *The Manchester School of Economic and Social Studies* 22: 139–191.

Leys, Colin. 1975. *Underdevelopment in Kenya: The Political Economy of Neo-Colonialism 1964–1971*. Berkeley: University of California Press.

Liedholm, Carl. 1990. "The Dynamics of Small-Scale Industry in Africa and the Role of Policy." GEMINI Paper No. 2. Washington, D.C.: GEMINI.

———. 1989. "Small Enterprise Dynamics and the Evolving Role of Informal Finance." Paper prepared for Conference on Informal Financial Markets in Development, Washington, D.C.

———, and Peter Kilby. 1989. "Nonfarm Activities in the Rural Economy." In *The Balance Between Industry and Agriculture in Economic Development*, Vol. 2, ed. J. Williamson and V. Panchamukhi. New York: St. Martin Press.

———, and Donald Mead. 1987. "Small Scale Industries in Developing Countries: Empirical Evidence and Policy Implications." MSU International Development Paper No. 9, Michigan State University.

———, and Joan Parker. 1989. "Small Scale Manufacturing Growth in Africa: Initial Evidence." MSU International Development Working Paper No. 33, Michigan State University.

Light, Ivan, and Edna Bonacich. 1988. *Immigrant Entrepreneurs*. Berkeley: University of California Press.

Lim, Linda. 1988. "Labor Standards and Development in Newly Industrializing Countries: The Case of Singapore." Paper presented at the Symposium on Labor Standards and Development organized by the U.S. Department of Labor, Georgetown University.

Lipton, Michael. 1980. *Manufacturing in the Backyard: Case Studies of Accumulation and Employment in Small Scale Brazilian Industry*. London: Frances Pinter.

Little, Ian M. D., Dipak Mazumdar, and John M. Page, Jr. 1987. *Small Manufacturing Enterprises: A Comparative Analysis of India and Other Economies*. London: Oxford University Press.

Llona, Agustín. 1983. "Pobreza, satisfacción de necesidades básicas e inserción productiva." Document SIU-13, mimeo. Caracas: CORDIPLAN-OIT.

Lomnitz, Larissa. 1978. "Mechanisms of Articulation Between Shantytown Settlers and the Urban System." *Urban Anthropology* 7: 185–205.

Long, Norman, and Bryan R. Roberts. 1985. *Miners, Peasants and Entrepreneurs*. Cambridge: Cambridge University Press.

———, and Bryan R. Roberts, eds. 1978. *Peasant Cooperation and Capitalist Expansion in the Highlands of Peru*. Austin, Tex.: University of Texas Press.

López Castaño, Hugo. 1984. "El Papel del Sector Informal: La Experiencia Colombiana." In *The Urban Informal Sector: Recent Trends in Research and Theory*. Conference Proceedings, pp. 139–159. Baltimore: Department of Sociology, The Johns Hopkins University.

Lycette, Margaret, and Karen White. 1989. "Improving Women's Access to Credit in Latin America and the Caribbean: Policy and Project Recommendations." In *Women's Ventures: Assistance to the Informal*

Sector in Latin America, ed. Marguerite Berger and Mayra Buvinič, pp. 19–44. West Hartford, Conn.: Kumarian Press.

Lynton, Rolf, and Udai Pareek. 1978. *Training for Development*. West Hartford, Conn.: Kumarian Press.

MacEwen Scott, Alison. 1991. *Class and Gender in the Andes*. Unpublished manuscript, Department of Sociology, University of Essex.

———. 1979. "Who Are the Self-Employed?" In *Casual Work and Poverty in Third World Cities*, ed. Ray Bromley and Chris Gerry, pp. 105–132. New York: Wiley.

———. 1977. "Notes on the Theoretical Status of Petty Commodity Production," Unpublished paper, University of Essex.

Maddala, G. S. 1977. *Econometrics*. New York: McGraw-Hill.

Main, Jeremy. 1989. "An Interview with Hernando de Soto" and "The Informal Route to Prosperity." *International Health and Development* 1, no. 1: 10–17.

Malloy, James. 1979. *The Politics of Social Security in Brazil*. Pittsburgh: University of Pittsburgh Press.

Management Systems International. 1988. "A Program Appraisal of Guatemala's Urban Microenterprise Multiplier System (SIMME)." Prepared for Office of Private Sector Programs of the U.S. Agency for International Development/Guatemala.

Mangin, William. 1967. "Squatter Settlements." *Scientific American* 217, no. 4: 21–29.

Márquez, Carlos. 1988. "La ocupación informal urbana en México: Un enfoque regional." Working document, Friedrich Ebert Foundation, Mexico City.

Márquez, Gustavo. 1991. "Venezuela. An Assessment of the Situation of Women." Report prepared for the World Bank. Caracas: IESA.

———. 1990. "Wage Differentials and Labor Market Equilibrium in Venezuela." Doctoral dissertation, Boston Univerity, Boston.

———, and Carmen Portela. 1991. "Los informales urbanos en Venezuela: ¿Pobres o eficientes?" In *La Economía Informal*, ed. Gustavo Márquez and Carmen Portela, pp. 1–41. Caracas: Institute for Advanced Management Studies (IESA).

Marroquín, Escoto, and Jorge Rolando. 1987. *El Sector Informal: Estudio Sobre el Sector Informal de Producción y Servicios en el Area Urbana Central de Guatemala*. Guatemala: Fundación FADES de Centroamérica.

Mars, Z. 1977. "Small-Scale Industry in Kerala," IDS Discussion Paper No. 105. Sussex: Institute of Development Studies, University of Sussex.

Marshall, Adrianna. 1987. "Non-Standard Employment Practices in Latin America." Discussion Paper OP/06/1987, International Institute for Labour Studies, Geneva.

Matos Mar, José. 1984. *Desborde Popular y Crisis del Estado*. Lima: Instituto de Estudios Peruanos.

Mazumdar, Dipak. 1976. "The Urban Informal Sector." *World Development* 4, no. 8: 655–679.

McDonald, Ian, and Robert Solow. 1985. "Wages and Employment in a Segmented Labor Market." *Quarterly Journal of Economics* 100, no. 4: 1115–1141.

McKean, Cressida S. 1987. "Small-Scale Manufacturing: The Potential and Limitations for Growth—the Case of Wood Products in Ecuador." Master's thesis, Institute of Development Studies, Sussex, United Kingdom.

———. 1985. "Evaluation of the Small and Medium Enterprise Project in the Philippines." Falls Church, Va.: Pragma Corporation.

McKee, Katherine. 1989. "Microlevel Strategies for Supporting Livelihoods, Employment, and Income Generation of Poor Women in the Third World: The Challenge of Significance." *World Development* 17, no. 7: 993–1006.

McNeil, D. 1983. "The Informal Sector: Concept and Method." Unpublished paper.

Mead, Donald, B. R. Bolnick, and R. C. Young. 1989. "Strategies for Small and Medium Enterprises in Malawi." Report submitted to USAID/ Malawi.

Medici, André Cezar. 1989. "Saude e crise na America Latina (impactos sociais e politicas de ajuste)." *Revista de Administración Pública* 23, no. 3: 7–98.

Mesa-Lago, Carmelo. 1990. "Protección del sector informal en América Latina y el Caribe por la seguridad social o medios alternativos." In *Más Allá de la Regulación: El sector informal en América Latina*, ed. PREALC, pp. 277–318. Santiago: PREALC.

———. 1986. "Social Security and Development in Latin America." *CEPAL Review* 28: 135–150.

———. 1983. "Social Security and Extreme Poverty in Latin America." *Journal of Development Economics* 12: 83–110.

———. 1978. *Social Security in Latin America: Pressure Groups, Stratification and Inequality*. Pittsburgh: University of Pittsburgh Press.

Mezzera, Jaime. 1991. "El excedente de oferta laboral: Teoría y propuestas de política." In *Economía Informal*, ed. Gustavo Márquez and Carmen Portela, pp. 65–96. Caracas: Ediciones IESA.

———. 1990. "Gasto del sector moderno e ingresos en el sector informal: Segmentación y relaciones económicas." In *Ventas Informales: Relaciones con el Sector Moderno*, ed. PREALC, pp. 1–41. Santiago: PREALC.

———. 1989. "Excess Labor Supply in the Urban Informal Sector: An Analytical Framework." In *Women's Ventures: Assistance to the Informal Sector in Latin America*, ed. Marguerite Berger and Mayra Buvinič, pp. 45–64. West Hartford, Conn.: Kumarian Press.

———. 1987. "Abundancia como efecto de la escasez: Oferta y demanda en el mercado laboral urbano." *Nueva Sociedad* 90: 106–117.

Michon, Francois. 1987. "Time and Flexibility: Working Time in the Debate on Flexibility." *Labor and Society* 12, no. 1: 3–17.

Middleton, Alan. 1979. "Poverty, Production and Power: The Case of Petty Manufacturing in Ecuador." Dissertation, University of Sussex.

Mingione, Enzo. 1991. *Fragmented Societies: A Sociology of Economic Life Beyond the Market Paradigm.* Oxford: Basil Blackwell.

Möller, Alois. 1979. "Los Vendedores Ambulantes en Lima." In *El Subempleo en América Latina,* ed. Victor Tokman and Emilio Klein, pp. 415–471. Buenos Aires: El Cid Editores.

Moser, Caroline O.N. 1984. "The Informal Sector Reworked: Viability and Vulnerability in Urban Development." *Regional Development Dialogue* 5, no. 2: 135–178.

——. 1982. "A Home of One's Own: Squatter Housing Strategies in Guayaquil, Ecuador." In *Urbanisation in Contemporary Latin America,* ed. Alan Gilbert, pp. 159–190. London: Wiley.

——. 1980. "Why the Poor Remain Poor: The Experience of Bogotá Market Traders in the 1970s." *Journal of Interamerican Studies and World Affairs* 22.

——. 1978. "Informal Sector or Petty Commodity Production: Dualism or Dependence in Urban Development?" *World Development* 6: 1041–1064.

Mosley, Paul. 1978. "Implicit Models and Policy Recommendations: Policy Towards the 'Informal Sector' in Kenya." *IDS Bulletin* 9, no. 3: 3–10.

Murphy, Martin F. 1990. "The Need for a Reevaluation of the Concept Informal Sector: The Dominican Case." In *The Informal Economy: Monographs in Economic Anthropology,* ed. M. Estelle Smith. Washington, D.C.: University Press of America.

Mussa, Michael. 1984. "The Adjustment Process and the Timing of Trade Liberalization." NBER Working Paper No. 1458.

Ngirabatware, Augustin, Leonidas Murembya, and Donald Mead. 1988. "Large Private Manufacturing Firms in Rwanda: Current Situation and Policy Impact." Draft paper. E. Lansing: Michigan State University.

Nihan, Georges, and Robert Jourdain. 1978. "The Modern Informal Sector in Nouakchott." *International Labour Review* 117, no. 6: 709–719.

North, Douglass C. 1990. *Institutions, Institutional Change, and Economic Performance.* New York: Cambridge University Press.

——. 1981. *Structure and Change in Economic History.* New York: W. W. Norton.

——, and Robert P. Thomas. 1973. *The Rise of the Western World.* Cambridge: Cambridge University Press.

Olivares, Mirtha. 1990. "Evaluación de Impacto Sobre los Usuarios de CEAPE, ADIM y Banco de la Mujer de Salvador." Report presented to UNICEF.

Olson, Mancur. 1982. *The Rise and Decline of Nations: Economic Growth, Stagflation, and Social Rigidities.* New Haven, Conn.: Yale University Press.

——. 1965. *The Logic of Collective Action: Public Goods and the Theory of Groups.* Cambridge, Mass.: Harvard University Press.

Osborne, David, and Ted Gaebler. 1992. *Reinventing Government*. Reading, Mass.: Addison-Wesley.

Otero, María. 1989. "Solidarity Group Programs: A Working Methodology for Enhancing the Economic Activities of Women in the Informal Sector." In *Women's Ventures: Assistance to the Informal Sector in Latin America*, ed. Marguerite Berger and Mayra Buvinič, pp. 83–101. West Hartford, Conn.: Kumarian Press.

———. 1988. "Micro-Enterprise Assistance Programs: Their Benefits, Costs, and Sustainability." Discussion Papers Series No. 2. Cambridge: ACCION International.

———. 1986. *The Solidarity Group Concept: Its Characteristics and Significance for the Urban Informal Sector*. New York: Private Agencies Cooperating Together.

———, and Robert Blayney. 1984. "An Evaluation of the Dominican Development Foundation's Program for the Development of Microenterprises (PRODEME)." Report prepared for USAID/Dominican Republic.

Padrón, Marisela, Pedro Castro, Hans Neumann, and Jesús E. Rodríguez. 1991. "La economía informal: ¿Qué hacer?" In *Economía Informal*, ed. Gustavo Márquez and Carmen Portela, pp. 139–148. Caracas: Ediciones IESA.

Paine, Thomas. 1915. *The Rights of Man*. London: J. M. Dent.

Pantelides, Edith. 1976. "Estudios de la población femenina economicamente activa en América Latina, 1950–1970, Serie C." Paper No. 161. Santiago: CELADE.

Paul, Samuel. 1988. "Governments and Grassroots Organizations: From Co-Existence to Collaboration." In *Strengthening the Poor: What Have We Learned?*, ed. John P. Lewis, pp. 61–71. New Brunswick, N.J.: Transaction Books.

PCP (Partido Comunista del Perú). 1989. *Entrevista al Presidente Gonzalo*. Lima: Ediciones Bandera Roja.

Peattie, Lisa R. 1990. "Real-World Economics." *Hemisphere* (Fall): 32–34.

———. 1987. "An Idea in Good Currency and How It Grew: The Informal Sector." *World Development* 15, no. 7: 851–860.

———. 1981. "What Is to Be Done with the 'Informal Sector': A Case Study of Shoe Manufacturers in Colombia." Manuscript, Department of City and Regional Planning, MIT.

Pedrero Nieto, Mercedes. 1990. "Evolución de la participación económica femenina en las ochenta." *Revista Mexicana de Sociología* 52, no. 1: 133–149.

Pérez Sáinz, Juan Pablo. 1991. "Informalidad urbana en América Latina: Enfoques y Problemáticas." Unpublished paper, FLACSO, Guatemala.

———. 1989. *Respuestas Silenciosas. Proletarización urbana y reproducción de la fuerza de trabajo en América Latina*. Caracas: Nueva Sociedad.

———, and Rafael Menjívar Larín. 1991. *Informalidad Urbana en Centroamerica*. Caracas: FLACSO.

Pinilla, Susana. 1985. "Experiencias y Perspectivas de la Promoción Empresarial en el SIU: El Caso Peruano." In *El Sector Informal en los Paises Andinos*, ed. Santiago Escobar, pp. 301–26. Quito, Ecuador: ILDIS/CEPESIU.

Pinto, Aníbal. 1965. "Concentración del progreso técnico y de sus frutos en el desarrollo económico latino-americano." *El Trimestre Económico* 32, no. 125: 3–69.

Piore, Michael J. 1988. "Labor Standards and Business Strategies." Paper presented at the Symposium on Labor Standards and Development organized by the U.S. Department of Labor, Georgetown University.

———, and Charles Sabel. 1984. *The Second Industrial Divide*. New York: Basic Books.

Placencia, María Mercedes. 1989. "Training and Credit Programs for Microentrepreneurs: Some Concerns about the Training of Women." In *Women's Ventures: Assistance to the Informal Sector in Latin America*, ed. Marguerite Berger and Mayra Buvinič, pp. 121–131. West Hartford, Conn.: Kumarian Press.

———. 1985. "La Promoción en el SIU Ecuadoriano: El Caso del Programa de Apoyo a la Microempresa en Guayaquil." In *El Sector Informal en los Paises Andinos*, ed. Santiago Escobar, pp. 275–300. Quito, Ecuador: ILDIS/CEPESIU.

PNUD (United Nations Programme for Development). 1988. *Base para una Estrategia y un Programa de Acción Regional*. Working Paper, Regional Project on Poverty Alleviation RLA/86/004, Bogotá.

Polinsky, A. Mitchell. 1989. *An Introduction to Law and Economics*, 2nd ed. Boston: Little, Brown.

Pollack, Molly. 1986. "Poverty and Labour Market in Costa Rica." PREALC Working Paper. Santiago: PREALC.

Portes, Alejandro. 1991. "An Informal Path to Development?" *Hemisphere* (Winter–Spring): 4–5.

———. 1989a. "Latin American Urbanization in the Years of the Crisis." *Latin American Research Review* 24, no. 3: 7–44.

———. 1989b. "La informalidad como parte integral de la economía moderna y no como indicador de atraso: Respuesta a Klein y Tokman." *Estudios Sociológicos de El Colegio de México* 7, no. 20: 369–374.

———. 1984. "Latin American Class Structures: Their Composition and Change During the Last Decades." Occasional Paper 3. Baltimore: Johns Hopkins University.

———. 1983. "The Informal Sector: Definition, Controversy and Relation to National Development." *Population and Development Review* (Summer).

———. 1978. "The Informal Sector and the World Economy: Notes on the Structure of Subsidized Labour." *IDS Bulletin* 9: 35–40.

———, and Lauren Benton. 1987. "Desarrollo industrial y absorción laboral." *Estudios Sociológicos de El Colegio de México* 5, no. 13: 111–137.

———, and Lauren Benton. 1984. "Industrial Development and Labor Absorption: A Reinterpretation." *Population and Development Review* 10: 589–611.

———, Manuel Castells, and Lauren A. Benton. 1989. "Conclusion: The Policy

Implications of Informality." In *The Informal Economy: Studies in Advanced and Less Developed Countries*, ed. Alejandro Portes, Manuel Castells, and Lauren A. Benton, pp. 298–311. Baltimore: Johns Hopkins University Press.

————, and Saskia Sassen-Koob. 1988. "Comparative Material on the Informal Sector in Western Market Economies." Mimeo. Baltimore: The John Hopkins University Press.

————, and Saskia Sassen-Koob. 1987. "Making it Underground: Comparative Material on the Informal Sector in Western Market Economies." *American Journal of Sociology* 93: 30–61.

————, and John Walton. 1981. *Labor, Class and the International System*. Orlando, Fla.: Academic Press.

Posner, Richard A. 1986. *The Economic Analysis of Law*, 3rd ed. Boston: Little, Brown.

Poundstone, William. 1992. *Prisoner's Dilemma*. Garden City, N.Y.: Doubleday.

PREALC (Regional Employment Programme for Latin America and the Caribbean). 1990. *Urbanización y Sector Informal en América Latina, 1960–1980*. Santiago: PREALC.

————. 1988. "La evolución del mercado laboral entre 1980 y 1987." Working Document 328. Santiago: PREALC.

————. 1987a. "El sector informal hoy: El imperativo de actuar." PREALC Document 314. Santiago: PREALC.

————. 1987b. *Pobreza y Mercado de Trabajo en cuatro países: Costa Rica, Venezuela, Chile y Perú*. Santiago: PREALC.

————. 1983. *Empleo y salarios*. Santiago: OIT.

————. 1982. *Mercado de trabajo en cifras 1950–1980*. Santiago: OIT.

————. 1979. "Acceso a recursos y creación de empleos en la pequeña industria Mexicana." Employment Studies No. 17. Santiago: PREALC.

————. 1978. *El sector informal: Funcionamiento y políticas*. Santiago: PREALC.

————. 1976. *The Employment Problem in Latin America*. Santiago: OIT.

Prigogine, Ilya, and Isabelle Stengers. 1984. *Order out of Chaos: Man's New Dialogue with Nature*. New York: Bantam Books.

PRODEM (Fundación para la Promoción y Desarrollo de la Micro-Empresa). 1990. "Financing Proposal for a Commercial Micro-Credit Bank in Bolivia." Bolivia: PRODEM.

Pruegl, Elisabeth. 1989. "The Politics of Micro-Enterprise Development." Paper presented at the meetings of the Association for Women in International Development, Washington, D.C.

Quijano, Aníbal. 1974. "The Marginal Pole of the Economy and the Marginalized Labor Force." *Economy and Society* 3, no. 4: 393–428.

Rahman, Atiur. 1986. "Consciousness Raising Efforts of the Grameen Bank." Unpublished paper. Dhaka, Bangladesh: Institute of Development Studies.

Rakowski, Cathy A. 1991. "Gender, Family, and Economy in a Planned, Industrial City: The Working- and Lower-Class Households of Ciudad Guayana." In *Gender, Family, and Economy: The Triple Overlap*, ed. Rae Lesser Blumberg, pp. 149–172. Newbury Park, Calif.: Sage Publications.

————. 1987. "Desventaja Multiplicada: La mujer en el sector informal." *Nueva Sociedad* 90: 134–146.

————. 1984. "El comportamiento de la mano de obra femenina y masculina en Ciudad Guayana con enfoque especial en el más reciente período de boom y post-boom," Ciudad Guayana, paper prepared for the Corporación Venezolana de Guayuana—CVG, mimeo.

————. 1983. "Estímulos y restricciones para el ingreso de la fuerza de trabajo al sector informal urbano: Los casos de la construcción y del transporte." Document published by CORDIPLAN and the United Nations as part of the Project PNUD/OIT/VEN/82/003. Caracas: Cordiplán and United Nations.

Rangel, Carlos. 1986. *Third World Ideology and Western Reality: Manufacturing Political Myth.* New Brunswick, N.J.: Transaction Books.

Razeto Migliaro, Luís. 1986. *Economía Popular de Solidaridad: Identidad y Proyecto en una Visión Integrada.* Santiago: ICECOOP.

Rees, Martha W., and Arthur D. Murphy. 1990. "Generative and Regulative Issues in Urbanization: To Plan or Not to Plan." *City and Society* 4, no. 2: 107–113.

Reichmann, Rebecca. 1989. "Women's Participation in Two PVO Credit Programs for Microenterprise: Cases from the Dominican Republic and Peru." In *Women's Ventures: Assistance to the Informal Sector in Latin America,* ed. Marguerite Berger and Mayra Buvinič, pp. 132–160. West Hartford, Conn.: Kumarian Press.

————. 1984a. "Women's Participation in ADEMI: The Association for the Development of Microenterprises, Inc." Cambridge: ACCION International/AITEC.

————. 1984b. "Women's Participation in Progreso: A Microenterprise Program Reaching the Smallest Businesses of the Poor in Lima, Peru." Cambridge: ACCION International/AITEC.

Reichmuth, Markus. 1978. "Dualism in Peru: An Investigation into the Interrelationships Between Lima's Informal Clothing Industry and the Formal Sector." Unpublished B. Litt. thesis, Oxford University.

Revere, Elspeth. 1990. "Guatemala: A Thriving Undertaking: Private and Public Programs Serving the Informal Sector." In *The Critical Connection: Governments, Private Institutions, and the Informal Sector in Latin America,* ed. Katherine Stearns and María Otero, pp. 89–109. Cambridge: ACCION International.

————. 1989. "An Impact Evaluation of the Microbusiness Promotion Project, Guatemala." Cambridge: ACCION International.

Rhyne, Elisabeth, and María Otero. 1990. "A Financial System Approach to Micro-Enterprise Development." Paper presented at GEMINI conference on microenterprise finance, Rosslyn, Virginia.

Roberts, Bryan R. 1993. "The Dynamics of Formal Employment in Mexico." In *Work without Protections,* ed. Gregory K. Schoepfle and Jorge Prez-López, pp. 101–125. Washington, D.C.: Bureau of International Labor Affairs, U.S. Department of Labor.

————. 1991. "Introducción." In *Informalidad Urbana en Centroamérica: Entre la acumulación y la subsistencia*, ed. Juan Pablo Pérez Sáinz and Rafael Menjívar Larín, pp. 13–20. San José, Costa Rica: Editorial Nueva Sociedad.

————. 1990. "The Informal Sector in Comparative Perspective." In *Perspectives on the Informal Economy*, ed. M. Estelle Smith, pp. 23–48. Lanham, Md.: University Press of America.

————. 1989a. "Employment Structure, Life Cycle, and Life Chances: Formal and Informal Sectors in Guadalajara." In *The Informal Economy: Comparative Studies in Advanced and Third World Countries*, ed. Alejandro Portes, Manuel Castells, and Lauren Benton, pp. 41–59. Baltimore: Johns Hopkins University Press.

————. 1989b. "The Other Working Class: Uncommitted Labor in Britain, Spain and Mexico." In *Cross-National Research in Sociology*, ed. Melvin L. Kohn, pp. 352–372. Newbury Park, Calif.: Sage Publications.

————. 1978. *Cities of Peasants*. London: Edward Arnold.

————. 1975. "Center and Periphery in the Development Process: The Case of Peru." In *Latin American Urban Research, Volume 5*, ed. Wayne Cornelius and Felicity Trueblood, pp. 77–106. Beverly Hills, Calif.: Sage Publications.

Rodgers, Gerry. 1987. "Labour Markets Mechanisms and Urban Poverty: A Review of Ten Studies." Discussion Paper 7. Geneva: International Institute for Labour Studies.

Rodríguez, Alfredo, Gustavo Riofrio, and Eileen Walsh. 1980. *De Invasores a Invadidos*. Lima: DESCO.

Roldán, Martha. 1985. "Industrial Outworking: Struggles for the Reproduction of Working-Class Families and Gender Subordination." in *Beyond Employment: Household, Gender and Subsistence*, ed. Nanneke Redclift and Enzo Mingione, pp. 248–285. Oxford: Basil Blackwell.

Rossini, R. G. and J. J. Thomas. 1990. "The Size of the Informal Sector in Peru: A Critical Comment on Hernando de Soto's *El Otro Sendero*." *World Development* 18: 125–135.

Rostow, Walter W. 1960. *The Stages of Economic Growth: A Non-Communist Manifesto*. Cambridge: Cambridge University Press.

Rutte, Alberto. 1976. *Simplemente Explotadas: El Mundo de las Empleadas Domésticas en Lima*. Lima: DESCO.

Sabot, R. H. 1988. "Labor Standards in a Small Low-Income Country: Tanzania." Paper presented at the Symposium on Labor Standards and Development organized by the U.S. Department of Labor, Georgetown University.

Safa, Helen I. 1987. "Urbanization, the Informal Economy, and State Policy in Latin America." In *The Capitalist City*, ed. Michael Smith and Joe Feagin, pp. 252–272. Cambridge: Basil Blackwell.

Saldanha, Rosangela, Rosane Mais, and José Marangoni Camargo. 1983. "Emprego e Salario no Sector Publico Federal." Discussion Paper No. 5. Brasilia: SES.

Sánchez León, Abelardo, Julio Calderón, and Paul Guerrero. 1978. *Paradero Final? El Transporte Público en Lima Metropolitana.* Lima: DESCO.

Sanchis, Enric, and José Miñana, eds. 1988. *La Otra Economía: Trabajo Negro y Sector Informal.* Valencia, Spain: Valencian Institute of Research.

Sandbrook, Richard. 1982. *The Politics of Basic Needs: Urban Aspects of Assaulting Poverty in Africa.* Toronto: University of Toronto Press.

Sassen-Koob, Saskia. 1984. "The New Labor Demand in Global Cities." In *Cities in Transformation: Class, Capital, and the State,* ed. Michael P. Smith, pp. 139–171. Beverly Hills, Calif.: Sage Publications.

——. 1983. "Labor Migration and the New Industrial Division of Labor." In *Women, Men, and the International Division of Labor,* ed. June Nash and María Patricia Fernández-Kelly, pp. 175–204. Albany: State University of New York Press.

Schmitz, Hubert. 1982a. "Growth Constraints on Small-Scale Manufacturing in Developing Countries: A Critical Review." *World Development* 10, no. 6: 429–450.

——. 1982b. *Manufacturing in the Backyard: Case Studies on Accumulation and Employment in Small-Scale Brazilian Industries.* London: Frances Pinter.

——. 1977. "Notes on the Theoretical Status of Petty Commodity Production." Unpublished paper.

Schuck, Peter, and Robert E. Litan. 1986. "Regulatory Reform in the Third World: The Case of Peru." *Yale Journal on Regulation* 4, no. 1: 51–78.

Schydlowsky, Daniel M. 1986. "The Tragedy of Lost Opportunity in Peru." In *Latin American Political Economy,* ed. Jonathon Hartlyn and Samuel A. Morley, pp. 217–242. Boulder, Colo.: Westview Press.

SEEP Network. 1991–. "NEXUS." Newsletter published by SEEP, New York, United Nations.

——. 1988. "PVO Programs in Small Enterprise Development: Potential and Limitations," Forum Report. Washington, D.C. and New York: PACT–United Nations.

Selby, Henry, Arthur D. Murphy, and Stephen A. Lorenzen. 1990. *The Mexican Urban Household: Organizing for Self-Defense.* Austin: University of Texas Press.

Sen, Amartya. 1982. *Choice, Welfare and Measurement.* Oxford: Basil Blackwell.

——. 1975. *Employment, Technology, and Development.* Oxford: Oxford University Press.

Serrano-García, Irma. 1984. "The Illusion of Empowerment: Community Development Within a Colonial Context." In *Studies in Empowerment: Steps Toward Understanding and Action,* ed. Julian Rappaport and Robert Hess, pp. 173–200. New York: The Haworth Press.

Sethuraman, S. V., ed. 1981. *The Urban Informal Sector in Developing Countries: Employment, Poverty and Environment.* Geneva: ILO.

——. 1976a. *Jakarta: Urban Development and Employment.* Geneva: ILO.

——. 1976b. "The Urban Informal Sector: Concepts, Measurement and Policy." *International Labour Review* 114, no. 1: 69–81.

Shahin, Wassim N. 1990. "Unorganized Loan Markets and Monetary Policy Instruments." *World Development* 18, no. 2: 325–332.

Sinclair, S. W. 1976. "The 'Intermediate' Sector in the Economy." *Manpower and Unemployment Research* 9, no. 2.

Smith, A. 1981. "The Informal Economy." *Lloyds Bank Review* (July): 45–60.

Smith, Adam. 1776. *An Inquiry into the Nature and Causes of the Wealth of Nations*, 2 vols. London: Strahan and Cadell.

SPP (Secretaría de Programación y Presupuesto). 1979. *La Ocupación Informal en Areas Urbanas 1976.* Mexico City: SPP

Souza, Paulo Renato and Victor E. Tokman. 1976. "The Informal Sector in Latin America." *International Labour Review* 114, no. 3: 355–365.

Standing, Guy. 1986. "Meshing Labour Flexibility with Security: An Answer to British Unemployment?" *International Labour Review* 125: 87–106.

Stanfield, J. R. 1989. "Recent U.S. Marxist Economics in Veblenian Perspective." In *Radical Institutionalism: Contemporary Voices*, ed. William M. Dugger, pp. 83–104. New York: Greenwood Press.

Stearns, Katherine, and María Otero, eds. 1990. *The Critical Connection: Governments, Private Institutions, and the Informal Sector in Latin America.* Cambridge: ACCION International.

Steel, William F. 1977. *Small-Scale Employment and Production in Developing Countries: Evidence from Ghana.* New York: Praeger Books.

————, and Leila Webster. 1990. "Ghana's Small Enterprise Sector Survey of Adjustment Response and Constraints." Industry and Energy Department Working Paper, Washington, D.C.

Stepick, Alex. 1989. "Miami's Two Informal Sectors." In *The Informal Economy: Advanced and Less Developed Countries*, ed. Alejandro Portes, Manuel Castells, and Lauren Benton, pp. 111–131. Baltimore: Johns Hopkins University Press.

Stewart, Frances, ed. 1987. *Macro-Policies for Appropriate Technology in Developing Countries.* Boulder, Colo.: Westview Press.

————. 1978. *Technology and Underdevelopment.* London: MacMillan.

STPS (Secretaría del Trabajo y Previsión Social). 1974. "Bases para una Política de Empleo hacia el Sector Informal o Marginal Urbano en México." Mexico City: PREALC Employment Planning Project Document.

Stretton, Alan. 1979. "Instability of Employment Among Building Industry Labourers in Manila." In *Casual Work and Poverty in Third World Cities*, ed. Ray Bromley and Chris Gerry, pp. 267–282. New York: Wiley.

Sullivan, John D. 1987. "Building Constituencies for Economic Change: Report on the International Conference on the Informal Sector." Washington, D.C.: Center for International Private Enterprise and USAID.

Tanzi, Vito, ed. 1982. *The Underground Economy in the United States and Abroad.* Lexington, Mass.: Lexington Books.

Tarazona-Sevillano, Gabriela. 1990. *Sendero Luminoso and the Threat of Narcoterrorism.* New York: Praeger Books.

Telles, Edward. 1988. "The Consequences of Employment Structure in Brazil: Earnings, Socio-Demographic Characteristics and Metropolitan Differences." Ph.D. dissertation, University of Texas at Austin.

Tendler, Judith. 1988. "The Remarkable Convergence of Fashion on Small Enterprises and the Informal Sector: What Does It Mean for Policy? A Proposal." Mimeo, Massachusetts Institute of Technology.

———. 1987. "What Ever Happened to Poverty Alleviation?" A report prepared for the mid-decade review of the Ford Foundation's Programs on Livelihood, Employment and Income Generation, New York.

———. 1983. "Ventures in the Informal Sector and How They Worked out in Brazil." AID Evaluation Special Study No. 12. Washington, D.C.: United States Agency for International Development (USAID).

———. 1982. "Turning Private Voluntary Organizations into Development Agencies: Questions for Evaluation." AID Program Evaluation Discussion Papers, No. 12. Washington, D.C.: United States Agency for International Development (USAID).

Thomas, George, and John Mayer. 1984. "The Expansion of the State." *Annual Review of Sociology* 10: 461–482.

Thomas, J. J. 1986. "Incorporating Informal Economic Activity into a Macroeconomic Model." Unpublished paper, London School of Economics.

Timberg, Tom. 1978. "Report on the Survey of Small-Scale Industry Units in Bombay." Washington, D.C.: World Bank Development Economic Department.

Timmer, C. Peter. 1980. "Public Policy for Improving Technological Choice," HIID Discussion Paper No. 84.

Tippett, Bruce, and Cressida S. McKean. 1987. "Evaluation of the Impact of A.I.D. on Small Business and Micro-enterprise in the Dominican Republic." Report Prepared for USAID/Dominican Republic. Washington, D.C.: International Science and Technology Institute.

Tokman, Victor E. 1991. "The Informal Sector in Latin America: From Underground to Legality." In *Towards Social Adjustment: Labor Market Issues in Structural Adjustment*, ed. Guy Standing and Victor Tokman, pp. 141–157. Geneva: ILO.

———. 1990. "Sector informal en América Latina: De subterráneo a legal." In *Más Allá de la Regulación: El sector informal en América Latina*, ed. PREALC, pp. 3–23. Santiago: PREALC.

———. 1989. "Policies for a Heterogeneous Informal Sector in Latin America." *World Development* 17, no. 7: 1067–1076.

———. 1987a. "El imperativo de actuar: El sector informal hoy." *Nueva Sociedad* 90 (July–August): 93–105.

———. 1987b. "El sector informal: Quince años después." PREALC Document 316. Santiago: PREALC.

———. 1978. "An Exploration into the Nature of Informal-Formal Sector Relationships." *World Development* 6, nos. 9–10: 1065–1075.

———, and Emilio Klein, eds. 1979. *El subempleo en América Latina*. Buenos Aires: CLACSO/El Cid Editor.

Toledo, Alejandro. 1991. "La economía informal: 'amortiguadora' de la crisis peruana." In *Las Otras Caras de la Sociedad Informal: Una Visión Multidisciplinaria*, ed. Alejandro Toledo and Alain Chanlat, pp. 71–131. Lima: ESAN, HEC.

———, and Alain Chanlat, eds. 1991. *Las Otras Caras de la Sociedad Informal: Una Visión Multidisciplinaria*. Lima: ESAN, HEC.

Trade and Development International. 1985. "Evaluation of Women's World Banking Program in the Dominican Republic and Colombia." Unpublished report.

Turner, John. 1968. "Housing Priorities, Settlement Patterns, and Urban Development in Modernizing Countries." *American Institute of Planners Journal* 34: 354–363.

———. 1967. "Barriers and Channels for Housing Development in Modernizing Countries." *American Institute of Planners Journal* 34: 167–181.

Uchimura, Kasuro. 1991. "Colombia—Informal Sector-Poverty Study." Washington, D.C.: The World Bank.

U.S. Agency for International Development. 1990. "A.I.D. Microenterprise Development Program." Report to Congress (March 30, 1990).

Universidad de San Buenaventura. n.d. "Evaluación de la Asesoría Brindada a Microempresas en el Marco del Convenio Universidad San Buenaventura." Colombia: Fundación Carvajal.

Urriola, Rafael. 1988. *Crítica a una Visión Neoliberal del Sector Informal*. Quito: CEPLAES, Centro de Planificación y Estudios Sociales.

Uthoff, Andras. 1986. "Changes in earnings inequality and labour market segmentation: Metropolitan Santiago 1969–1978." *Journal of Development Studies* 22, no. 2.

Uzzell, J. Douglas. 1990. "Dissonance Between Formal Planners and the Informal Sector: Can Formal Planners Do Bricolage?" *City and Society* 4, no. 2: 114–130.

———. 1987. "A Homegrown Mass Transit System in Lima, Peru: A Case of Generative Planning." *City and Society* 1, no. 1: 6–34.

———. 1980a. "Mixed Strategies and the Informal Sector: Three Faces of Reserve Labor." *Human Organization* 39, no. 1: 40–49.

———. 1980b. "Which Region? Whose Context?: Problems of Defining the Regional Context of Frontera, Texas." In *Cities in a Larger Context*, ed. Thomas W. Collins, pp. 34–52. Athens: University of Georgia Press.

———. 1976. "From Play Lexicons to Disengagement Spheres in Peru's Social Structure." Rice University Program for Development Studies Paper No. 72.

———. 1974a. "Cholos and Bureaus in Lima: Case History and Analysis." *International Journal of Comparative Sociology* 15, no. 3: 23–30.

———. 1974b. "A Strategic Analysis of Social Structure in Lima, Using the Concept of 'Plays'." *Urban Anthropology* 3, no. 1: 34–46.

———. 1972. "Bound for Places I'm Not Known To: Adaptation of Migrants and Residence in Four Irregular Settlements in Lima, Peru." Ph.D. dissertation, University of Texas at Austin.

Valecillos, Hector. 1986. "Proceso y crisis de la inversión privada en Venezuela." Unpublished paper, prepared for Ministry of Labor, Caracas.

Van Wijnbergen, Sweder. 1983. "Credit Policy, Inflation and Growth in a Financially Repressed Economy," *Journal of Development Economics* 13, no. 1: 45–65.

Verdusco, Gustavo. 1990. "Zamora." Unpublished manuscript, Center for Sociological Research, Colegio de Mexico.

von Hayek, Friedrich A. 1973–1979. *Law, Legislation and Liberty.* 3 vols. Chicago: University of Chicago Press.

———. 1960. *The Constitution of Liberty.* Chicago: University of Chicago Press.

Waisman, Carlos. 1987. *Reversal of Development in Argentina.* Princeton, N.J.: Princeton University Press.

Walton, John. 1985. "The Third 'New' International Division of Labour." In *Capital and Labour in the Urbanized World,* ed. John Walton, pp.3–14. London: Sage.

Ward, Kathryn, ed. 1990. *Women Workers and Global Restructuring.* Ithaca, N.Y.: ILR Press, School of Labor Relations, Cornell University.

Watanabe, Susumu. 1971. "Subcontracting, Industrialization and Employment Creation." *International Labour Review* 104, nos. 1–2: 51–76.

Weeks, John. 1975. "Policies for Expanding Employment in the Informal Sector of Developing Countries." *International Labour Review* 111, no. 1: 1–13.

Williamson, Oliver E. 1975. *Markets and Hierarchies: Analysis and Antitrust Implications.* New York: Free Press.

Wilson, Patricia. 1989. "The New Maquiladoras: Flexible Production in Low Wage Regions." *Texas Papers on Mexico* 89–01, Mexican Center, University of Texas at Austin.

Winters, Carolyn. 1991. "Venezuela 1989, Country Report." In *Women's Employment and Pay in Latin America: A Regional Study.* Washington, D.C.: The World Bank.

World Bank. 1990a. *Poverty, World Development Report.* Washington, D.C.: The World Bank.

———. 1990b. *World Development Report.* New York: Oxford University Press.

———. 1989. *World Development Report.* New York: Oxford University Press.

———. 1988. *World Development Report, 1988.* New York: Oxford University Press.

You, Jong-il. 1988. "Labor Standards and Economic Development: The South Korean Experience." Paper presented at the Symposium on Labor Standards and Development organized by the U.S. Department of Labor, Georgetown University.

Yudelman, Sally. 1987. *Hopeful Openings: A Study of Five Women's Development Organizations in Latin America and the Caribbean.* West Hartford, Conn.: Kumarian Press.

Yunus, Muhammad. 1989. "Grameen Bank: Organization and Operation." In *Microenterprises in Developing Countries: Papers and Proceeding of an International Conference*, ed. Jacob Levitsky, pp. 144–161. London: Intermediate Technology.

Contributors

Ray Bromley is Professor of Planning, Geography, and Latin American Studies at the State University of New York at Albany. He has authored numerous articles on urban, regional, and national development issues, and he edited *The Urban Informal Sector: Critical Perspectives* (1979), *Casual Work and Poverty in Third World Cities* (with Chris Gerry, 1979), and *Planning for Small Enterprises in Third World Cities* (1985).

Vanessa Cartaya is Researcher at the Center for Economic and Social Research and Assistant Professor of Urban Studies at the Simón Bolívar University in Caracas. She is author of many books and articles on Venezuela's and Latin America's labor markets and social policy issues, including "Employment and labour conditions in Venezuela's public sector" (in W. van Ginneken ed. *Government and its Employees*, Geneva: ILO, 1991), "The Costs of Becoming Legal for Informal Firms" (in Victor E. Tokman ed. *Beyond Regulation* (Boulder and London: Lynne Rienner, 1992), and *Pobreza en Venezuela* (Caracas: CESAP-CISOR, 1991), co-authored with Yolanda D'Elia.

Orlandina de Oliveira is chairperson of the Center for Sociological Studies at El Colegio de México and co-author of many books and articles on labor markets, family, and gender relations, including *Households and Workers in Mexico*.

Jeffrey R. Franks has recently completed his Ph.D. in Political Economy and Government at Harvard University. He has conducted research and written on the economics and politics of the informal sector in Peru and Bolivia. He is currently an economist at the International Monetary Fund.

Carl Liedholm is Professor of Economics at Michigan State University and the author of numerous articles and books on micro and small enterprises, including *Small Scale Industries in Developing Countries* and

Employment and Growth in Small Scale Industry. He has conducted research on this topic in over two dozen countries in Latin America, Asia, and Africa.

Gustavo A. Márquez is Associate Professor of Labor Economics at the Instituto de Estudios Superiores de Administración (IESA) in Caracas, Venezuela, and author of *Economía Informal* (Ed. IESA, Caracas, 1991), *Gestión fiscal y distribución del ingreso en Venezuela* (Ed. IESA, Caracas, 1993), and compiler of *La regulación del mercado de trabajo en América Latina* (forthcoming, ICEG).

Cressida S. McKean is an economist with the Center for Development Information and Evaluation (CDIE) of the U.S. Agency for International Development (A.I.D.), where she assesses A.I.D.'s experience with development finance institutions, microenterprise development, and trade promotion. Her most recent publication is "Export and Investment Promotion Services: Do They Make a Difference? Assessment Synthesis Report" for A.I.D.

Caroline O. N. Moser is Senior Urban Social Policy Specialist in the Urban Development Division, World Bank. Washington D.C. She has written a number of articles on the informal sector, is co-editor of *Women, Human Settlements and Housing,* and author of *Gender Planning and Development: Theory, Practice and Training.*

María Otero is the Associate Director of ACCION International, a U.S. based organization specializing in microenterprise development. Previously she served as ACCION director in Honduras, as an economist in A.I.D.'s Women in Development Office, and as a management training coordinator for the Centre for Development and Population Activities. Her recent publications include *The New World of Microenterprise Finance* (with Elisabeth Rhyne) and she has written numerous monographs on microenterprise development.

Alejandro Portes is John Dewey Professor of Sociology and Chair at the Johns Hopkins University. He is co-editor (with Manuel Castells and Lauren Benton) of *The Informal Economy: Studies in Advanced and Less Developed countries* (Johns Hopkins University Press); co-author (with Rubén G. Rumbaut) of *Immigrant America, a Portrait* (University of California Press 1990); and co-author (with Alex Stepick) for *City on the Edge: The Transformation of Miami* (University of California Press, 1993).

Cathy A. Rakowski is Assistant Professor at the Center for Women's Studies and the Department of Agricultural Economics and Rural Sociology at The Ohio State University. She has conducted research on the informal sector, women and development, and the social impacts of large projects since 1979. Her current research focuses on social and cultural change in a region of forestry-based development, and the social dimensions of ecotourism.

Bryan R. Roberts is C. B. Smith Sr. Chair in U.S.-Mexico Relations at the University of Texas at Austin. He is author of several books and edited collections on regional development and urbanization, including *Cities of Peasants*. Recently, he has written extensively on the informal economy, particularly the case of Mexico.

Douglas Uzzell has studied development issues in Mexico, Peru, and the United States. In recent publications he has formulated and amplified the concept of "generative" planning in and out of the informal sector. His work led to a special issue of City and Society on the concept in 1990. Now a psychotherapist, he manages psychiatric outpatient programs at St. Joseph's Hospital in Tampa, Florida, and is in private practice.

Author Index

Subject Index

Cheap labor strategy, 22, 61, 125, 167.
See also Subcontracting
Children: impact on women's
employment, 65–69, 134, 167, 201,
206, 209, 229–30, 232, 243–44;
workers, 133, 146
Chile, 53, 55, 59, 120, 122
Cities, and labor markets, 13–16,
25–28, 42, 44, 56–69, 86, 117–18,
121, 147, 155, 177, 180
Class: and informality, 20–21, 26, 53,
57, 106, 138, 148, 229, 233–34,
253–54; restructuring, 57, 61, 229;
struggle, 24, 36, 114, 234, 276
Clothing, 23, 56–57
Colombia, 15, 19, 25, 53–55, 59, 95,
115, 118, 120–21, 132, 164, 182–83,
188, 190–91, 202, 214–16
Commerce, 21, 32, 35, 54, 55, 61, 64,
93, 135, 158, 162, 165, 169, 179,
200, 205, 207, 217, 237–41; petty,
240, 243, 274
Comparative advantage, 167, 282
Competition: among NGOs, 187;
between firms, 9, 23, 25, 64, 67, 69,
106, 116, 165–66, 215, 246, 258,
261, 265, 277–81; international, 7,
60, 76, 114–15, 118, 245; in labor
markets, 65, 159, 241
Construction, 21, 23, 55–56, 118, 147,
166, 238, 248, 284
Corruption, 48, 137, 140, 143–44, 146,
192–93, 196
Costa Rica, 61, 149, 188, 190
Cost: of credit, 81, 185–86, 203–9, 217,
283; of labor, 13, 28, 38, 52, 58, 64,
83, 114, 118, 170, 209, 224, 241; of
legalization, 40–42, 64, 84, 136–37,
148; of production, 19, 22, 27, 40,
181, 185, 209–11, 234, 282; of transactions, 204, 252, 255–68
Crafts, 40, 53, 56, 59, 60, 63, 134, 216
Credit: access to, 16, 23–24, 40, 46–47,
60, 62, 64, 69, 78, 82, 87, 96, 127–28,
134, 137, 145, 161–62, 164, 167, 183,
244–46, 277, 281; impact on macro-

economic policy, 96–97, 104; programs and policies, 9, 12, 18, 43,
46, 48, 69, 81, 87–88, 96–97, 102–3,
137, 146, 163, 166–71, 182–87,
191–93, 195, 199–218, 244–46, 257,
281, 183–84
Criminal activities, 93, 95, 133, 145–47
Crisis, economic, 7–8, 13, 31–32, 34,
36, 61–62, 66–67, 101, 103, 108,
140, 142, 149, 160–62, 168, 179,
181, 224–26, 232, 246

de Soto, Hernando, 6, 8, 10, 39, 40,
42, 43–44, 126, 128, 131–49,
161–63, 166, 168, 180, 256, 285
Domestic service, 4, 35, 52–53, 55–57,
61, 66, 120–21, 147, 158, 238, 242
Dominican Republic, 188, 190, 204,
215, 216
Drug trafficking, 95, 140, 144–47
Dualism: economic, 32, 36, 40, 58,
156; labor market, 122, 126–28

Ecuador, 132, 149, 182, 187–91, 215
Efficiency, 19, 23, 26, 31, 41, 43, 47–48,
99, 104, 107, 114, 125, 144, 169,
277–78
Entrepreneurship, small scale: 3, 6–7,
13, 19, 22, 25, 32–40, 42–43, 47,
55–56, 58, 61, 63–64, 68–69, 76,
92–93, 96, 103, 126–28, 134, 136–39,
142, 146, 148–49, 161–62, 164–66,
179, 181, 183–84, 189–91, 193, 196,
201–2, 205, 211, 213, 215, 217,
223–24, 237, 240, 242–44, 246, 251,
254, 257, 262, 265, 275, 281, 283

Financial services, 178, 184, 191, 194
Firm size, 6, 19, 35, 42, 48, 78–80, 83,
85–88, 158, 166, 170, 172, 209–10,
217, 224–26, 234, 241, 254, 277
Fiscal policy, 18, 77–79, 93, 96, 103–4
Flexibility: in production and hiring,
8, 19, 24, 28, 36, 62, 102, 105, 123,
126–28, 171, 210, 245, 275, 282; in
support programs for informal
sector, 184, 277, 280